Chef Paul Prudhomme's
Fiery Foods
That I Love

Also by Chef Paul Prudhomme

Chef Paul Prudhomme's Louisiana Kitchen

The Prudhomme Family Cookbook
(with the Prudhomme Family)

Chef Paul Prudhomme's Seasoned America

Chef Paul Prudhomme's Fork in the Road

Chef Paul Prudhomme's Pure Magic

Chef Paul Prudhomme's

Fiery Foods
That I Love

William Morrow and Company, Inc.
New York

It is the policy of William Morrow and Company, Inc., and its imprints and affiliates, recognizing the importance of preserving what has been written, to print the books we publish on acid-free paper, and we exert our best efforts to that end.

Library of Congress Cataloging-in-Publication Data

Prudhomme, Paul.
    Chef Paul Prudhomme's fiery foods that I love / Paul Prudhomme.
      p. cm.
    ISBN 0-688-12153-5
    1. Cookery, American. 2. Cookery (Herbs) 3. Spices. I. Title.
  TX715.P9476 1995
  641.6´ 384—dc20   95-34370
                                                CIP

Printed in the United States of America

First Edition

1 2 3 4 5 6 7 8 9 10

ILLUSTRATIONS BY DAVE ALBERS

BOOK DESIGN BY RENATO STANISIC

I dedicate this book to everyone who's reading it right now.

When I decide to dedicate a book to someone, I put a lot of emotion and thought into the process, because I feel a dedication is very important and should express sincere feelings.

In the past I've adapted family and regional recipes, or re-created dishes that I've tasted in other parts of the country, but these recipes were developed out of the experiences that I've had over the past twenty or so years. And in these years my education has been made possible only by you—all of you who have eaten at my restaurant, bought my products, bought and used my cookbooks, watched me on television, and written to me with your comments and questions. I very honestly believe that your feedback has been vital to my growth as a cook, and in many ways I feel that the book you're holding in your hands is a very special one, containing as it does so many totally new flavor combinations. You've made these recipes possible, and therefore I want to dedicate this book to you. It's my way of saying "Thank you."

My mission, my job, is simply to make your dinner better. And with your continued help, I'll keep on getting better at my job.

Acknowledgments

A huge undertaking like a cookbook is not a one-person project—it takes the time and talents of many individuals, some of whom worked very long hours and made personal sacrifices to make the book the best it could be. My heartfelt thanks go to . . .

Shawn Granger McBride, the life force in all my projects. Her boundless energy and valuable critiques push the work forward at a rapid pace and, at the same time, help ensure that it is done correctly.

Sean O'Meara, my kitchen and computer guru. He was in the kitchen with me every day, not only prepping every vegetable and piece of meat and washing every pot, but in his "spare time" keeping the computers on line.

Patricia Kennedy Livingston, our New Orleans editor. She recooked all the dishes, suggested and rewrote headnotes, methods, and other material, and helped make the whole thing work with her persistence and sense of humor.

Marty Cosgrove, a man of many abilities. Marty worked day and night to make the dishes look good for the photographs in this book and for the television series based on these recipes, in addition to many other assignments.

My grandnephew Troy Brocato. He was here every step of the way and was especially helpful with the television shows. *My grandniece, Monica Tatis,* was a pinch hitter in the test kitchen, saving the day more than once.

Glen Prevost, a lifelong friend. He worked miracles keeping everything in order—a great job with the reconstruction of the test kitchen (and my house)—so that I could devote my attention and time to developing the recipes for this book.

And *Gail Bonomo*, Glen's partner in life, was always ready to pitch in when someone was sick or everyone else was gone.

Paula LaCour, John Alexander, David Hickey, Margie Noonan Blaum, and John McBride, all at Magic Seasoning Blends. Paula manages to make sure there's enough money for any project and offers advise and assistance along the way. John A. and David were tremendously helpful in finding rare ingredients and special items we needed, and Margie, who remained serene amid the chaos, kept us on an even keel as she kept up with my complicated schedules. While John McB. was not directly involved with this book, he contributed mightily to the work by his patient acceptance of Shawn's long hours, and by his efforts to keep us well fed during some of our marathon meetings.

Kate Ross, our bit of sunshine. This sweet-tempered lady, in the city just for the summer, was ready to do anything at any time, and helped very much with several aspects of the project.

Paul Rico, our super-talented photographer. He has done many beautiful shots for us over the years—his pictures are magnificent and he is really great to work with.

Our friends at the Elite Spice Company. Isaac Samuels, president, and his brother Anton Samuels, executive vice president, jumped through hoops to get us things that were unusual and to help us make them work for the mass market.

Thanks to all of you, for without every one of you this book would not have been possible.

Contents

Introduction

Food is my passion, and my mission in life is to make your dinner better!

I could talk for days, but my message would come down to just that, because it's the truth. I could never imagine eating a meal, whether it's something I cooked myself or ordered at a restaurant, that isn't exciting, that doesn't have emotion and several levels of taste. It's this feeling and multiple layers of taste that I mean when I talk about "fiery."

When I first wanted to name this book, my staff was concerned, and I heard from other people that the title *Fiery Foods* would make people automatically assume that what I meant was very hot. But by fiery I don't mean a dish that's unbearably hot but one that lights the fires of your emotions and consumes your attention to the point that you think of nothing else but the pleasure the flavors give you.

Now, how to achieve this kind of taste? I get (and you can too) the kind of results I want through the use of herbs and spices and by the high-heat cooking called for in most of my recipes. Whether this is the first of my cookbooks you've picked up or you've been a friend through my recipes for many years, it's pretty obvious that I love to season with all kinds of herbs and spices—in my mind seasonings are "where it's at"!

You must be surfing the same flavor wave, because I've noticed that grocery stores and supermarkets are stocking a better supply and selection of herbs and spices than they did even ten years ago. For instance, when I first started using red pepper in recipes, back in the eighties, it was hard to find; only a very few grocery stores outside Louisiana and a scattering of small ethnic stores around the country had it. Now all the national spice companies package red pepper, and it's readily available to you.

You'll notice that many of these recipes contain either fresh or dried and ground chile peppers. I know in my heart that chiles are going to be the next great ingredient find and will become a permanent part of the way we cook. There is no doubt in my mind that in ten or fifteen years chile peppers are going to be just as common as salt and black pepper and white pepper and red pepper are now. That's because they give a wonderful, romantic jolt to the recipes they're used in; they should be used so that instead of overpowering a dish's flavor, they add an underlying taste that is simply awesome.

Different kinds of chiles create their own distinctive kinds of taste. If you've not used them before, then you're about to discover the incredible depth of flavor and amazing taste combinations that can be achieved with chiles. Because I feel so strongly about chiles, I've added a section on them in "Notes from the Test Kitchen."

In this book we've tried to use herbs and spices that will be easy for you to find. You may have to search around to find some of the seasonings we've used and some of the major ingredients too, but for the most part everything will be right on the shelves of your supermarket. Any that you might be unfamiliar with are described in the Glossary.

Besides using a lot of different herbs and spices, the other way I achieve the kind of taste that excites me is to cook with dry high heat. You can cook with a lot of moisture, but you're not going to develop a depth of flavor that way. When you cook at a high temperature, you evaporate the moisture on the surface of the food, changing its color and then its flavor—that's why we love grilling so much. Think of a piece of wood burning in your fireplace or in a campfire. As it burns it constantly changes color, until it becomes a glowing coal and then is reduced to ash. Well, we don't want our food to go that far, but we do want it to change color, because that's when it changes taste, reaching a second, third, even fourth dimension of the same flavor. The repeated evaporation of liquid is part of what produces the complex flavors that I love so much. Reducing the liquids in the pan until they are almost gone, and doing it again and again, gives us a way to cook that is hot, dry, and controlled.

I've been lucky to travel a lot in the work I do, and when I travel I take cooking lessons from local chefs who really love and respect their own cultures. I also get a chance to eat a lot of wonderful, different foods. I really enjoy the surprises, whether in a new country or a new city (and actually even in a new restaurant across town), and have been thinking of using some of these flavors in recipes for you. For years now I've been remembering these dishes and daydreaming about them, so you might say this book is a summary of flavors that I've tasted in the past.

Some of these flavors come from the seasonings, and others come from the exciting ingredients we use, such as lemon grass, coconut milk, pine nuts, and so forth. Now, the ideal situation would be to use only fresh ingredients that grow nearby, for flavor is best when the food doesn't have to travel far. With uncommon ingredients, however, that isn't always possible. Take lemon grass as an example; the lemon grass in dishes I tasted in the Orient was very different from the lemon grass that is available to me in America. We can and do use it in our recipes, but the flavor is different from the lemon grass I encountered in Hong Kong. If there are communities originally from Asia or Latin America near where you live, as there are in some cities in the United States, you will find many of these ingredients in the markets that serve them.

When I write a book, my goal is to try to explain clearly what I've learned and what I'm currently feeling about what's going on in the kitchens of the world. When you and I discuss food and recipes, whether in person or through letters or phone calls, I feel very close to you. When we share that special emotion, it inspires me to work even harder for you.

Are you ready to be fired up by a trip through *Chef Paul Prudhomme's Fiery Foods That I Love*? Put on your apron, sharpen your knives, and let's get to cooking!

> Good cooking,
> Good eating,
> Good loving,

Notes
from the Test
Kitchen

Chile Peppers are, to me, one of the most important additions you can make to a recipe. While some of the dishes in this book may be what you would call spicy or hot, in most of them I add chiles to bring out the other flavors in the food. Rather than overpowering or changing the taste of a dish, when they're used well, chile peppers add an awesome underlying taste.

There are hundreds of varieties of chiles; we use many different ones, most especially ancho, guajillo, árbol, and chipotle. With the exception of chipotle, whose smoked flavor is totally different from all the others, it doesn't matter so much which ones you use as that you use several different kinds. Taste and choose until you find three or four varieties of chiles that you really like, and use those in various combinations and proportions.

Some fresh chiles can be very hot and these peppers do require special handling if you're not accustomed to them. Always wear protective gloves (we get disposable vinyl gloves—100 to a box—from the pharmacy) when handling fresh hot chiles, and be careful to wash the gloves (or throw them away), knife, and cutting board after use.

A number of these recipes call for ground dried chile peppers. The good news is that most supermarkets and a lot of neighborhood groceries sell dried chile peppers these days, but the bad news is that they'll probably not be ground. An inexpensive coffee grinder takes care of that problem—just remember to keep it for chiles only, or clean it very carefully if you want to grind coffee later!

The chile peppers that we used in creating the dishes for this book may be obtained from my company, Magic Seasoning Blends. At this suburban New Orleans plant, experienced professionals do their utmost to control the heat level of each package of dried, ground chile peppers, and make sure that every variety remains unsullied by other types. To place an order or for more information, write or call:

Chef Paul Prudhomme's Magic Seasoning Blends®
824 Distributors Row
Harahan, LA 70123
(504) 731-3590
(800) 457-2857

Chile peppers also may be purchased from:

Coyote Cafe General Store
132 W. Water Street
Santa Fe, NM 87501
(505) 982-2454
(800) 866-HOWL

La Fiesta Food Products. Inc.
940 McLaughlin Avenue
San Jose, CA 95122-2611
(408) 292-1729
(408) 292-1799

Don't let the chile peppers in these recipes scare you. Be excited about them. I mean really be excited because they're going to make your food different, they're going to add sunshine to your dishes!

Cilantro, if it's wet when you chop it, will cling together and fill up your measuring cup more densely than it would if it were dry. So to measure accurately, dry the cilantro by squeezing it gently in a paper towel and set it aside. This is an important step because our recipes were developed using fresh cilantro that we rinsed and dried, and if you use wet, you'll add more of it than we did, which will result in a much stronger flavor than our versions.

Cook Chicken Skin Side Down First because when the fat just under the skin starts to melt, the water in the fat evaporates, leaving behind the essence of the chicken—we call it "chicken goodness."

Cook Uncovered unless the recipe specifically directs you to cover the pot.

Diced Canned Tomatoes are an ingredient you'll see in several of these recipes. Now, you know me, I always use fresh ingredients whenever possible (my restaurant, K-Paul's, doesn't even have a freezer!), but the tomatoes in the supermarket can sometimes be pretty unappealing. If poor-quality fresh ones are all that's available, then a great-quality canned product is far preferable. We've found that Hunt's Choice-Cut Diced Tomatoes are excellent and work really well in these dishes.

Grinding Peanuts is a little tricky, but they add such a nice taste and texture to a number of our recipes that I hope you'll give it a try. The simplest way is to use a small coffee grinder, and the only difficult thing is to stop before you make peanut butter! Put a few peanuts in, turn the grinder on for no more than 1 or 2 seconds, and check to see if the peanuts are ground. If not, turn it on for a split second longer and check again. An alternative method is to chop the peanuts very fine, but this is more difficult and time-consuming.

High Heat on your stove may be more or less hot than on the stoves we used to test our recipes. In many cases we brown the food to bring out its natural sweetness, but there's a huge difference between browned and burned. Never leave a pot over high heat untended; watch it carefully, and if the food seems in danger of burning, reduce the heat or remove from the heat as necessary. Your stove may be a dragon or a wimp, and you'll need to adjust accordingly.

Readers sometimes ask me what special pots and pans they should buy to cook with such high heat. Well, I learned to cook, and to cook over really high heat, using cast iron pots, and if you want to know a secret, they're still my favorites, although too heavy to use on a daily basis. As long as they're properly seasoned they're non-stick, and they're practically indestructible. There are many more modern kinds of cookware on the market, though, so you shouldn't have a problem with selection. Just choose pots that are sturdy and whose handles are well attached. And read the manufacturer's instructions for their proper care—no point spending a bundle on good cookware and then ruining your pieces by not taking good care of them.

A pot has two missions—one is to contain the ingredients in one location so that you can manage them. The second is to transfer heat. A well-made pot will heat the ingredients evenly, not just directly over where the fire strikes the pot. If you want to test the quality of your cookware, put about two inches of tap water in the pan and put it over high heat. If the first bubbles appear around the edges of the water, your pot is transferring properly. If the bubbles first appear closer to the center than the outside, then this pot transfers heat unevenly.

Julienne means cutting the vegetables in long, thin pieces. For example, julienne bell peppers refers to pieces cut approximately 2½ inches long by about ¼ inch wide.

Roasting Bell Peppers, Onions, or Garlic gives them a wonderful, unique flavor and is very impressive if your company is watching you cook (practice first!). You should know, too, that when you roast onions and garlic, their thin skins are going to blow around your kitchen. This will make a little mess, but the resulting enhanced flavors are well worth the necessary cleanup. If you have a gas stove, simply place the vegetable(s) right on the burner, in a high flame, and roast, turning with tongs, until the outer skin is charred all around. If your range is electric, you can roast in a pre-heated 500° oven. Plunge the roasted vegetables into ice water to stop the cooking, then rub off the black, charred skin under running water. It should slip right off, but if there are stubborn spots, just remove them with a sharp knife.

When roasting garlic, first remove the loose outer papery skin. After roasting, gently remove the cloves by pulling off the burned outer husk, which will be fairly hard and can be removed like a shell. The cloves inside will be a rich brown color and fairly soft. Removing the cloves is easy if you work from the bottom of the garlic head, gently prying the head open with your fingers and removing the cloves one at a time.

Roasting Onions

Scalloping meat is not difficult, but you need to pay close attention to the method the first time or two you do it. Think of the scallop as a slice of potato—thin and more or less oval. That's the shape you're working toward. Start with the meat in front of you on a firm surface, with the grain running from left to right. When you cut with the grain, you'll have long stringy pieces of beef (the meat looks kind of striped). When you cut against the grain, you'll see lots of little dots within the flesh. In some cuts of meat, such as the flank steak we use for meat scallops, the grain is much more pronounced than in others.

Use a sharp, heavy knife, holding it almost parallel to the surface. Slide the knife through the meat about 1/4 inch below the surface, at about a 30-degree angle to the meat's grain, and cut off a piece that measures about 2 by 3 inches. Make the next cut right next to the first one, also about 30 degrees from the meat's grain, but in the opposite direction. Continue removing thin ovals down the length of the meat, then through the thickness. Don't hurry, and try to keep the scallops as nearly the same size as possible so they'll cook in about the same amount of time.

Sticks Hard is a phrase you'll see in several of these recipes, because I like to cook vegetables, especially those used for seasoning, such as onions and bell peppers, over high heat until they brown and caramelize. This brings out their natural sweetness, which adds a unique flavor to the dishes. Every color change that the food goes through changes its flavor, giving your dish a different taste of that ingredient. You want to brown the food, which will make it stick hard to the bottom of the pot, but don't let it burn, for goodness' sake. Reduce the heat if you need to, or cut the time a little bit. Your cooktop may develop more or less heat than the ones we've used to test these recipes.

Stock is so far preferable over water as a cooking liquid that I want to stand on a box and shout: "*Water is just for washing!!!*" Believe me, making stock is not a big deal, and if you start it before you begin the rest of the recipe, in most cases it will be ready by the time you need it. A few recipes have so little preparation that you'll need to make the stock ahead of time, but even then it's well worth the effort for the richer flavor you'll develop in your dishes.

For 1 quart stock, start with 2 quarts cold water. Simmer with the trimmings from the vegetables in the recipe or a stalk or two of celery, an unpeeled quartered onion, and two unpeeled chopped cloves of garlic. If you're making vegetable stock, add a scrubbed carrot or two, and if you're making chicken stock, put in the giblets (but never the liver) and neck. If you're making meat stock, add the bones or scraps trimmed from the meat (or inexpensive pieces bought just for the stock), and add the shells and trimmings from seafood for seafood stock. Simmer as long as possible, adding water only if the quantity drops below 1 quart. Even if you can cook your stock for only 30 minutes, that's better than using water, but if you can let it simmer for 4 or 5 hours, that's even better!

If you first brown the bones in a 350° oven, your stock will be even more flavorful and have a deeper, richer color. Just like browning ingredients in a pot before adding other ingredients, this step caramelizes the sugars in the bones.

If you have a real stockpot—one that is taller than it is wide—this is the time to bring it out. You can make stock in any container large enough to hold it, but the narrower diameter of a stockpot means there is less liquid surface, thus slowing evaporation.

Stock freezes well, so you can always have it on hand. You can reduce it even further to make it really rich, and if you reduce it before you freeze it, it'll take up less space in your freezer.

That's all there is to it! Just remember never to add liver, salt, spices, or bell peppers (they might make the stock spoil quicker).

Symbols are my way to indicate recipes that are special favorites of some of the people who worked on this book. My picks are indicated by the oval with the cap inside . Shawn McBride's symbol is a wedge of Swiss cheese , and Sean O'Meara's is, appropriately, a shamrock . The recipes that Patricia Livingston loves are marked by a heart . My mythical friend Mrs. Podunk likes well-seasoned dishes, but not as much pepper as I do!

Toasting grits, cornmeal, nuts, and seeds or browning flour enhances the flavor and is simple to do. Just place the amount called for in a skillet over high heat and stir constantly as it browns (a heat-resistant flat spatula works best), being careful to mix the grains thoroughly so that all brown evenly. As soon as the desired shade of brown is achieved, immediately transfer from the hot skillet to a bowl to stop the toasting action.

Breads from My Head

Make 'n' Bake Basic Bread
Golden Rosemary Bread
Jalapeño Corn Bread
Okra Corn Bread

Fire-Roasted Vegetable Breads

Fire-Roasted Onion Bread
Fire-Roasted Garlic Bread
Fire-Roasted Golden Pepper Bread

Filled Breads

Black Bean Bread
Red Bean Bread
Lentil Bread
Mushroom Bread
Apple Raisin Spice Bread

Fried Breads

Ham Pockets
Roasted Veggy Pockets
Skillet Breads and Seasoned Butters

Muffin Cups

Andouille and Egg Muffin Cups
Ground Beef–Filled Muffin Cups
Spicy Cheese–Filled Muffin Cups
Zucchini-Filled Muffin Cups

Make 'n' Bake Basic Bread

MAKES 1 LARGE LOAF

This bread is incredibly light, airy, and very fragrant. It rises so much that you may think it's about to explode! It produces a crust that is delicate and soft, and the recipe is very versatile, as you can see from the number of other recipes based upon it. For best results, always flour your hands well and frequently when working with bread dough to help prevent sticking. The dough can be kept, tightly sealed in plastic wrap, for several days in the refrigerator, or it can be frozen. Because it doesn't contain any preservatives, the bread is best if eaten within two or three days. In most households I know, homemade bread hardly lasts two or three hours, so that probably won't be a problem for you!

2 large eggs

1 teaspoon salt

1 cup 2 percent fat milk

1 package active dry yeast

1 tablespoon sugar

3$\frac{1}{4}$ to 3$\frac{1}{2}$ cups all-purpose flour

Vegetable oil spray

Whisk the eggs in a bowl until they are frothy, then whisk in the salt.

Heat the milk to 110° in a microwave or on top of the stove and stir in the yeast and sugar.

Combine the eggs and the milk mixture in the bowl of an electric food mixer equipped with a dough hook. Stir briefly to combine, then with the mixer set on slow, gradually add 3$\frac{1}{4}$ cups of the flour. Increase the speed to medium and process for 10 minutes. The dough should cling to the dough hook and be fairly elastic. If the dough is soft and sticky, add the remaining $\frac{1}{4}$ cup flour.

Reduce the speed to medium slow and continue to process for 5 more minutes, or until the dough is smooth, very elastic, and clinging to the dough hook.

Flour your hands well, then gather the dough into a ball. Place the dough in a heavy mixing bowl (a thick porcelain bowl is best) that has been lightly sprayed with vegetable spray. Very lightly spray the top of the dough, then put the dough in a warm, draft-free place. (We use the top of our stove, with the oven set at 300°. Or, if you have a gas oven with a pilot light, and you're not using the oven for anything else, put the dough in the unlighted oven, for the pilot light alone generates just enough warmth to encourage rising, and with the door closed, the oven is completely draft-free.) Cover the bowl with a kitchen towel and let the dough rise until doubled in volume, about 1 hour. When the dough has risen, it's so light you'll think it is about ready to fly away! Push the top down very gently—it will collapse easily.

Spray a 5 × 8-inch bread pan lightly but evenly with vegetable oil spray. Form the dough into a loaf shape and place it in the prepared pan. Try to get the top as even as possible, for the shape of the finished bread depends upon how even it is as it rises and bakes.

Preheat the oven to 325°.

Bake until the top is browned and the loaf sounds hollow when lightly struck, about 1 hour. Cool the bread in the pan for 5 minutes, then remove from the pan and cool to room temperature on a wire rack before slicing.

Golden Rosemary Bread

MAKES 1 LARGE LOAF

This is one of the most beautiful breads you'll ever see, and it is just as great to eat as it is to look at! It makes the world's best turkey sandwiches, it's great with pork chops and gravy, it's fantastic spread with cream cheese and chutney, and it will be the star of your buffet table.

2 cups chicken stock (see Notes, page 10)

1 package active dry yeast

1 tablespoon sugar

2 large eggs

1 teaspoon salt

2 teaspoons dried rosemary leaves

1 teaspoon ground savory

¾ teaspoon ground turmeric

3¼ to 3½ cups all-purpose flour

Vegetable oil spray

2 tablespoons melted unsalted butter

Simmer the stock over medium heat until it is reduced to 1 cup. Let it cool to 110°, then stir in the yeast and sugar.

Whisk the eggs in a bowl until they are frothy, then whisk in the salt.

Combine the stock mixture and the eggs in the bowl of an electric food mixer equipped with a dough hook. Stir briefly to combine, then add the rosemary, savory, and turmeric. With the mixer set on slow, gradually add 3¼ cups of the flour. Increase the speed to medium and process for 10 minutes. The dough should cling to the dough hook and be fairly elastic. If the dough is soft and sticky, add the remaining ¼ cup flour.

Reduce the speed to medium slow and continue to process for 5 more minutes, or until the dough is smooth, very elastic, and clinging to the dough hook.

Flour your hands well, then gather the dough into a ball. Place the dough in a heavy mixing bowl (a thick porcelain bowl is best) that has been lightly sprayed with vegetable oil. Very lightly spray the top of the dough, then place the dough in a warm, draft-free place. (We use the top of our stove, with the oven set at 300°; if you have a gas oven with a pilot light, and you're not using the oven for anything else, this makes a great place to let dough rise.) Cover the bowl with a kitchen towel and let the dough rise until doubled in volume, about 1 hour.

Spray a 5 × 8-inch bread pan lightly but evenly with vegetable oil spray. Form the dough into a loaf shape and place it in the prepared pan. Try to get the top as even as possible, for the shape of the finished bread depends upon how even it is as it rises and bakes.

Preheat the oven to 325°.

Bake until the top is browned and the loaf sounds hollow when lightly struck, about 40 minutes. Remove from the pan and brush the top with the melted butter. Cool to room temperature on a wire rack before slicing.

Jalapeño Corn Bread

MAKES 8 OR 9 SERVINGS

In spite of the jalapeño peppers, this corn bread is not uncomfortably hot. Even my wimpy friend Mrs. Podunk enjoys it without shedding a single tear. And one of our testers likes it so much he has it for breakfast, soaked with cane syrup.

Seasoning Mix

1 teaspoon salt

½ teaspoon garlic powder

½ teaspoon onion powder

½ teaspoon ground dried chipotle chile peppers (see Notes, page 6)

½ teaspoon dried thyme leaves

¼ teaspoon cayenne

¼ teaspoon ground cinnamon

¼ teaspoon ground nutmeg

¼ teaspoon white pepper

¼ teaspoon black pepper

✳

Vegetable oil spray

½ cup cornmeal

½ cup corn flour (see Glossary, page 293)

½ cup all-purpose flour

3 tablespoons baking powder

1 tablespoon medium packed dark brown sugar

2 large eggs

1 cup milk

¼ cup cane syrup (see Glossary, page 298)

4 tablespoons (½ stick) melted unsalted butter

¼ pound grated sharp Cheddar cheese

¼ cup finely diced fresh jalapeño chile peppers (see Notes, page 6)

1 cup roasted unsalted peanuts

Preheat the oven to 350°.

Lightly coat a 9-inch square baking pan with vegetable oil spray.

Combine—it's not necessary to sift—the seasoning mix ingredients with the cornmeal, corn flour, all-purpose flour, baking powder, and brown sugar in a large mixing bowl.

Lightly beat the eggs with the milk and add to the dry ingredients, along with the syrup and butter, and stir just until the dry ingredients are moistened. Stir in the cheese, jalapeño chile peppers, and peanuts, being careful not to overmix, and pour the mixture into the oiled pan. Bake until the top is lightly browned and firm in the center, about 40 to 45 minutes. Cool slightly and cut into squares to serve.

Okra Corn Bread

MAKES 12 TO 15 SERVINGS

We could have named this recipe "Coo-Coo," which is a Caribbean name for any cooked side dish, many of which contain cornmeal, or even "Surprise," since the result is totally different from what you might expect when you start to prepare it. At first it resembles vegetable stew with cornmeal mush added, but what comes out of the oven is a wonderful corn bread, high-lighted with colorful bits of vegetables. Serve as a surprising appetizer at an informal dinner party or a perfect side dish for roasts. Some of my cooks enjoy it for lunch, accompanied by only a sliced tomato salad. When buying okra, choose young, tender pods that are no more than 5 inches long.

Seasoning Mix

2 tablespoons medium packed light brown sugar

2 teaspoons salt

2 teaspoons dried savory leaves

1 teaspoon garlic powder

1 teaspoon onion powder

½ teaspoon cayenne

½ teaspoon black pepper

½ teaspoon white pepper

✳

2 tablespoons unsalted butter

4 ounces finely diced bacon

1 pound okra, sliced into ¼-inch rounds

1 small sweet potato, peeled, sliced, and each slice quartered

1 medium red bell pepper, cut into julienne strips

1 (4-ounce) can green chiles, cut into strips

1½ cups all-purpose flour

1¾ cups yellow cornmeal

½ cup sugar

4 tablespoons baking powder

1 large egg

1½ cups milk

Vegetable oil spray

Combine the seasoning mix ingredients in a small bowl.

Preheat the oven to 350°.

Melt the butter in a 3-quart pot over high heat, add the bacon, and cook just until the bacon begins to brown. Add the vegetables and seasoning mix, cover, reduce the heat to low, and cook, stirring occasionally, until the sweet potatoes are just beginning to get tender, about 10 to 12 minutes. Remove from the heat. At this point the mixture is beautiful to look at and very fragrant.

Mix the flour, cornmeal, sugar, and baking powder together—no need to sift— in a large bowl. Whisk the egg and milk until frothy and combine thoroughly with the dry ingredients.

Lightly coat a 9 × 13-inch baking pan with vegetable oil spray. Gently but thoroughly combine the vegetables with the cornmeal mixture, being careful not to over-mix, and transfer to the pan. Bake until done (dry in the center) and browned around the edges, about 45 minutes. Let cool for 5 minutes, then cut into squares to serve.

Fire-Roasted Vegetable Breads

Fire-roasting goes back many years, to when cooking began, when whole animals and vegetables were cooked over an open fire. The taste it delivers is really wonderful. If you've never tasted fire-roasted garlic, onion, or bell pepper, you're living too sheltered a life and should definitely try one of these recipes, or better, all three.

Fire-Roasted Onion Bread

MAKES 1 LARGE LOAF

Bread dough

2 large eggs

1 teaspoon salt

1 cup 2 percent fat milk

1 package active dry yeast

1 tablespoon sugar

3¼ to 3½ cups all-purpose flour

Vegetable oil spray

Onion filling

Seasoning Mix

2 teaspoons sugar

1½ teaspoons onion powder

1 teaspoon cayenne

1 teaspoon ground fenugreek
(See Glossary, page 294)

1 teaspoon garlic powder

1 teaspoon salt

✳

2 medium onions, peeled and sliced in half

2 tablespoons unsalted butter

Egg wash

1 egg

1 tablespoon sugar

½ cup water

Assembly

Vegetable oil spray

2 tablespoons melted unsalted butter

BREAD DOUGH: Whisk the eggs in a bowl until they are frothy, then whisk in the salt.

Heat the milk to 110° in a microwave or on top of the stove and stir in the yeast and sugar.

Combine the eggs and the milk mixture in the bowl of an electric food mixer equipped with a dough hook. Stir briefly to combine, then with the mixer set on slow, gradually add 3¼ cups of the flour. Increase the speed to medium and process for 10 minutes. The dough should cling to the dough hook and be fairly elastic. If the dough is soft and sticky, add the remaining ¼ cup flour.

Reduce the speed to medium slow and continue to process for 5 more minutes, or until the dough is smooth, very elastic, and clinging to the dough hook.

Flour your hands well, then gather the dough into a ball. Place the dough in a heavy mixing bowl (a thick porcelain bowl is best) that has been lightly sprayed with vegetable spray. Very lightly spray the top of the dough, then put the dough in a warm, draft-free place. (We use the top of our stove, with the oven set at 300°. Or, if you have a gas oven with a pilot light, and you're not using the oven for anything else, put the dough in the unlighted oven, for the pilot light alone generates just enough warmth to encourage rising, and with the door closed the oven is completely draft-free.) Cover the bowl with a kitchen towel and let the dough rise until doubled in volume, about 1 hour.

ONION FILLING: Combine the seasoning mix ingredients in a small bowl.

Roast the onion halves: if you have a gas range, simply place the onion right on the burner, in a high flame, and roast, turning with tongs, until the outer skin is charred all the way around. If your range is electric, you can roast in a preheated 500° oven. Plunge the roasted onions into ice water to stop the cooking, then rub off the black, charred skin under running water. It should slip right off, but if there are stubborn spots, just remove them with a sharp knife. Cut the onions into very thin julienne strips—you should get about 1 cup.

Melt the butter in a 10-inch skillet over high heat, and as soon as it starts to sizzle, stir in the seasoning mix and the onions. Cook, stirring frequently, until the onions begin to stick. Add 1 or 2 tablespoons of water if necessary to loosen the brown bits. Set aside until cool enough to handle.

EGG WASH: Blend the egg, sugar, and water together.

ASSEMBLY: Lightly spray a 5 × 8-inch bread pan with vegetable oil spray.

continued

After the dough has risen in the mixing bowl to double its bulk, gently punch it down and turn it out onto a well-floured surface. Roll out the dough into a rectangle about 12 inches wide and 20 to 24 inches long. Brush the dough lightly with the egg wash, but leave a 6-inch-wide section unbrushed at one of the 12-inch ends. Spread the onion filling on the dough, except for the 6-inch-wide section that was not brushed with the egg wash, and leave a ½-inch unfilled border on the other 3 sides. Starting at the narrow filled end, roll the dough up, jelly-roll fashion, until only 1 inch of the unbrushed section is still sticking out. Brush this 1-inch flap with egg wash and close the roll, making sure that all the layers meet and there is no gap on the sides.

Place the rolled dough in the prepared pan, seam side down. Cover with a towel and let the loaf rise until doubled in volume, about 1 hour.

Preheat the oven to 325°.

Bake until the top is browned and crisp, about 40 minutes. Remove from the oven, then gently remove the loaf from the pan and brush the top with the melted butter. Let cool slightly, preferably on a wire rack, before slicing.

Fire-Roasted Garlic Bread

MAKES 1 LARGE LOAF

Bread dough

2 large eggs

1 teaspoon salt

1 cup 2 percent fat milk

1 package active dry yeast

1 tablespoon sugar

$3\frac{1}{4}$ to $3\frac{1}{2}$ cups all-purpose flour

Vegetable oil spray

Garlic filling

Seasoning Mix

2 teaspoons salt

2 teaspoons sugar

$1\frac{1}{2}$ teaspoons garlic powder

1 teaspoon dried thyme leaves

$\frac{1}{2}$ teaspoon onion powder

✳

2 whole garlic heads

2 tablespoons unsalted butter

Egg wash

1 egg

1 tablespoon sugar

$\frac{1}{2}$ cup water

Assembly

Vegetable oil spray

2 tablespoons melted unsalted butter

BREAD DOUGH: Whisk the eggs in a bowl until they are frothy, then whisk in the salt.

Heat the milk to 110° in a microwave or on top of the stove and stir in the yeast and sugar.

Combine the eggs and the milk mixture in the bowl of an electric food mixer equipped with a dough hook. Stir briefly to combine, then with the mixer set on slow, gradually add $3\frac{1}{4}$ cups of the flour. Increase the speed to medium and process for 10 minutes. The dough should cling to the dough hook and be fairly elastic. If the dough is soft and sticky, add the remaining $\frac{1}{4}$ cup flour.

Reduce the speed to medium slow and continue to process for 5 more minutes, or until the dough is smooth, very elastic, and clinging to the dough hook.

Flour your hands well, then gather the dough into a ball. Place the dough in a heavy mixing bowl (a thick porcelain bowl is best) that has been lightly sprayed with

vegetable spray. Very lightly spray the top of the dough, then put the dough in a warm, draft-free place. (We use the top of our stove, with the oven set at 300°. Or, if you have a gas oven with a pilot light, and you're not using the oven for anything else, put the dough in the unlighted oven, for the pilot light alone generates just enough warmth to encourage rising, and with the door closed the oven is completely draft-free.) Cover the bowl with a kitchen towel and let the dough rise until doubled in volume, about 1 hour.

GARLIC FILLING: Combine the seasoning mix ingredients in a small bowl.

To roast the garlic heads, first remove the papery outer skin. Place them over an open flame on your stove or grill and roast until the heads are completely black and charred on the outside. Plunge them into water with ice in it, peel the charred cloves, and mince them.

Melt the butter in a 10-inch skillet over high heat, and as soon as it starts to sizzle, stir in the seasoning mix and the garlic. Cook, stirring frequently, until the garlic begins to stick. Add 1 or 2 tablespoons of water if necessary to loosen the brown bits. Set aside until cool enough to handle.

EGG WASH: Blend the egg, sugar, and water together.

ASSEMBLY: Lightly spray a 5 × 8-inch bread pan with vegetable oil spray.

After the dough has risen in the mixing bowl to double its bulk, gently punch it down and turn it out onto a well-floured surface. Roll out the dough into a rectangle about 12 inches wide and 20 to 24 inches long. Brush the dough lightly with the egg wash, but leave a 6-inch-wide section unbrushed at one of the 12-inch ends. Spread the garlic filling on the dough, except for the 6-inch-wide section that was not brushed with the egg wash, and leave a 1/2-inch unfilled border on the other 3 sides. Starting at the narrow filled end, roll the dough up, jelly-roll fashion, until only 1 inch of the unbrushed section is still sticking out. Brush this 1-inch flap with egg wash and close the roll, making sure that all the layers meet and there is no gap on the sides.

Place the rolled dough in the prepared pan, seam side down. Cover with a towel and let the loaf rise until doubled in volume, about 1 hour.

Preheat the oven to 325°.

Bake until the top is browned and crisp, about 40 minutes. Remove from the oven, then gently remove the loaf from the pan and brush the top with the melted butter. Let cool slightly, preferably on a wire rack, before slicing.

Fire-Roasted Golden Pepper Bread

MAKES 1 LARGE LOAF

Bread dough

2 large eggs

1 teaspoon salt

1 cup 2 percent fat milk

1 package active dry yeast

1 tablespoon sugar

$3\frac{1}{4}$ to $3\frac{1}{2}$ cups all-purpose flour

Vegetable oil spray

Golden pepper filling

Seasoning Mix

2 teaspoons salt

2 teaspoons sugar

2 teaspoons ground dried ancho chile peppers (see Notes, page 6)

$1\frac{1}{2}$ teaspoons garlic powder

1 teaspoon dried oregano leaves

$\frac{3}{4}$ teaspoon ground cumin

✳

2 medium-sized yellow bell peppers

2 tablespoons unsalted butter

Egg wash

1 egg

1 tablespoon sugar

$\frac{1}{2}$ cup water

Assembly

Vegetable oil spray

2 tablespoons melted unsalted butter

BREAD DOUGH: Whisk the eggs in a bowl until they are frothy, then whisk in the salt.

Heat the milk to 110° in a microwave or on top of the stove and stir in the yeast and sugar.

Combine the eggs and the milk mixture in the bowl of an electric food mixer equipped with a dough hook. Stir briefly to combine, then with the mixer set on slow, gradually add $3\frac{1}{4}$ cups of the flour. Increase the speed to medium and process for 10 minutes. The dough should cling to the dough hook and be fairly elastic. If the dough is soft and sticky, add the remaining $\frac{1}{4}$ cup flour.

Reduce the speed to medium slow and continue to process for 5 more minutes, or until the dough is smooth, very elastic, and clinging to the dough hook.

Flour your hands well, then gather the dough into a ball. Place the dough in a heavy mixing bowl (a thick porcelain bowl is best) that has been lightly sprayed with

vegetable spray. Very lightly spray the top of the dough, then put the dough in a warm, draft-free place. (We use the top of our stove, with the oven set at 300°. Or, if you have a gas oven with a pilot light, and you're not using the oven for anything else, put the dough in the unlighted oven, for the pilot light alone generates just enough warmth to encourage rising, and with the door closed the oven is completely draft-free.) Cover the bowl with a kitchen towel and let the dough rise until doubled in volume, about 1 hour.

GOLDEN PEPPER FILLING: Combine the seasoning mix ingredients in a small bowl.

Roast the peppers by placing them over an open flame on your range or grill. Roast until all sides are black, then plunge them into water with ice in it and rub off the charred black parts. Cut the peppers into very thin julienne strips—you should get about $1\frac{1}{2}$ cups.

Melt the butter in a 10-inch skillet over high heat, and as soon as it starts to sizzle, stir in the seasoning mix and the peppers. Cook, stirring frequently, until the peppers begin to stick. Add 1 or 2 tablespoons of water if necessary to loosen the brown bits. Set aside until cool enough to handle.

EGG WASH: Blend the egg, sugar, and water together.

ASSEMBLY: Lightly spray a 5 × 8-inch bread pan with vegetable oil spray.

After the dough has risen in the mixing bowl to double its bulk, gently punch it down and turn it out onto a well-floured surface. Roll out the dough into a rectangle about 12 inches wide and 20 to 24 inches long. Brush the dough lightly with the egg wash, but leave a 6-inch-wide section unbrushed at one of the 12-inch ends. Spread the pepper filling on the dough, except for the 6-inch-wide section that was not brushed with the egg wash, and leave a $\frac{1}{2}$-inch unfilled border on the other 3 sides. Starting at the narrow filled end, roll the dough up, jelly-roll fashion, until only 1 inch of the unbrushed section is still sticking out. Brush this 1-inch flap with egg wash and close the roll, making sure that all the layers meet and there is no gap on the sides.

Place the rolled dough in the prepared pan, seam side down. Cover with a towel and let the loaf rise until doubled in volume, about 1 hour.

continued

Preheat the oven to 325°.

Bake until the top is browned and crisp, about 40 minutes. Remove from the oven, gently remove the loaf from the pan and brush the top with the melted butter. Let cool slightly, preferably on a wire rack, before slicing.

Filled Breads

Black Bean Bread

MAKES 1 LARGE LOAF

For centuries people have been combining starches by dipping bread into bean juices. This recipe does it all for you, by baking the beans right into the bread. We used 3 cups of the Devilishly Deliciously Black Beans and liquid drained from the beans. If you don't have enough liquid to make the cup called for, you can put some of the beans in a strainer and run a little water through them—the liquid that comes out will be more flavorful than plain water. Or you can use vegetable stock to complete the cup of liquid.

You can use leftover beans, or you can make the recipe just for the bread and eat the beans you don't use over hot white rice. Or make the whole recipe and use it for several loaves of bread, freezing any that you don't plan to enjoy right away. For best results, freeze the loaves before baking—place them in a zipper bag and put them into the freezer just as soon as you form them but before letting the loaves rise. When you're ready to use them, defrost, let them rise, and bake as usual.

Bread dough

2 large eggs

1 teaspoon salt

1 cup liquid drained from Devilishly Delicious Black Beans (page 244)

1 package active dry yeast

1 tablespoon sugar

3¼ to 3½ cups all-purpose flour

Vegetable oil spray

Egg wash

1 egg

1 tablespoon sugar

½ cup water

Assembly

Vegetable oil spray

3 cups drained Devilishly Delicious Black Beans

2 tablespoons melted unsalted butter

continued

BREAD DOUGH: Whisk the eggs in a bowl until they are frothy, then whisk in the salt.

Heat the drained bean cooking liquid to 110° in a microwave or on top of the stove and stir in the yeast and sugar.

Combine the eggs and the bean liquid mixture in the bowl of an electric food mixer equipped with a dough hook. Stir briefly to combine, then with the mixer set on slow, gradually add 3¹⁄4 cups of the flour. Increase the speed to medium and process for 10 minutes. The dough should cling to the dough hook and be fairly elastic. If the dough is soft and sticky, add the remaining ¹⁄4 cup flour.

Reduce the speed to medium slow and continue to process for 5 more minutes, or until the dough is smooth, very elastic, and clinging to the dough hook.

Flour your hands well, then gather the dough into a ball. Place the dough in a heavy mixing bowl (a thick porcelain bowl is best) that has been lightly sprayed with vegetable spray. Very lightly spray the top of the dough, then put the dough in a warm, draft-free place. (We use the top of our stove, with the oven set at 300°. Or, if you have a gas oven with a pilot light, and you're not using the oven for anything else, put the dough in the unlighted oven, for the pilot light alone generates just enough warmth to encourage rising, and with the door closed the oven is completely draft-free.) Cover the bowl with a kitchen towel and let the dough rise until doubled in volume, about 1 hour.

EGG WASH: Blend the egg, sugar, and water together.

ASSEMBLY: Lightly spray a 5 × 8-inch bread pan with vegetable oil spray.

After the dough has risen in the mixing bowl to double its bulk, turn it out onto a well-floured surface. Roll out the dough into a rectangle about 12 inches wide and 20 to 24 inches long. Brush the dough lightly with the egg wash, but leave a 6-inch-wide section unbrushed at one of the 12-inch ends. Spread the black beans on the dough, except for the 6-inch-wide section that was not brushed with the egg wash, and leave a ¹⁄2-inch unfilled border on the other 3 sides. Starting at the narrow filled end, roll the dough up, jelly-roll fashion, until only 1 inch of the unbrushed section is still sticking out. Brush this flap with egg wash and close the roll, making sure that all layers meet and there is no gap on the sides. It is very important to roll the dough evenly so it will rise evenly and you'll have a loaf of bread that looks as good as it tastes.

Place the rolled dough in the prepared pan, seam side down. Cover with a towel and let the dough rise until doubled in volume, about 1 hour.

Preheat the oven to 325°.

Bake until the top is browned and crisp, about 40 minutes. Remove from the oven, gently remove the loaf from the pan, and brush the top with the melted butter. Let cool slightly, preferably on a wire rack, before slicing.

Red Bean Bread

MAKES 1 LARGE LOAF

Use 3 cups of Yo' Mama's Red Beans and 1 cup of the liquid to make this wonderfully different bread. Either use leftover beans or make the red beans recipe just for the bread and eat those you don't use over hot white rice. Another alternative is to make several loaves of bread and freeze the extra loaves. For best results, freeze the loaves before you bake them—as soon as they've finished rising, place them in a zipper bag and put into the freezer immediately.

If you can't drain enough liquid from the beans to equal the cup called for, either use vegetable stock to make up the difference, or put some of the beans in a strainer and run a little water through them. The liquid that drains out will be better than plain water.

Bread dough

2 large eggs

1 teaspoon salt

1 cup liquid drained from Yo' Mama's Red Beans (page 247)

1 package active dry yeast

1 tablespoon sugar

3¼ to 3½ cups all-purpose flour

Vegetable oil spray

Egg wash

1 egg

1 tablespoon sugar

½ cup water

Assembly

Vegetable oil spray

3 cups drained Yo' Mama's Red Beans

2 tablespoons melted unsalted butter

BREAD DOUGH: Whisk the eggs in a bowl until they are frothy, then whisk in the salt.

Heat the drained bean cooking liquid to 110° in a microwave or on top of the stove and stir in the yeast and sugar.

Combine the eggs and the bean liquid mixture in the bowl of an electric food mixer equipped with a dough hook. Stir briefly to combine, then with the mixer set on slow, gradually add 3¼ cups of the flour. Increase the speed to medium and process for 10 minutes. The dough should cling to the dough hook and be fairly elastic. If the dough is soft and sticky, add the remaining $1/4$ cup flour.

Reduce the speed to medium slow and continue to process for 5 more minutes, or until the dough is smooth, very elastic, and clinging to the dough hook.

Flour your hands well, then gather the dough into a ball. Place the dough in a heavy mixing bowl (a thick porcelain bowl is best) that has been lightly sprayed with vegetable spray. Very lightly spray the top of the dough, then put the dough in a warm, draft-free place. (We use the top of our stove, with the oven set at 300°. Or, if you have a gas oven with a pilot light, and you're not using the oven for anything else, put the dough in the unlighted oven, for the pilot light alone generates just enough warmth to encourage rising, and with the door closed the oven is completely draft-free.) Cover the bowl with a kitchen towel and let the dough rise until doubled in volume, about 1 hour.

EGG WASH: Blend the egg, sugar, and water together.

ASSEMBLY: Lightly spray a 5 × 8-inch bread pan with vegetable oil spray.

After the dough has risen in the mixing bowl to double its bulk, turn it out onto a well-floured surface. Roll out the dough into a rectangle about 12 inches wide and 20 to 24 inches long. Brush the dough lightly with the egg wash, but leave a 6-inch-wide section unbrushed at one of the 12-inch ends. Spread the red beans on the dough, except for the 6-inch-wide section that was not brushed with the egg wash, and leave a $1/2$-inch unfilled border on the other 3 sides. Starting at the narrow filled end, roll the dough up, jelly-roll fashion, until only 1 inch of the unbrushed section is still sticking out. Brush this flap with egg wash and close the roll, making sure that all layers meet and there is no gap on the sides. It is very important to roll the dough evenly, so it will rise evenly and you'll have a loaf of bread that looks as good as it tastes.

Place the rolled dough in the prepared pan, seam side down. Cover with a towel and let the dough rise until doubled in volume, about 1 hour.

Preheat the oven to 325°.

Bake until the top is brown and crisp, about 40 minutes. Remove from the oven, gently remove the loaf from the pan, and brush the top with the melted butter. Let cool slightly, preferably on a wire rack, before slicing.

Lentil Bread

MAKES 1 LARGE LOAF

You've probably never heard of baking a salad inside bread before. Well, now you have! Don't decide it's a crazy idea without even trying it; I think once you taste a slice, this recipe will become one of your favorites. Remember to make the Lentil Salad first so you will have it available when you need it for the bread. You'll have about 5 cups of the salad left over, so you're almost ready for another meal!

Bread dough

  2 large eggs

  1 teaspoon salt

  1 cup liquid drained from Lentil
     Salad (page 252)

  1 package active dry yeast

  1 tablespoon sugar

  3¼ to 3½ cups all-purpose flour

  Vegetable oil spray

Egg wash

  1 egg

  1 tablespoon sugar

  ½ cup water

Assembly

  Vegetable oil spray

  3 cups drained Lentil Salad

  2 tablespoons melted unsalted butter

BREAD DOUGH: Whisk the eggs in a bowl until they are frothy, then whisk in the salt.

Heat the lentil salad liquid to 110° in a microwave or on top of the stove and stir in the yeast and sugar.

Combine the eggs and the lentil liquid mixture in the bowl of an electric food mixer equipped with a dough hook. Stir briefly to combine, then with the mixer set on slow, gradually add 3¼ cups of the flour. Increase the speed to medium and process for 10 minutes. The dough should cling to the dough hook and be fairly elastic. If the dough is soft and sticky, add the remaining ¼ cup flour.

Reduce the speed to medium slow and continue to process for 5 more minutes, or until the dough is smooth, very elastic, and clinging to the dough hook.

Flour your hands well, then gather the dough into a ball. Place the dough in a heavy mixing bowl (a thick porcelain bowl is best) that has been lightly sprayed with vegetable spray. Very lightly spray the top of the dough, then put the dough in a warm, draft-free place. (We use the top of our stove, with the oven set at 300°. Or, if you have a gas oven with a pilot light, and you're not using the oven for anything else, put the dough in the unlighted oven, for the pilot light alone generates just enough warmth to encourage rising, and with the door closed the oven is completely draft-free.) Cover the bowl with a kitchen towel and let the dough rise until doubled in volume, about 1 hour.

EGG WASH: Blend the egg, sugar, and water together.

ASSEMBLY: Lightly spray a 5 × 8-inch bread pan with vegetable oil spray.

After the dough has risen in the mixing bowl to double its bulk, about 1 hour, turn it out onto a well-floured surface. Roll out the dough into a rectangle about 12 inches wide and 20 to 24 inches long. Brush the dough lightly with the egg wash, but leave a 6-inch-wide section unbrushed at one of the narrow ends. Spread the lentil salad on the dough, except for the 6-inch-wide section that was not brushed with the egg wash, and leave a ½-inch unfilled border on the other 3 sides. Starting at the narrow filled end, roll the dough up, jelly-roll fashion, until only 1 inch of the unbrushed section is still sticking out. Brush this flap with egg wash and close the roll, making sure that all layers meet and there is no gap on the sides. It is very important to roll the dough evenly so it will rise evenly and you'll have a loaf of bread that looks as good as it tastes.

Place the rolled dough in the prepared pan, seam side down. Cover with a towel and let the dough rise until doubled in volume, about 1 hour.

Preheat the oven to 325°.

Bake until the top is browned and crisp, about 40 minutes. Remove from the oven, gently remove the loaf from the pan, and brush the top with the melted butter. Let cool slightly, preferably on a wire rack, before slicing.

Mushroom Bread

MAKES 1 LARGE LOAF

This bread is a winner for entertaining—the seasonings we've chosen really bring out the flavor of the mushrooms, and the spiral of the filling looks good when you lay out the slices. It's great alone, but I think it really shines with cream cheese. Because the bread does not contain any preservatives, it's best to eat it within a couple of days. Keep it in a tightly closed plastic bag. Even though this appears to be a long recipe, don't be intimidated—we just wanted to explain it well.

Mushroom filling

Seasoning Mix

2 tablespoons sugar

1 teaspoon dried basil leaves

1 teaspoon cayenne

1 teaspoon salt

¾ teaspoon white pepper

½ teaspoon garlic powder

½ teaspoon onion powder

½ teaspoon black pepper

½ teaspoon ground dried árbol chile peppers (see Notes, page 6)

½ teaspoon ground savory

½ teaspoon dried tarragon leaves

✳

2 tablespoons unsalted butter

1 cup finely diced onions

1 cup finely diced green bell peppers (or use ⅓ cup each of finely diced green, red, and yellow bell peppers)

½ cup finely diced celery

8 ounces sliced fresh mushrooms

1½ cups vegetable stock, in all (see Notes, page 10)

Bread dough

2 large eggs

1 teaspoon salt

1 cup liquid drained from the mushroom filling

1 package active dry yeast

1 tablespoon sugar

3¼ to 3½ cups all-purpose flour

Vegetable oil spray

Egg wash

1 egg

1 tablespoon sugar

½ cup water

Assembly

Vegetable oil spray

2 tablespoons melted unsalted butter

MUSHROOM FILLING: Combine the seasoning mix ingredients in a small bowl.

Heat the butter in a 4-quart pot until it sizzles. Add the onions, bell peppers, and celery and cook, stirring frequently, until the vegetables are wilted, turning brown, and beginning to stick to the pot bottom, about 10 minutes. Add the mushrooms and the seasoning mix. Stir and scrape the pot bottom thoroughly. Add $1/2$ cup of the stock and cook, scraping the sides and bottom of the pot, until almost all the liquid evaporates, about 15 minutes. Add the remaining stock, bring just to a boil and remove from the heat.

Strain the liquid from the mixture into a large bowl. You will probably need to press with the back of a spoon to extract all the liquid. You'll need 1 cup of liquid, so if you don't get that much from the mushrooms, add enough additional stock to equal the cup. Use this cup of liquid and all the mushroom filling for this bread.

BREAD DOUGH: Whisk the eggs in a bowl until they are frothy, then whisk in the salt.

Heat the drained liquid from the mushroom filling to 110° in a microwave or on top of the stove and stir in the yeast and sugar.

Combine the eggs and the mushroom liquid mixture in the bowl of an electric food mixer equipped with a dough hook. Stir briefly to combine, then with the mixer set on slow, gradually add $3^{1/4}$ cups of the flour. Increase the speed to medium and process for 10 minutes. The dough should cling to the dough hook and be fairly elastic. If the dough is soft and sticky, add the remaining $1/4$ cup flour.

Reduce the speed to medium slow and continue to process for 5 more minutes, or until the dough is smooth, very elastic, and clinging to the dough hook.

Flour your hands well, then gather the dough into a ball. Place the dough in a heavy mixing bowl (a thick porcelain bowl is best) that has been lightly sprayed with vegetable spray. Very lightly spray the top of the dough, then put the dough in a warm, draft-free place. (We use the top of our stove, with the oven set at 300°. Or, if you have a gas oven with a pilot light, and you're not using the oven for anything else, put the dough in the unlighted oven, for the pilot light alone generates just enough warmth to encourage rising, and with the door closed the oven is completely draft-free.) Cover the bowl with a kitchen towel and let the dough rise until doubled in volume, about 1 hour. *continued*

EGG WASH: Blend the egg, sugar, and water together.

ASSEMBLY: Lightly spray a 5 × 8-inch bread pan with vegetable oil spray.

After the dough has risen in the mixing bowl to double its bulk, turn it out onto a well-floured surface. Roll out the dough into a rectangle about 12 inches wide and 20 to 24 inches long. Brush the dough lightly with the egg wash, but leave a 6-inch-wide section unbrushed at one of the 12-inch ends. Spread the mushroom filling on the dough, except for the 6-inch-wide section that was not brushed with the egg wash, and leave a 1/2-inch unfilled border on the other 3 sides. Starting at the narrow filled end, roll the dough up, jelly-roll fashion, until only 1 inch of the unbrushed section is still sticking out. Brush this 1-inch flap with egg wash and close the roll, making sure that all layers meet and there is no gap on the sides. It is very important to roll the dough evenly so it will rise evenly and you'll have a loaf of bread that looks as good as it tastes.

Place the rolled dough in the prepared pan, seam side down. Cover with a towel and let the dough rise until doubled in volume, about 1 hour.

Preheat the oven to 325°.

Bake until the top is browned and crisp, about 40 minutes. Remove from the oven, gently remove the loaf from the pan, and brush the top with the melted butter. Let cool slightly, preferably on a wire rack, before serving.

Apple Raisin Spice Bread

MAKES 1 LARGE LOAF

You can walk into any grocery store and buy ordinary raisin bread, but this loaf is about as far from ordinary bread as you can get! It's so chock full of good things—pecans and apples as well as raisins—that it might take a little longer than other breads to rise. Check it after an hour, and let it continue to rise if it hasn't doubled in volume. Buy pecans already chopped if you can, or chop them yourself after toasting, as soon as they are cool enough to handle comfortably.

Bread dough

1 cup pecans, toasted (instructions follow) and chopped

2 cups apple juice

1 package active dry yeast

2 large eggs

1 teaspoon salt

2 tablespoons lightly packed dark brown sugar

$3/4$ teaspoon ground cinnamon

$1/2$ teaspoon ground nutmeg

$3\frac{1}{4}$ to $3\frac{1}{2}$ cups all-purpose flour

2 cups raisins

4 tablespoons grated Romano cheese

Vegetable oil spray

Egg wash

1 egg

1 tablespoon sugar

$1/2$ cup water

Assembly

Vegetable oil spray

2 medium apples, finely diced (about $1\frac{1}{2}$ cups)

2 tablespoons melted unsalted butter

BREAD: Toast the pecans by heating them in a 10-inch skillet over high heat. Stir constantly to prevent scorching, and as soon as they begin to darken, remove them from the skillet to stop the toasting.

Simmer the apple juice over medium heat until it is reduced to 1 cup. Cool the reduced juice to 110° and stir in the yeast.

Whisk the eggs in a bowl until they are frothy, then whisk in the salt.

Combine the eggs and the juice mixture in the bowl of an electric food mixer equipped with a dough hook. Add the brown sugar, cinnamon, and nutmeg, and stir briefly to combine. With the mixer set on slow, gradually add 3¹/₄ cups of the flour. Increase the speed to medium and process for 10 minutes. The dough should cling to the dough hook and be fairly elastic. If the dough is soft and sticky, add the remaining ¹/₄ cup flour.

Reduce the speed to medium slow, add the pecans, raisins, and cheese, and continue to process for 5 more minutes, or until the dough is smooth, very elastic, and clinging to the dough hook.

Flour your hands well, then gather the dough into a ball. Place the dough in a heavy mixing bowl (a thick porcelain bowl is best) that has been lightly sprayed with vegetable spray. Very lightly spray the top of the dough, then put the dough in a warm, draft-free place. (We use the top of our stove, with the oven set at 300°. Or, if you have a gas oven with a pilot light, and you're not using the oven for anything else, put the dough in the unlighted oven, for the pilot light alone generates just enough warmth to encourage rising, and with the door closed the oven is completely draft-free.) Cover the bowl with a kitchen towel and let the dough rise until doubled in volume, about 1 hour.

EGG WASH: Blend the egg, sugar, and water together.

ASSEMBLY: Lightly spray a 5 × 8-inch bread pan with vegetable oil.

After the dough has risen in the mixing bowl to double its bulk, turn it out onto a well-floured surface. Roll out the dough evenly into a rectangle about 12 inches wide and 20 to 24 inches long. This step is very important—the more even the dough is at this stage, the more evenly it will rise for a nice-looking finished loaf of bread. Brush the dough lightly with the egg wash, but leave a 6-inch-wide section unbrushed at one of the narrow ends. Spread the diced apples over the dough, except for the 6-inch-wide section that was not brushed with the egg wash, and leave a ¹/₂-inch unfilled border on the other 3 sides. Starting at the narrow filled end, roll the dough up, jelly-roll fashion, until only 1 inch of the unbrushed section is still sticking out. Brush this flap with egg wash and close the roll, making sure that all layers meet and there is no gap on the sides.

Place the rolled dough in the prepared pan, seam side down. Cover with a towel and let the dough rise until doubled in volume, at least 1 hour, longer if necessary because of the filling.

Preheat the oven to 325°.

Bake until the top is browned and crisp, about 40 minutes. Remove from the oven, gently remove the loaf from the pan, and brush the top with the melted butter. Let cool, preferably on a wire rack, before slicing.

Fried Breads
Ham Pockets

MAKES 6 TO 8 BREAD POCKETS

You can use sliced ham from the deli or slice your own leftover baked ham—either one will com-bine with the homemade bread and roasted onions and bell peppers to make an unforgettable light lunch or supper.

Bread dough

2 large eggs

1 teaspoon salt

1 cup 2 percent fat milk

1 package active dry yeast

1 tablespoon sugar

3¼ to 3½ cups all-purpose flour

Vegetable oil spray

Egg wash

1 egg, beaten lightly

¼ cup milk

Filling

¾ cup finely diced roasted onions (instructions follow)

¾ cup finely diced roasted green bell peppers (instructions follow)

¾ pound thinly sliced baked ham

✳

4 tablespoons melted unsalted butter

BREAD DOUGH: Whisk the eggs until they are frothy, then whisk in the salt.

Heat the milk to 110° in a microwave or on top of the stove and stir in the yeast and sugar.

Combine the eggs and the milk mixture in the bowl of an electric food mixer equipped with a dough hook. Stir briefly to combine, then with the mixer set on slow, gradually add 3¼ cups of the flour. Increase the speed to medium and process for 10 minutes. The dough should cling to the dough hook and be fairly elastic. If the dough is soft and sticky, add the remaining ¼ cup flour.

Reduce the speed to medium slow and continue to process for 5 more minutes, or until the dough is smooth, very elastic, and clinging to the dough hook.

Flour your hands well, then gather the dough into a ball. Place the dough in a heavy mixing bowl (a thick porcelain bowl is best) that has been lightly sprayed with

vegetable spray. Very lightly spray the top of the dough, then put the dough in a warm, draft-free place. (We use the top of our stove, with the oven set at 300°. Or, if you have a gas oven with a pilot light, and you're not using the oven for anything else, put the dough in the unlighted oven, for the pilot light alone generates just enough warmth to encourage rising, and with the door closed the oven is completely draft-free.) Cover the bowl with a kitchen towel and let the dough rise until doubled in volume, about 1 hour.

When the dough has risen, push the top of the dough down very gently—it will collapse easily. Turn the dough onto a floured surface. With your hands, rolling pin, and working surface well floured, separate the dough into 12 to 16 balls each about the size of a golf ball (the amount of dough produced by the recipe will vary depending upon the hardness of the wheat in the flour and the size of the eggs, among other factors) and roll them out to circles about 5 to 6 inches in diameter. Place the rounds on a sheet pan or cookie pan, layers separated by foil, plastic wrap, or waxed paper, and refrigerate them (to stop the rising) until ready to use.

EGG WASH: Combine the beaten egg with the milk.

FILLING: Roast the onions and bell peppers to give them a wonderful, unique flavor. The technique isn't difficult and is very impressive if your company is watching you cook (practice first!). If you have a gas range, simply place the vegetables right on the burner, in a high flame, and roast, turning with tongs, until the outer skin is charred all around. If your range is electric, you can roast in a preheated 500° oven. Plunge the roasted vegetables into ice water to stop the cooking, then rub off the black, charred skin under running water. It should slip right off, but if there are stubborn spots, just remove them with a sharp knife.

Combine the roasted onions and bell peppers in a bowl.

ASSEMBLY: Brush one side of each dough round with the egg wash. Divide the onions, bell peppers, and ham among half the dough rounds with the egg-washed side up, and top with the remaining dough rounds, egg-washed side down. Seal the edges all the way around, coat the outer surfaces with the melted butter, and fry, turning frequently, on a griddle or in a skillet over medium heat (about 250°) until golden brown. Keep the first bread pockets warm while you fry the others so you can serve everyone at the same time.

Roasted Veggy Pockets

MAKES 6 BREAD POCKETS

There is absolutely no substitute for roasting the onions, bell peppers, and garlic in this recipe because the smoky flavor cannot be obtained any other way. Fire-roasting goes back to the beginning of man, but it's popular today because of its unique, awesome flavor. Like any new thing, if you haven't done it before, it may seem time-consuming. However, once you understand the process, you're probably going to want to enjoy the taste every time you use onions, garlic, and bell peppers.

Bread dough

2 large eggs

1 teaspoon salt

1 cup 2 percent fat milk

1 package active dry yeast

1 tablespoon sugar

3¼ to 3½ cups all-purpose flour

Vegetable oil spray

Egg wash

1 egg, lightly beaten

¼ cup milk

Filling

1¼ cups finely diced roasted onions (instructions follow)

½ cup finely diced roasted green bell peppers (instructions follow)

½ cup finely diced roasted red bell peppers (instructions follow)

½ cup finely diced roasted yellow bell peppers (instructions follow)

¼ cup finely diced roasted garlic (instructions follow)

✳

4 tablespoons melted unsalted butter

BREAD DOUGH: Whisk the eggs in a bowl until they are frothy, then whisk in the salt.

Heat the milk to 110° in a microwave or on top of the stove and stir in the yeast and sugar.

Combine the eggs and the milk mixture in the bowl of an electric food mixer equipped with a dough hook. Stir briefly to combine, then with the mixer set on slow, gradually add 3¼ cups of the flour. Increase the speed to medium and process for 10 minutes. The dough should cling to the dough hook and be fairly elastic. If the dough is soft and sticky, add the remaining ¼ cup flour.

Reduce the speed to medium slow and continue to process for 5 more minutes, or until the dough is smooth, very elastic, and clinging to the dough hook.

Flour your hands well, then gather the dough into a ball. Place the dough in a heavy mixing bowl (a thick porcelain bowl is best) that has been lightly sprayed with vegetable spray. Very lightly spray the top of the dough, then place the dough in a warm, draft-free place. (We use the top of our stove, with the oven set to 300°, or if you have a gas oven with a pilot light, and you're not using the oven for anything else, this makes a great place to let dough rise.) Cover the bowl with a kitchen towel and let the dough rise until doubled in volume, about 1 hour.

Push the top down very gently—it will collapse easily. Turn the dough onto a floured surface. With your hands, rolling pin, and working surface well floured, separate the dough into 12 to 16 balls each about the size of a golf ball (the amount of dough produced by the recipe will vary depending upon the hardness of the wheat in the flour and the size of the eggs, among other factors) and roll them out to circles about 5 to 6 inches in diameter. Place the rounds on a sheet pan or cookie pan, layers separated by foil, plastic wrap, or waxed paper, and refrigerate them (to stop the rising) until ready to use.

EGG WASH: Combine the beaten egg with the milk.

FILLING: To roast the onions, bell peppers, and garlic, if you have a gas range, simply place the vegetables right on the burner, in a high flame, and roast, turning with tongs, until the outer skin is charred all around. If your range is electric, you can roast in a preheated 500° oven. Plunge the roasted vegetables into ice water to stop the cooking, then rub off the black, charred skin under running water. It should slip right off, but if there are stubborn spots, just remove them with a sharp knife.

When roasting garlic, first remove the loose outer papery skin. After roasting, gently remove the cloves by pulling off the burned outer husk, which will be fairly hard and can be removed like a shell. The cloves will be a rich brown color and fairly soft inside. Removing the cloves is easy if you work from the bottom of the garlic head, gently prying the head open with your fingers.

Make the filling by combining the roasted onions, bell peppers, and garlic in a bowl.

continued

ASSEMBLY: Brush one side of each dough round with the egg wash. Divide the filling among half of the dough rounds with the egg-washed side up, and top with the remaining dough rounds, egg-washed side down. Seal the edges all the way around, coat the outer surfaces with the melted butter, and fry, turning often, on a griddle or in a skillet over medium heat (about 250°) until golden brown. Keep the first bread pockets warm while you fry the others so you can serve everyone at the same time.

Skillet Breads and Seasoned Butters

MAKES ABOUT 6 ROUNDS

In different cultures around the world, I've seen many versions of flat bread. The dough we use here and the ways we flavor it are, I think, unique to this book. The herb and spice butters that we use to fry the different versions truly make these skillet breads versatile and interesting. These unusual and delicious bread rounds make great snacks all by themselves, they go well with a salad for a light meal, and when cooked very crisp, they are wonderful as party treats. Cook them at the last minute to serve at the table with dinner. These butters can be used a lot of other ways—brush them on sliced bread, dip vegetables (raw or cooked) in them, or serve them with cold meat and crackers.

Bread rounds

2 large eggs

1 teaspoon salt

1 cup 2 percent fat milk

1 package active dry yeast

1 tablespoon sugar

3¼ to 3½ cups all-purpose flour

Vegetable oil spray

Whisk the eggs in a bowl until they are frothy, then whisk in the salt.

Heat the milk to 110° in a microwave or on top of the stove and stir in the yeast and sugar.

Combine the eggs and the milk mixture in the bowl of an electric food mixer equipped with a dough hook. Stir briefly to combine, then with the mixer set on slow, gradually add 3¼ cups of the flour. Increase the speed to medium and process for 10 minutes. The dough should cling to the dough hook and be fairly elastic. If the dough is soft and sticky, add the remaining ¼ cup flour.

Reduce the speed to medium slow and continue to process for 5 more minutes, or until the dough is smooth, very elastic, and clinging to the dough hook.

Flour your hands well, then gather the dough into a ball. Place the dough in a heavy mixing bowl (a thick porcelain bowl is best) that has been lightly sprayed with vegetable spray. Very lightly spray the top of the dough, then place the dough in a warm, draft-free place. (We use the top of our stove, with the oven set at 300°, or if you have a gas oven with a pilot light, and you're not using the oven for anything else, this makes a great place to let dough rise.) Cover the bowl with a kitchen towel and let the dough rise until doubled in volume, about 1 hour. Push the top down very gently—it will collapse easily.

On a floured surface, roll out a piece of the dough about the size of a baseball into a circle about 6 to 8 inches across. Use plenty of flour and turn as you roll. If the round starts to stick, add more flour. Brush both sides of the dough round lightly with your choice of the seasoned butters (recipes follow) and set aside on a piece of baker's parchment paper. Let rise until doubled in bulk. Preheat a 9- or 10-inch skillet over very high heat for 4 minutes, then reduce the heat to medium-high to keep it hot while frying the bread. A nonstick electric skillet set at 350° would be ideal for these bread rounds. Fry the rounds, turning them several times, until crisp and nicely browned, about 3 to 5 minutes in all.

Seasoned Butters

These butters are simple to prepare—simply melt the butter in a small skillet over medium heat, add the seasonings, stir well to combine, and cook for about 2 minutes. Remove from the heat. To use, brush on just the seasoned liquid on top of the mixture, leaving the actual seasonings behind to continue flavoring the remaining butter.

Because these are seasoned butters, not just dry seasoning mixes, you want them to be nice and liquid, so add more butter if necessary. You can store any leftover butter in the refrigerator and remelt when ready to use again, adding additional butter to replace what was used.

Garlic bread butter

4 tablespoons melted unsalted butter (or more if necessary, see above)

2 tablespoons minced fresh garlic

1 tablespoon grated Parmesan cheese

1 tablespoon white balsamic vinegar (see Glossary, page 299)

1¾ teaspoons dried oregano leaves

1 teaspoon cayenne

1 teaspoon onion powder

1 teaspoon black pepper

1 teaspoon white pepper

½ teaspoon garlic powder

Peppery-sweet butter

4 tablespoons melted unsalted butter (or more if necessary, see above)

1 tablespoon sugar

1 teaspoon dried oregano leaves

1 teaspoon ground dried chipotle chile peppers (see Notes, page 6)

1 teaspoon salt

½ teaspoon ground cumin

½ teaspoon ground dried ancho chile peppers (see Notes, page 6)

½ teaspoon dried thyme leaves

Spice cake butter

4 tablespoons melted unsalted butter (or more if necessary, see above)

3 tablespoons lightly packed light brown sugar

1 teaspoon ground ginger

1 teaspoon ground dried árbol chile peppers (see Notes, page 6)

1 teaspoon salt

¾ teaspoon ground cinnamon

¾ teaspoon ground nutmeg

½ teaspoon ground mace

Muffin Cups

Andouille and Egg Muffin Cups

MAKES ABOUT 24 MUFFIN CUPS

A plateful of these on your breakfast table would be a terrific way to start the day! They have bread, andouille, and egg all in one. Or serve them as a light lunch. If you don't have very small eggs, you can use several large ones, beat them together, and spoon them over the top.

Timing is important with this recipe. You don't want the cups to rise after they're made (or there won't be room for the filling), so time the filling to be ready as the muffin cups are finished rising, or place the muffin tin in the refrigerator to stop the rising while you prepare the filling.

Muffin cups

2 large eggs

1 teaspoon salt

1 cup 2 percent fat milk

1 package active dry yeast

1 tablespoon sugar

$3\frac{1}{4}$ to $3\frac{1}{2}$ cups all-purpose flour

Flour for dusting

Vegetable oil spray

Andouille filling

Seasoning Mix

2 teaspoons paprika

2 teaspoons ground dried chipotle chile peppers (see Notes, page 6)

2 teaspoons salt

$1\frac{1}{2}$ teaspoons garlic powder

1 teaspoon ground allspice

1 teaspoon ground fenugreek (see Glossary, page 294)

1 teaspoon ground mace

1 teaspoon dry mustard

✳

6 tablespoons unsalted butter, in all

2 pounds diced andouille (see Glossary, page 292) or your favorite smoked sausage

2 cups finely diced onions

$1\frac{1}{2}$ cups finely diced green bell peppers

1 cup finely diced celery

2 cups beef stock, in all (see Notes, page 10)

6 tablespoons all-purpose flour

2 dozen very small eggs

continued

MUFFIN CUPS: Whisk the eggs in a bowl until they are frothy, then whisk in the salt.

Heat the milk to 110° in a microwave or on top of the stove and stir in the yeast and sugar.

Combine the eggs and the milk mixture in the bowl of an electric food mixer equipped with a dough hook. Stir briefly to combine, then with the mixer set on slow, gradually add 3¼ cups of the flour. Increase the speed to medium and process for 10 minutes. The dough should cling to the dough hook and be fairly elastic. If the dough is soft and sticky, add the remaining ¼ cup flour.

Reduce the speed to medium slow and continue to process for 5 more minutes, or until the dough is smooth, very elastic, and clinging to the dough hook.

Flour your hands well, then gather the dough into a ball. Place the dough in a heavy mixing bowl (a thick porcelain bowl is best) that has been lightly sprayed with vegetable spray. Very lightly spray the top of the dough, then put the dough in a warm, draft-free place. (We use the top of our stove, with the oven set at 300°. Or, if you have a gas oven with a pilot light, and you're not using the oven for anything else, put the dough in the unlighted oven, for the pilot light alone generates just enough warmth to encourage rising, and with the door closed the oven is completely draft-free.) Cover the bowl with a kitchen towel and let the dough rise until doubled in volume, about 1 hour.

Take a piece of dough roughly the size of a golf ball, flour it on all sides, and place it on a floured surface. Gently roll the dough out, working one direction at a time and rotating, turning, and flouring the dough frequently. When the dough is circular in shape and very thin, it is ready. Be sure that the thickness of the dough is even, especially at the edges.

Fold the circle of dough in half, then in half again, and drop the point into a cup of a muffin tin. Unfold the circle and, keeping the edges as even as possible, arrange the edges into a decorative, crinkly shape. Repeat with the remaining dough and put the tin into the refrigerator to keep the dough from rising while you prepare the filling.

ANDOUILLE FILLING: Combine the seasoning mix ingredients in a small bowl.

Heat a 4-quart pot over high heat for 4 minutes. Add 4 tablespoons of the butter and the andouille, onions, bell peppers, celery, and seasoning mix and cook, stirring frequently, until the mixture begins to stick to the pan bottom, about 10 minutes. Add 1/2 cup of the stock and scrape to loosen the brown bits. Sprinkle the flour evenly over the mixture and stir until the white of the flour is no longer visible. Continue to cook, stirring constantly, until the mixture begins to stick to the pan, about 3 to 4 minutes. Add the remaining stock, scrape the pan bottom thoroughly to loosen any brown bits, and cook, scraping the pan frequently, for 10 minutes.

Preheat the oven to 325°.

Melt the remaining butter.

Divide the andouille filling evenly among the cups and break 1 egg on top of each. Brush the edges with the melted butter and bake until the edges are browned and the filling is heated through, about 15 to 20 minutes. Serve piping hot, and if you should happen to have leftovers, freeze them to enjoy another time.

Ground Beef–Filled Muffin Cups

MAKES ABOUT 24 MUFFIN CUPS

There's a little surprise at the bottom of every one of these little meat pies—a portion of melted cheese! I think you'll like the way the chile pepper, caraway, and mace really bring out the ground beef flavor. These are great for appetizers, party snacks, at picnics and barbecues, and to stick in your pocket for a rainy day.

Timing is important with this recipe. You don't want the cups to rise after they're made (or there won't be room for the filling), so time the filling to be ready as the muffin cups are finished rising, or place the muffin tin in the refrigerator to stop the rising while you prepare the filling.

Muffin cups

2 large eggs

1 teaspoon salt

1 cup 2 percent fat milk

1 package active dry yeast

1 tablespoon sugar

3¼ to 3½ cups all-purpose flour

Flour for dusting

Vegetable oil spray

Ground beef filling

Seasoning Mix

1 tablespoon salt

2 teaspoons onion powder

2 teaspoons dried oregano leaves

2 teaspoons ground dried árbol chile peppers (see Notes, page 6)

1½ teaspoons garlic powder

1 teaspoon cayenne

1 teaspoon caraway seeds

1 teaspoon black pepper

1 teaspoon white pepper

½ teaspoon ground mace

✳

6 tablespoons unsalted butter, in all

2 pounds lean ground beef

2 cups finely diced onions

2 cups finely diced green bell peppers

2 cups finely diced celery

2 cups finely diced green bell peppers

6 tablespoons all-purpose flour

2 cups beef stock (see Notes, page 10)

3 cups grated Monterey Jack cheese

MUFFIN CUPS: Whisk the eggs in a bowl until they are frothy, then whisk in the salt.

Heat the milk to 110° in a microwave or on top of the stove and stir in the yeast and sugar.

Combine the eggs and the milk mixture in the bowl of an electric food mixer equipped with a dough hook. Stir briefly to combine, then with the mixer set on slow, gradually add 3¼ cups of the flour. Increase the speed to medium and process for 10 minutes. The dough should cling to the dough hook and be fairly elastic. If the dough is soft and sticky, add the remaining ¼ cup flour.

Reduce the speed to medium slow and continue to process for 5 more minutes, or until the dough is smooth, very elastic, and clinging to the dough hook.

Flour your hands well, then gather the dough into a ball. Place the dough in a heavy mixing bowl (a thick porcelain bowl is best) that has been lightly sprayed with vegetable spray. Very lightly spray the top of the dough, then put the dough in a warm, draft-free place. (We use the top of our stove, with the oven set at 300°. Or, if you have a gas oven with a pilot light, and you're not using the oven for anything else, put the dough in the unlighted oven, for the pilot light alone generates just enough warmth to encourage rising, and with the door closed the oven is completely draft-free.) Cover the bowl with a kitchen towel and let the dough rise until doubled in volume, about 1 hour.

Take a piece of dough roughly the size of a golf ball, flour it on all sides, and place it on a floured surface. Gently roll the dough out, working one direction at a time and rotating, turning, and flouring the dough frequently. When the dough is circular in shape, and very thin, it is ready. Be sure that the thickness of the dough is even, especially at the edges.

Fold the circle of dough in half, then in half again, and drop the point into a cup of a muffin tin. Unfold the circle and, keeping the edges as even as possible, arrange the edges into a decorative, crinkly shape. Repeat with the remaining dough and put the tin into the refrigerator to keep the dough from rising while you prepare the filling.

GROUND BEEF FILLING: Combine the seasoning mix ingredients in a small bowl.

Melt 4 tablespoons of the butter in a 4-quart pot over high heat. When the butter sizzles, add the meat and cook, stirring to break up any clumps, until nicely browned, about 5 to 6 minutes. Add the seasoning mix, onions, bell peppers, and celery and cook, stirring occasionally, for 10 minutes. Sprinkle the flour evenly over the mixture, then stir the flour into the beef juices until the white of the flour is no longer visible. Cook, continuing to stir and scrape and press down on the mixture to incorporate the flour into the meat mixture, until the mixture begins to stick to the pan bottom, about 3 to 4 minutes. Scrape the pan to loosen all the browned bits, then stir in the stock and scrape again to dissolve any remaining brown bits. Reduce the heat to medium and simmer, stirring and scraping the pan bottom frequently, until the mixture thickens, about 15 minutes.

Preheat the oven to 325°.

Melt the remaining butter.

Fill each muffin cup with 1 tablespoon grated cheese and divide the meat filling evenly among the cups. Brush the edges with the melted butter and bake until the edges are browned and the filling is heated through, about 15 to 20 minutes. Immediately remove from the oven and remove the muffin cups from the pan. Cool slightly and enjoy.

Spicy Cheese-Filled Muffin Cups

MAKES ABOUT 24 MUFFIN CUPS

Real men, and real women too, love to eat these miniature cheese cups. Serve them with drinks, as an appetizer, or with side dishes as a light meal.

Timing is important with this recipe. You don't want the cups to rise after they're made (or there won't be room for the filling), so time the filling to be ready as the muffin cups are finished rising, or place the muffin tin in the refrigerator to stop the rising while you prepare the filling.

Muffin cups

2 large eggs

1 teaspoon salt

1 cup 2-percent-fat milk

1 package active dry yeast

1 tablespoon sugar

3$\frac{1}{4}$ to 3$\frac{1}{2}$ cups all-purpose flour

Flour for dusting

Vegetable oil spray

Filling

1 pound ricotta cheese

12 ounces cream cheese

$\frac{3}{4}$ cup cane syrup (see Glossary, page 298)

$\frac{3}{4}$ cup heavy cream

4 large eggs

1 tablespoon plus 1$\frac{1}{2}$ teaspoons dried basil leaves

1$\frac{1}{2}$ teaspoons ground dried chipotle chile peppers (see Notes, page 6)

1$\frac{1}{2}$ teaspoons vanilla extract

✳

2 tablespoons melted unsalted butter

MUFFIN CUPS: Whisk the eggs until they are frothy, then whisk in the salt.

Heat the milk to 110° in a microwave or on top of the stove and stir in the yeast and sugar.

Combine the eggs and the milk mixture in the bowl of an electric food mixer equipped with a dough hook. Stir briefly to combine, then with the mixer set on slow, gradually add 3$\frac{1}{4}$ cups of the flour. Increase the speed to medium and process for 10 minutes. The dough should cling to the dough hook and be fairly elastic. If the dough is soft and sticky, add the remaining $\frac{1}{4}$ cup flour.

continued

Reduce the speed to medium slow and continue to process for 5 more minutes, or until the dough is smooth, very elastic, and clinging to the dough hook.

Flour your hands well, then gather the dough into a ball. Place the dough in a heavy mixing bowl (a thick porcelain bowl is best) that has been lightly sprayed with vegetable spray. Very lightly spray the top of the dough, then put the dough in a warm, draft-free place. (We use the top of our stove, with the oven set at 300°. Or, if you have a gas oven with a pilot light, and you're not using the oven for anything else, put the dough in the unlighted oven, for the pilot light alone generates just enough warmth to encourage rising, and with the door closed the oven is completely draft-free.) Cover the bowl with a kitchen towel and let the dough rise until doubled in volume, about 1 hour.

FILLING: Process all the filling ingredients in a blender or food processor until smooth.

ASSEMBLY: Take a piece of dough roughly the size of a golf ball, flour it on all sides, and place it on a floured surface. Gently roll the dough out, working one direction at a time and rotating, turning, and flouring the dough frequently. When the dough is circular in shape and very thin, it is ready. Be sure that the thickness of the dough is even, especially at the edges.

Fold the circle of dough in half, then in half again, and drop the point into a cup of a muffin tin. Unfold the circle and, keeping the edges as even as possible, arrange the edges into a decorative, crinkly shape. Repeat with the remaining dough.

Preheat the oven to 325°.

Divide the filling among the muffin cups and brush the edges with the melted butter. Bake until the cheese filling rises and turns golden brown, about 15 minutes. Immediately remove from the oven, remove the muffin cups from the pan, and serve.

Zucchini-Filled Muffin Cups

MAKES ABOUT 24 MUFFIN CUPS

These delicious little muffin cups can be served as an appetizer, a side dish, or the main course of a light lunch or supper. If you're in the mood to get creative with the dough, you can make the edges very decorative. I especially like the contrast between the chile peppers and the cinnamon and coriander; the combination is not uncomfortably hot, but it's spicy and unusual.

Timing is important with this recipe. You don't want the cups to rise after they're made (or there won't be room for the filling), so time the filling to be ready as the muffin cups are finished rising, or place the muffin tin in the refrigerator to stop the rising while you prepare the filling.

Muffin cups

 2 large eggs

 1 teaspoon salt

 1 cup 2 percent fat milk

 1 package active dry yeast

 1 tablespoon sugar

 3¼ to 3½ cups all-purpose flour

 Flour for dusting

 Vegetable oil spray

Filling

Seasoning Mix

 1½ teaspoons dried oregano
    leaves

 1 teaspoon dried basil leaves

 1 teaspoon garlic powder

 1 teaspoon paprika

 1 teaspoon ground dried guajillo
    chile peppers (see Notes,
    page 6)

 1 teaspoon salt

 ¾ teaspoon onion powder

 ½ teaspoon cayenne

 ½ teaspoon ground cinnamon

 ½ teaspoon ground coriander
    (see Glossary, page 293)

 ½ teaspoon black pepper

    *

 4 tablespoons unsalted butter, in all

 1¼ cups finely diced onions

 1¼ cups finely diced green bell
    peppers

 ½ cup finely diced celery

 1 (14½-ounce) can diced tomatoes
    (see Notes, page 7)

 2 tablespoons loosely packed
    dark brown sugar

 1 pound finely diced zucchini

continued

MUFFIN CUPS: Whisk the eggs in a bowl until they are frothy, then whisk in the salt.

Heat the milk to 110° in a microwave or on top of the stove and stir in the yeast and sugar.

Combine the eggs and the milk mixture in the bowl of an electric food mixer equipped with a dough hook. Stir briefly to combine, then with the mixer set on slow, gradually add 3¼ cups of the flour. Increase the speed to medium and process for 10 minutes. The dough should cling to the dough hook and be fairly elastic. If the dough is soft and sticky, add the remaining ¼ cup flour.

Reduce the speed to medium slow and continue to process for 5 more minutes, or until the dough is smooth, very elastic, and clinging to the dough hook.

Flour your hands well, then gather the dough into a ball. Place the dough in a heavy mixing bowl (a thick porcelain bowl is best) that has been lightly sprayed with vegetable spray. Very lightly spray the top of the dough, then put the dough in a warm, draft-free place. (We use the top of our stove, with the oven set at 300°. Or, if you have a gas oven with a pilot light, and you're not using the oven for anything else, put the dough in the unlighted oven, for the pilot light alone generates just enough warmth to encourage rising, and with the door closed the oven is completely draft-free.) Cover the bowl with a kitchen towel and let the dough rise until doubled in volume, about 1 hour.

Take a piece of dough roughly the size of a golf ball, flour it on all sides, and place it on a floured surface. Gently roll the dough out, working one direction at a time and rotating, turning and flouring the dough frequently. When the dough is circular in shape, about 5 to 6 inches in diameter, and very thin, it is ready. Be sure that the thickness of the dough is even, especially at the edges.

Fold the circle of dough in half, then in half again, and drop the point into a cup of a muffin tin. Unfold the circle and, keeping the edges as even as possible, arrange the edges into a decorative, crinkly shape. Repeat with the remaining dough and put the tin into the refrigerator to keep the dough from rising while you prepare the filling.

FILLING: Combine the seasoning mix ingredients in a small bowl.

Melt 2 tablespoons of the butter in a 12-inch skillet or 4-quart pot over high heat. When the butter sizzles, add the onions, bell peppers, celery, and seasoning mix. Cook, stirring and scraping the pan bottom frequently, until the mixture is a uniform dark brown and sticks hard to the bottom of the pan, about 8 minutes. Stir in the diced tomatoes and brown sugar. Reduce the heat to low and cook, scraping the pan bottom frequently, for 10 minutes. Stir in the zucchini, remove from the heat, and stir until all the ingredients are combined.

Preheat the oven to 325°.

Melt the remaining butter.

Divide the filling among the muffin cups and brush the edges with the melted butter. Bake until the edges are browned and the filling is heated through, about 20 minutes. Immediately remove from the oven, remove the muffin cups from the pan, and serve.

Ladles
of
Love

Fire-Roasted Garlic Soup

MAKES ABOUT 8 CUPS

Roasting the garlic and onions gives this soup a distinctive flavor that you can't get any other way, and the soup is hearty and satisfying without being heavy. Serve it with well-buttered freshly baked bread and a mixed green salad for a fine meal for family or friends.

Seasoning Mix

2 teaspoons salt

1½ teaspoons garlic powder

1 teaspoon dried basil leaves

1 teaspoon cayenne

1 teaspoon dry mustard

1 teaspoon onion powder

1 teaspoon white pepper

½ teaspoon black pepper

✳

2 onions, roasted (instructions follow) and chopped

3 heads garlic, roasted (instructions follow) and chopped

¼ cup olive oil

½ cup couscous (see Glossary, page 294)

6 tablespoons all-purpose flour

¼ cup white balsamic vinegar (see Glossary, page 299)

¼ cup tamari (see Glossary, page 299)

5 cups vegetable stock, in all (see Notes, page 10)

¼ cup honey

2 (13½-ounce) cans unsweetened coconut milk (see Glossary, page 293)

Combine the seasoning mix ingredients in a small bowl.

To roast the onions and garlic, if you have a gas range, simply place them right on the burner, in a high flame, and roast, turning with tongs, until the outer skin is charred all the way around. If your range is electric, you can roast in a preheated 500° oven. Plunge the roasted vegetables into ice water to stop the cooking, then rub off the black, charred skin under running water. It should slip right off, but if there are stubborn spots, just remove them with a sharp knife.

When roasting garlic, first remove the loose outer papery skin. After roasting, gently remove the cloves by pulling off the burned outer husk, which will be fairly hard and can be removed like a shell. The cloves inside will be a rich brown color and fairly soft. Removing the cloves is easy if you work from the bottom of the garlic head, gently prying the head open with your fingers and removing the cloves one at a time.

Heat the olive oil in a 5-quart pot over high heat just until it begins to smoke, about 3 to 4 minutes. Add the couscous and flour. Lower the heat to medium and cook, stirring constantly, for 3 minutes. Add the seasoning mix, onions, garlic, vinegar, and tamari and continue to cook, stirring and scraping the bottom of the pot constantly, for 2 minutes. Add 1 cup of the stock and cook, stirring constantly, for 4 minutes. Add 2 cups stock and cook, stirring frequently, for 8 minutes, then remove from the heat.

Purée the mixture in a blender or food processor, then return the mixture to the pot and stir in 1 cup stock. Bring to a boil, reduce the heat to low, and simmer, stirring occasionally, for 10 minutes. Add the remaining stock, the honey, and the coconut milk and simmer for 20 minutes. Stir gently and serve.

Greens Stew

MAKES ABOUT 10 CUPS

This recipe will work with just about any kind of greens, so choose your favorites or use your imagination and come up with a brand new combination! When I make dishes like this, I always like to use at least three different kinds of greens for a well-balanced flavor. Suggestions include spinach, cabbage, kale (if you can find purple and white, they make a pretty stew), mustard, turnip, and collards. If you use tough greens, use your judgment and add them a little earlier than we specify.

Seasoning Mix

2 teaspoons salt

1½ teaspoons dried basil leaves

1½ teaspoons garlic powder

1½ teaspoons onion powder

1¼ teaspoons ground coriander
(see Glossary, page 293)

1¼ teaspoons dry mustard

1¼ teaspoons ground turmeric

1 teaspoon ground fenugreek
(see Glossary, page 294)

1 teaspoon white pepper

1 teaspoon ground dried pasilla
chile peppers (see Notes,
page 6)

¾ teaspoon ground anise

¾ teaspoon ground ginger

¾ teaspoon black pepper

½ teaspoon cayenne

✳

10 tablespoons grits, toasted
(instructions follow)

8 ounces ground salt pork

2 cups chopped onions

1 cup chopped celery

8 cups vegetable stock, in all
(see Notes, page 10)

4 tablespoons unsalted butter

12 cups chopped greens, at least
3 varieties

8 ounces grated mozzarella cheese

Combine the seasoning mix ingredients in a small bowl.

Toast the grits in a small skillet over high heat, stirring constantly so all the grains will brown evenly, just until the grits are light golden brown. Immediately remove from the hot skillet to stop the toasting.

Boil the salt pork in just enough water to cover it for 10 minutes. Drain thoroughly.

Cook the drained salt pork in a 5-quart pot over high heat until the pork is nicely browned, about 5 to 6 minutes. Add the onions, celery, 2 tablespoons of the seasoning mix, and ½ cup of the stock. Cook, stirring occasionally, for 15 minutes, then add the remaining stock, the remaining seasoning mix, and the grits. Cook, stirring occasionally, until the grits are cooked, about 12 to 15 minutes. Add the butter and the greens, stir just until the butter melts, then add the cheese. Cook and stir until the cheese melts and the soup is smooth. Serve immediately.

Lemon Custard Soup

MAKES ABOUT 7 CUPS

Lemon is a great flavor in soup—just ask anyone from Greece, where egg and lemon soup is regular fare. This soup uses the same ingredients but takes them in an entirely new direction by making them into a custard. The soup is comforting when served hot and refreshing when slightly chilled.

Seasoning Mix

50 strands saffron (see Glossary, page 298)

2 teaspoons salt

1 teaspoon cayenne

1 teaspoon dill weed

1 teaspoon ground dried guajillo chile peppers (see Notes, page 6)

1 teaspoon dried thyme leaves

1 teaspoon ground turmeric

3/4 teaspoon white pepper

1/2 teaspoon garlic powder

1/2 teaspoon onion powder

1/2 teaspoon black pepper

1/2 teaspoon dried rosemary leaves

2 bay leaves

＊

7 tablespoons unsalted butter, in all

1 1/2 cups finely diced leeks, white parts only

Juice of 2 lemons (about 1/4 cup juice)

5 large egg yolks

2 tablespoons sugar

2 (5-ounce) cans evaporated milk

3 cups heavy cream

Combine the seasoning mix ingredients in a small bowl.

Set aside 4 tablespoons of the butter to allow it to soften.

Melt the remaining butter in a small skillet over high heat just until it sizzles, then add the leeks and cook, stirring frequently, for 3 minutes. Add the lemon juice and continue cooking until the liquid is reduced almost entirely, about 4 to 5 minutes, then remove from the heat.

In a large bowl, combine the egg yolks, softened butter, and sugar. Whisk until the mixture is frothy and all the sugar dissolves.

Combine the milk and cream in the top of a double boiler over 2 inches of boiling water and heat for 5 minutes. Remove $1/2$ cup of the milk-cream mixture and whisk it into the yolks. Return the yolk mixture to the cream, add the leek mixture from the skillet and the seasoning mix, and cook, stirring constantly, just until the soup begins to thicken and coat the back of a spoon, about 8 to 10 minutes. Remove from the heat and serve, or chill and serve.

Elixir of Portobello

MAKES 12 CUPS, ENOUGH FOR 12 APPETIZERS OR 6 MAIN-DISH SERVINGS

We used cane syrup the first several times we cooked this soup. Knowing that cane syrup may be hard to find in some parts of the country, and that some readers may want to try the recipe before they have a chance to find it, I wondered if it might work equally well with maple syrup. What a pleasant surprise! It's great with maple, but if this is your choice, use just 1/2 cup instead of the 3/4 cup called for with cane syrup. And do use pure maple syrup, not maple-flavored pancake syrup. The syrup, whichever variety you choose, is essential to reach the emotional highs that this soup creates, and the combination of other ingredients and seasonings brings out the special flavor of the portobello mushrooms.

Seasoning Mix

2 teaspoons paprika

2 teaspoons salt

1½ teaspoons dried basil leaves

1½ teaspoons ground dried chipotle chile peppers (see Notes, page 6)

1 teaspoon cayenne

1 teaspoon garlic powder

1 teaspoon onion powder

1 teaspoon white pepper

1 teaspoon ground dried guajillo chile peppers (see Notes, page 6)

1 teaspoon dried tarragon leaves

1 teaspoon dried rosemary leaves

½ teaspoon black pepper

＊

1 large onion, roasted (instructions follow) and chopped

8 ounces finely diced bacon

2 pounds medium-diced fresh portobello mushrooms, in all (see Glossary, page 296)

1 cup chopped green bell peppers

1 cup chopped red bell peppers

1 cup chopped celery

¾ cup cane syrup (see Glossary, page 298)

¼ cup all-purpose flour

6 cups beef stock (see Notes, page 10)

Combine the seasoning mix ingredients in a small bowl.

To roast the onion, if you have a gas range, simply place the onion right on the burner, in a high flame, and roast, turning with tongs, until the outer skin is charred all the way around. If your range is electric, you can roast in a preheated 500° oven. Plunge the roasted onion into ice water to stop the cooking, then rub off the black, charred skin under running water. It should slip right off, but if there are stubborn spots, just remove them with a sharp knife.

Render the bacon in a 5-quart pot over high heat until crisp, about 8 minutes. Add 1 pound of the mushrooms, all the bell peppers, the celery, and onion and cook, stirring occasionally, for 5 minutes. Add the syrup, flour, and seasoning mix and stir until the flour is completely absorbed. Stir in the stock and scrape the pot bottom thoroughly. Bring to a boil, add the remaining mushrooms, reduce the heat to medium-low, and cook at a brisk simmer for 30 minutes. Remove from the heat and serve.

Saucy Bell Pepper Soup

MAKES 7 CUPS

Here is a soup with all the rich flavor of a sauce. The brown flour taste is delicious when paired with beautiful bell peppers. If you are one of those people who use a spoon to get every drop of gravy, this soup is definitely for you.

Seasoning Mix

2 teaspoons salt

1½ teaspoons garlic powder

1 teaspoon dried basil leaves

1 teaspoon cayenne

1 teaspoon onion powder

1 teaspoon dry mustard

1 teaspoon white pepper

1 teaspoon ground dried guajillo chile peppers (see Notes, page 6)

1 teaspoon ground dried ancho chile peppers (see Notes, page 6)

½ teaspoon paprika

＊

½ cup vegetable oil

1 cup all-purpose flour

1 cup chopped green bell peppers

2 cups chopped red bell peppers

1 cup chopped yellow bell peppers

2 cups chopped onions

5 cups vegetable stock (see Notes, page 10)

Combine the seasoning mix ingredients in a small bowl.

Heat the oil in a heavy 5-quart pot just until the oil begins to smoke, about 4 minutes. Add the flour and whisk constantly, scraping the bottom of the pot, until the roux turns the color of milk chocolate. Be very careful not to let the flour brown too much, or it will become bitter. Also, at this point the roux is very hot, so be careful not to spatter any on yourself. (Notice we add the vegetables before the stock, to help prevent spatters.) Add all the bell peppers, the onions, the seasoning mix, and the stock. Whisk thoroughly until the roux is completely dissolved into the stock. Bring to a boil, reduce the heat to low, and simmer for 20 minutes. Remove from the heat and serve.

Squash Soup

MAKES ABOUT 12 CUPS

This soup is wonderful any time of year that you can find butternut squash, but it seems to me it's absolutely perfect on a cold day, with buttered dark bread right out of the oven (or bread-maker). If you want to serve a crowd, the recipe can be doubled or tripled, as long as you have a pot big enough to hold it.

Seasoning Mix

1 teaspoon salt

¾ teaspoon ground dill seeds

¾ teaspoon ground ginger

¾ teaspoon dry mustard

¾ teaspoon paprika

¾ teaspoon ground dried California Beauty chile peppers (see Notes, page 6)

¾ teaspoon ground dried guajillo chile peppers (see Notes, page 6)

½ teaspoon cayenne

½ teaspoon onion powder

½ teaspoon black pepper

½ teaspoon ground cinnamon

½ teaspoon garlic powder

½ teaspoon ground nutmeg

½ teaspoon white pepper

*

1 cup pine nuts (see Glossary, page 297)

4 tablespoons unsalted butter

1 cup chopped onions

1 cup medium-diced daikon (see Glossary, page 294)

1 cup chopped red bell peppers

1½ teaspoons minced fresh garlic

1½ teaspoons finely diced fresh jalapeño chile peppers (see Notes, page 6)

½ cup medium-packed finely chopped fresh parsley

4 cups fresh spinach, washed, stemmed, and chopped

1 medium butternut squash, peeled and diced into 1-inch cubes (about 4 to 5 cups)

1 cup vegetable stock (see Notes, page 10)

½ cup white grape juice

1 (12-ounce) can evaporated milk

1 cup heavy cream

Combine the seasoning mix ingredients in a small bowl.

Toast the pine nuts in a small skillet over high heat, stirring and shaking constantly until the nuts turn a rich golden brown without burning. Remove from the heat and set aside.

continued

Melt the butter in a heavy 5-quart pot over high heat. When the butter sizzles, add the onions, daikon, bell peppers, garlic, jalapeño peppers, parsley, spinach, squash, pine nuts, and seasoning mix. Reduce the heat to low and cook, stirring and scraping frequently, for 35 minutes. Remove from the heat and purée the mixture with the stock in a food processor or blender. Return the puréed mixture to the pot and stir in the grape juice and evaporated milk. Bring just to a boil, reduce the heat to low, and simmer for 25 minutes. Stir in the heavy cream, return just to a boil, remove from the heat, and serve.

Tomatillo Soup

MAKES ABOUT 7 CUPS

Although this soup is not overwhelmingly hot and peppery, it is well seasoned and can add a zesty international touch to your next entertainment. You may be able to buy your pumpkin seeds already toasted, but if they're also salted, reduce the salt in the seasoning mix by 1/2 teaspoon.

Seasoning Mix

2 teaspoons salt

1 teaspoon ground allspice

1 teaspoon dried basil leaves

1 teaspoon cayenne

1 teaspoon ground cumin

1 teaspoon ground fenugreek (see Glossary, page 294)

1 teaspoon garlic powder

1 teaspoon dried oregano leaves

¾ teaspoon onion powder

¾ teaspoon black pepper

½ teaspoon white pepper

✳

½ cup pumpkin seeds, toasted (instructions follow)

¼ cup cornmeal, toasted (instructions follow)

15 tomatillos (see Glossary, page 299), husks removed, parboiled for 10 minutes, and drained

3 cups vegetable stock (see Notes, page 10)

2 cups chopped red bell peppers

1 cup chopped yellow bell peppers

2 cups chopped onions

2 teaspoons tamari (see Glossary, page 299)

2 teaspoons white balsamic vinegar (see Glossary, page 299)

¼ cup honey

Combine the seasoning mix ingredients in a small bowl.

Toast the pumpkin seeds and cornmeal, separately, by placing them in a small skillet over high heat and stirring constantly until they reach the desired color. The pumpkin seeds should have light brown markings, and the cornmeal should be speckled light gray-brown. As soon as they are toasted, remove them from the hot skillet to stop the toasting.

Purée the tomatillos with the pumpkin seeds in a blender or food processor.

Place a 5-quart pot over high heat and add the puréed mixture and the seasoning mix, cornmeal, stock, bell peppers, onions, tamari, and vinegar. Cover and bring to a boil, then reduce the heat to low and simmer, stirring occasionally, for 1 hour. Stir in the honey and cook 5 minutes longer. Remove from the heat and serve.

Fennel and Split Pea Soup

MAKES ABOUT 8½ CUPS, ENOUGH FOR 8 APPETIZERS
OR 4 MAIN-DISH SERVINGS

The old saw about appearances being deceiving is true here—at first glance this soup looks exactly like the kind your grandma used to make. It's smooth and creamy, and just the right shade of green. But we've added fresh fennel (did you know it's also called anise, and its feathery leaves are used as an herb?) and several other nontraditional seasonings. If powdered hickory smoke is unavailable, use bottled smoke flavoring and add it the first time you add stock.

Seasoning Mix

1 teaspoon salt

1 teaspoon ground dried ancho chile peppers (see Notes, page 6)

1 teaspoon ground dried guajillo chile peppers (see Notes, page 6)

¾ teaspoon dried basil leaves

½ teaspoon dry mustard

½ teaspoon onion powder

½ teaspoon ground dried chipotle chile peppers (see Notes, page 6)

½ teaspoon dried thyme leaves

¼ teaspoon ground allspice

¼ teaspoon cayenne

¼ teaspoon ground coriander (see Glossary, page 293)

¼ teaspoon ground mace

¼ teaspoon black pepper

¼ teaspoon white pepper

¼ teaspoon powdered hickory smoke

✳

2 tablespoons vegetable oil

1 cup chopped onions

1 cup chopped green bell peppers

1½ cups chopped fresh fennel (1 whole bulb)

1 pound cooked ham, diced into ½-inch cubes

7 cups chicken stock, in all (see Notes, page 10)

1 pound dried green split peas, picked over and washed

2 cups heavy cream

Combine the seasoning mix ingredients in a small bowl.

Heat the oil in a 5-quart pot over high heat just until the oil begins to smoke, about 4 minutes. Add the onions, bell peppers, fennel, ham, and seasoning mix. Cover and cook, stirring frequently, for 15 minutes. Stir in 4 cups of the stock, the bottled smoke flavoring if using, and the peas. Cook, covered, for 20 minutes and stir in the remaining stock. Cover, bring just to a boil, reduce the heat to low, and simmer for 1½ hours. While the soup is cooking, don't go off and read a book—check it occasionally for sticking, and lower the heat even more if necessary. When the soup is done, stir in the cream and return just to a simmer before serving.

Lima Bean Soup

MAKES ABOUT 20 CUPS

This soup can be made any time of year, as long as fresh cilantro is available, for you can always find onions, celery, and garlic, and the main ingredients are dried lima beans and ham. If you have leftovers, this soup freezes very well. Be prepared—soak the beans the day before you plan to cook.

Seasoning Mix

2 teaspoons garlic powder

2 teaspoons dried oregano leaves

2 teaspoons salt

2 teaspoons dried tarragon leaves

1½ teaspoons onion powder

1½ teaspoons ground dried chipotle chile peppers (see Notes, page 6)

1 teaspoon ground allspice

1 teaspoon cayenne

1 teaspoon ground coriander (see Glossary, page 293)

¾ teaspoon black pepper

½ teaspoon ground cloves

½ teaspoon white pepper

✳

1 pound dried large lima beans, rinsed and picked over

3 cups chopped onions

2 cups chopped celery

1 pound cooked ham, diced into ½-inch cubes

½ cup medium-packed chopped fresh cilantro (see Notes, page 7, Glossary, page 293)

2 tablespoons minced fresh garlic

8 cups chicken stock (see Notes, page 10)

Day 1: Add enough water to the lima beans to cover them by 3 or 4 inches and soak overnight in the refrigerator.

Day 2: Drain but do not rinse the beans.

Combine the seasoning mix ingredients in a small bowl.

Place the beans, onions, celery, ham, cilantro, garlic, seasoning mix, and stock in a 5-quart pot over high heat. Cover and bring to a boil, then reduce the heat to low and simmer until the beans are tender and start to break up, about 1 hour. Remove from the heat and serve.

Pasta and Bean Soup

MAKES ABOUT 8 CUPS

It's hard to believe something that tastes so good can also be good for you, but it's true! This dish cries out for some hearty hot bread and a salad made of every kind of greens you can find at the market. Notice that the beans are to be soaked overnight, so plan ahead.

Seasoning Mix

2 teaspoons dry mustard

2 teaspoons paprika

2 teaspoons salt

1½ teaspoons dried basil leaves

1½ teaspoons onion powder

1½ teaspoons ground dried pasilla chile peppers (see Notes, page 6)

1 teaspoon garlic powder

1 teaspoon dried oregano leaves

1 teaspoon ground dried ancho chile peppers (see Notes, page 6)

1 teaspoon dried thyme leaves

¾ teaspoon black pepper

½ teaspoon cayenne

½ teaspoon white pepper

✳

1 pound dried lima beans

8 ounces finely diced bacon

2 cups chopped onions

1 cup chopped green bell peppers

4 cups chicken stock (see Notes, page 10)

2 cups cooked rotini or your favorite pasta

Day 1: Add enough water to the beans to cover them by 3 to 4 inches and soak overnight in the refrigerator.

Day 2: Combine the seasoning mix ingredients in a small bowl.

Drain but do not rinse the beans.

Render the bacon in a 5-quart pot over high heat until the bacon is browned. Add the onions, bell peppers, and seasoning mix and cook until the vegetables are wilted and beginning to brown, about 10 to 12 minutes. Add the beans and stock, bring to a boil, reduce the heat to low, and cover. Simmer, stirring occasionally, for 30 minutes. Remove 1 cup of the beans and purée them in a food processor or blender. Return the puréed mixture to the pot and stir until blended into the soup. Add the cooked pasta and simmer just until the pasta is heated through, about 2 minutes. Remove from the heat and serve.

Glutinous Rice Soup

This is probably the most surprising of all the dishes that I created for this book—the simple ingredients created a taste both unexpected and satisfying. I truly could have this as a soothing snack before bedtime or to calm me when I'm thinking bad thoughts about being late for any schedule. If you can't find glutinous rice, use regular (not instant) rice, then purée at the end of the recipe to develop the starches. This will produce less flavor than glutinous rice, but will still be very satisfying. I can't believe I cooked this recipe with water and stock instead of just stock, but it's one of the few that really works well with plain old water.

Seasoning Mix

2 tablespoons lightly packed light
    brown sugar

2 teaspoons salt

¾ teaspoon cayenne

½ teaspoon garlic powder

½ teaspoon onion powder

½ teaspoon white pepper

＊

3 tablespoons unsalted butter

2 cups chopped onions

4 cups chopped butternut squash
    (1 medium squash, about 1½
    pounds)

3 cups chicken stock (see Notes, page 10)

1 cup glutinous rice (see Glossary,
    page 297)

4 cups water, in all

½ cup cane syrup (see Glossary,
    page 298)

Combine the seasoning mix ingredients in a small bowl.

Melt the butter in a 4-quart pot over high heat. As soon as the butter sizzles, add the onions, squash, and seasoning mix. Cook, stirring occasionally, for 13 minutes, then remove from the heat and transfer the mixture to a blender or food processor. Purée the mixture and return it to the pot. Add the stock, bring to a boil, and add the rice. Reduce the heat to low and simmer for 30 minutes. Add 1 cup of the water and simmer for 30 minutes longer. Add 2 cups water and simmer for 15 minutes. Add the remaining water and the cane syrup, simmer for 5 more minutes, remove from the heat, and serve.

Oyster and Plantain Soup

MAKES 6 CUPS, ENOUGH FOR 6 APPETIZERS OR 3 MAIN-DISH SERVINGS

Unless you're exceptionally well traveled or have an unusually adventurous palate, the combination of ingredients in this dish is likely to seem peculiar at best and downright impossible at worst. Just say yes. One taste and you'll discover a blend of flavors that is admittedly unusual, yet works incredibly well.

Seasoning Mix

2 teaspoons salt

1½ teaspoons garlic powder

1½ teaspoons white pepper

1 teaspoon dried basil leaves

1 teaspoon cayenne

1 teaspoon onion powder

1 teaspoon dried tarragon leaves

1 teaspoon ground dried ancho chile peppers (see Notes, page 6)

½ teaspoon dried thyme leaves

＊

1 tablespoon all-purpose flour

1 cup chicken stock, in all (see Notes, page 10)

2 tablespoons unsalted butter

1 cup chopped onions

2 ripe plantains, peeled and finely diced (see Glossary, page 297)

2 (13½-ounce) cans unsweetened coconut milk (see Glossary, page 293)

1 cup heavy cream

1 pint fresh shucked oysters in their liquor (liquid inside the shell)

Combine the seasoning mix ingredients in a small bowl.

Dissolve the flour in 2 tablespoons of the stock.

Melt the butter in a heavy 5-quart pot over high heat. When it sizzles, add the onions and plantains and cook, stirring constantly, until the onions begin to brown and the plantains are tender, about 8 minutes. Add the remaining stock and deglaze the pot (that's just a fancy professional chef's term for scraping and using the liquid to loosen the brown bits). Add the seasoning mix, flour-stock mixture, and coconut milk. Stir well, then stir in the heavy cream. Bring just to a boil, stirring constantly, and add the oysters and their liquor. Return to a gentle boil, reduce the heat to medium, and cook, stirring occasionally, just until the oysters are heated through, about 3 minutes. Remove from the heat and serve.

Scallop and Lemon Grass Soup

MAKES ABOUT 8½ CUPS

Someone called this soup a convention of textures, with its firm but delicate mushrooms, crunchy celery, soft papayas, and the muscular scallops. The ingredients' flavors are something of a mixed bag too, but one bite will tell you how well they all work together.

Seasoning Mix

1 teaspoon ground dried ancho chile peppers (see Notes, page 6)

1 teaspoon salt

¾ teaspoon ground cardamom

¾ teaspoon cayenne

½ teaspoon garlic powder

½ teaspoon onion powder

½ teaspoon white pepper

¼ teaspoon ground coriander (see Glossary, page 293)

¼ teaspoon ground fenugreek (see Glossary, page 294)

¼ teaspoon black pepper

✳

2 ripe papayas, peeled, seeded, and chopped (see Glossary, page 297)

2 cups heavy cream

2 tablespoons plus 2 teaspoons minced fresh ginger, in all

2 teaspoons olive oil

4 tablespoons unsalted butter

2 cups chopped onions

1½ cups chopped celery

1 stalk lemon grass, cut diagonally into ½-inch pieces (see Glossary, page 295)

8 ounces oyster mushrooms, quartered (see Glossary, page 296)

2 teaspoons minced fresh garlic

1½ cups seafood stock, in all (see Notes, page 10)

1 pound fresh bay scallops

¼ cup finely chopped fresh cilantro (see Notes, page 7, Glossary, page 293)

Combine the seasoning mix ingredients in a small bowl.

Purée the papayas, cream, and 2 tablespoons of the ginger in a blender and set aside.

Heat the oil and butter in a 5-quart pot over high heat just until it begins to smoke, about 3 to 4 minutes. Add the onions, celery, lemon grass, and seasoning mix. Cook, stirring and scraping the pan bottom frequently, for 6 minutes. Add the oyster mushrooms, garlic, remaining ginger, and 1/2 cup of the stock. Cook, stirring frequently, for 5 minutes, then stir in the remaining stock and the puréed mixture. Cook, stirring occasionally, until the soup comes to a boil. Add the scallops, return to a boil, add the cilantro, and remove from the heat. Remove the lemon grass before serving.

Thu's Wonderful Soup

MAKES 5 CUPS, ENOUGH FOR 4 TO 5 APPETIZERS OR 2 MAIN-DISH SERVINGS

Visiting Hawaii, I always look forward to at least one meal at the home of Jerry Kringel, a cousin of Shawn McBride. Shawn and I always request Thu's Wonderful Soup.

Seasoning Mix

1½ teaspoons salt

1 teaspoon cayenne

1 teaspoon onion powder

1 teaspoon ground ancho chile peppers (see Notes, page 6)

¾ teaspoon garlic powder

¾ teaspoon black pepper

½ teaspoon white pepper

✳

2 tablespoons unsalted butter

2 cups sliced fresh mushrooms

1 medium stalk lemon grass, cut in diagonal slices (see Glossary, page 295)

2 teaspoons finely chopped fresh garlic

2 teaspoons finely chopped fresh serrano chile peppers (see Notes, page 6)

4 tablespoons lemon juice

2 tablespoons lime juice

3 tablespoons Thu's Fish Sauce (page 115)

4 cups chicken stock (see Notes, page 10)

½ pound peeled shrimp

1 tablespoon lightly packed chopped parsley

Combine the seasoning mix ingredients in a small bowl.

Melt the butter in a 4-quart pot over high heat. As soon as the butter begins to sizzle, add the mushrooms, lemon grass, garlic, serranos, and the seasoning mix. Cook, stirring frequently, and when the mixture begins to stick, about 2 minutes, add the lemon juice, lime juice, and fish sauce. Cook for 5 minutes over high heat until the liquid barely covers the bottom of the pan and is thick. Add the chicken stock, cover, and bring to a full boil. Add the shrimp and parsley, return to a full, rolling boil, remove from the heat and serve immediately.

Bacon, Lettuce, and Tomato Soup

MAKES ABOUT 9 CUPS

For those who love the unexpected, this is a perfect recipe! If you were having a Backwards Party or a lunch for April Fool's Day, you could serve this soup, Lentil Bread (page 36), and a dessert that looks like a fried egg (a poached apricot or peach half in a round mound of vanilla ice cream on a toasted slice of pound cake).

On the serious side, this is a seriously great soup—wonderful color, wonderful texture, and a very emotional taste.

Seasoning Mix

2 teaspoons salt

1½ teaspoons garlic powder

1½ teaspoons onion powder

1 teaspoon dried basil leaves

1 teaspoon caraway seeds

1 teaspoon cayenne

1 teaspoon dry mustard

1 teaspoon ground dried árbol chile peppers (see Notes, page 6)

1 teaspoon ground dried ancho chile peppers (see Notes, page 6)

½ teaspoon dried thyme leaves

2 bay leaves

✳

8 ounces finely diced bacon

2 cups chopped onions

1 cup chopped green bell peppers

1 cup chopped red bell peppers

1 cup chopped yellow bell peppers

4 cups chopped fresh tomatoes

2 cups vegetable stock (see Notes, page 10)

1 cup heavy cream

4 cups chopped lettuce, green-leaf or Boston preferred (not iceberg)

12 ounces grated sharp Cheddar cheese

Combine the seasoning mix ingredients in a small bowl.

Render the bacon in a 5-quart pot over high heat until it is browned, about 8 minutes, then add the onions, bell peppers, and 2 tablespoons of the seasoning mix.

continued

Cook, stirring frequently, until the vegetables wilt and start to brown, about 12 minutes. Add the tomatoes and the remaining seasoning mix and cook, stirring frequently, for 10 minutes, then add the stock. Bring to a boil, then reduce the heat to low, cover, and simmer for 30 minutes. Stir in the heavy cream and lettuce. Increase the heat to high and return the soup to a boil. Add the cheese, remove from the heat, and serve immediately.

Fire-Roasted Onion Bread

Apple Raisin Spice Bread

The technique for rolling filled breads is the same
whether using onions, black beans (above),
or any other ingredient

Ham Pockets

Skillet Breads

Ground Beef-Filled Muffin Cups

Fennel and Split Pea Soup

Lemon Custard Soup

Cucumber Salad with Yogurt Dressing

Hot and Sour Beef with Jicama Salad

Western Chili

T.J.'s Spring Rolls

Hot and Sour Shrimp

Curried Shrimp

Scallops and Eggplant

Fried Orange Roughy

Crawfish in Tomato-Sugar Snap Pea Gravy

Shrimp-Stuffed Poblanos

The Best Damned Grilled Chicken I Ever Ate!

Chicken in a Fruit Sauce

Coffee-Nut Chicken

Zucchini and Chicken Casserole

Tomato Cream Chicken

Fenugreek Chicken

Patricia's Pork Roast

King Midas Rice, Flank Steak with Black Mushrooms

Enchilada Casserole

Western Chili

MAKES ALMOST 10 CUPS, ENOUGH FOR 10 APPETIZERS OR
5 MAIN-DISH SERVINGS

This is the best chili recipe I've ever done. It brings you to the edge of ecstacy, of danger, of alarm, of excitement. If you like chili and don't cook this, you may not get into heaven!

Seasoning Mix

4 tablespoons ground dried
California Beauty chile peppers (see Notes, page 6)

1 tablespoon plus 2 teaspoons salt

2 teaspoons cayenne

2 teaspoons ground cumin

2 teaspoons garlic powder

2 teaspoons onion powder

2 teaspoons dried oregano leaves

2 teaspoons white pepper

2 teaspoons ground dried guajillo
chile peppers (see Notes,
page 6)

2 teaspoons dried thyme leaves

1½ teaspoons ground cinnamon

1½ teaspoons ground nutmeg

1½ teaspoons ground dried ancho
chile peppers (see Notes,
page 6)

1½ teaspoons ground dried pasilla
chile peppers (see Notes, page 6)

1 teaspoon ground coriander
(see Glossary, page 293)

1 teaspoon black pepper

＊

½ cup yellow cornmeal, toasted
(instructions follow)

3 tablespoons vegetable oil

2 pounds beef chuck, cut into ½-inch
cubes

1½ cups finely diced fresh Anaheim
chile peppers (see Notes, page 6)

4 cups chopped onions, in all

5 cups beef stock, in all (see Notes,
page 10)

1½ cups chopped green bell peppers

1½ cups chopped red bell peppers

1½ cups chopped yellow bell peppers

Combine the seasoning mix ingredients in a small bowl.

Toast the cornmeal in a 6- to 8-inch skillet over high heat, stirring constantly, until it turns light brown, about 10 minutes.

continued

Heat the oil in a 5-quart pot over high heat just until the oil begins to smoke, about 4 minutes. Add the meat and 4 tablespoons of the seasoning mix. Cook, stirring frequently, until the meat begins to brown, about 4 minutes. Stir in the fresh Anaheim peppers and 2 cups of the onions. Cook, stirring and scraping occasionally, for 7 minutes. Add the cornmeal and 1½ cups of the stock, vigorously stir and scrape the pan bottom, then add all the bell peppers and the remaining onions. Stir and scrape the pan bottom and stir in the remaining stock and the remaining seasoning mix. Bring to a boil, then reduce the heat to low, cover, and simmer, stirring occasionally, until the meat is tender and the chili is thick, about 1½ hours.

Remove from the heat and serve.

Little
Dishes

Fritters

Black-eyed Fritters
Potato and Daikon Fritters
White Bean Fritters

This 'n' That

T. J.'s Spring Rolls
Beef and Peanut Wrap
Fried Eggplant
Twice-Fried Plantain Chips
Chickpea Spread
Fresh Pickles
Marinated Roasted Peppers
Spiced Apples
Beet and Daikon Salad
Cucumber Salad with Yogurt Dressing
Jicama Salad
Homemade Noodles

Sauces

Greens Sauce
Spring Roll Dipping Sauce
Thu's Fish Sauce
Herbal Brown Sugar Dipping Sauce
Tamari Ginger Dipping Sauce

Fritters

Black-eyed Fritters

MAKES ABOUT 40 FRITTERS

The batter for these fritters will be a little sticky, so don't worry if they're not perfectly even around the edges—they'll still taste wonderful! I think they're perfect with drinks, as an appetizer, or as a side dish with spicy chicken or fish. If you're having a party, scoop the batter with a teaspoon to make the smaller size. They'll take longer to form but will cook a little quicker. Remember to soak the black-eyed peas the day before, to save cooking time.

Seasoning Mix

2½ teaspoons onion powder

2 teaspoons dried basil leaves

2 teaspoons garlic powder

2 teaspoons dry mustard

2 teaspoons black pepper

2 teaspoons salt

1 teaspoon cayenne

1 teaspoon ground cumin

1 teaspoon ground ginger

1 teaspoon dried thyme leaves

½ teaspoon white pepper

✳

½ pound dried black-eyed peas

¼ cup bacon drippings, preferred, or a combination of bacon drippings and butter or vegetable oil

1 cup chopped onions

½ cup chopped green bell peppers

1 tablespoon minced fresh ginger

1 teaspoon minced fresh garlic

2 cups chicken stock (see Notes, page 10)

1 large egg, slightly beaten

½ cup heavy cream

3½ cups all-purpose flour

3 tablespoons baking powder

2 cups vegetable oil

Day 1: Add enough water to the black-eyed peas to cover them by 3 or 4 inches and soak in the refrigerator overnight.

Day 2: Combine the seasoning mix ingredients in a small bowl.

Drain but do not rinse the black-eyed peas.

Heat the bacon drippings in a 3-quart pot over high heat for 4 minutes. Add the onions, bell peppers, ginger, garlic, seasoning mix, and black-eyed peas. Cook, stirring and scraping frequently, for 10 minutes. The vegetables and some of the peas will brown a little—this mixture looks and smells good enough to eat right now! Stir in the stock, scrape up the brown bits on the bottom of the pot, cover, and bring to a boil. Reduce the heat to low and simmer, stirring occasionally, for 30 minutes. Remove from the heat and let cool.

Combine the beaten egg with the heavy cream. Combine with the flour, baking powder, and cooled cooked vegetable mixture in a food processor and process until well blended. Refrigerate until well chilled.

Heat enough vegetable oil to measure 1 inch deep in a large skillet to 325° (use an electric or a regular skillet over high heat and a cooking thermometer, adjusting the heat as necessary).

With a large tablespoon, scoop up some of the batter to form a patty about 2½ inches across and ½ inch thick or shape the patties with well-floured hands. Fry in the hot oil until golden brown, turning frequently until done, about 6 to 8 minutes in all. We found that a slotted spoon, plus a spatula if necessary, works well for turning and removing the patties from the oil. Drain on paper towels before serving.

Potato and Daikon Fritters

These fritters are crunchy on the outside and tender-crisp inside. They make a great snack, especially if you give them a New York touch with a dollop of sour cream or applesauce on the side. An electric skillet is the perfect appliance for cooking these delicious fritters because it's so easy to control the temperature of the oil.

Seasoning Mix

2 teaspoons salt

1 teaspoon garlic powder

1 teaspoon onion powder

1 teaspoon ground dried ancho chile peppers (see Notes, page 6)

1/2 teaspoon dried basil leaves

1/2 teaspoon dried oregano leaves

1/2 teaspoon black pepper

1/2 teaspoon white pepper

1/2 teaspoon ground dried chipotle chile peppers (see Notes, page 6)

✳

2 cups grated potatoes

1 cup grated daikon (see Glossary, page 294)

1/2 cup chopped onions

2 large eggs

1 cup all-purpose flour

2 tablespoons medium packed dark brown sugar

2 cups vegetable oil

Combine the seasoning mix in a large bowl, then add all the remaining ingredients except the oil and mix thoroughly.

Heat the oil to 350° in a large skillet over high heat. When the oil is hot, drop spoonfuls—about 2 ounces each, enough to form a fritter about 3 inches in diameter—of the batter into the oil. Cook, turning the fritters several times, until golden brown, about 3 minutes. Drain on paper towels and serve immediately.

White Bean Fritters

MAKES ABOUT 24 FRITTERS

The raisins in these fritters give them a slightly sweet taste, so I think of them when I can't decide between a main course and a dessert. They're really great party food too. Remember to soak the beans the day before you want to make the fritters because that will cut the cooking time by more than half.

Seasoning Mix

1 tablespoon medium packed dark brown sugar

1 tablespoon salt

2 teaspoons dry mustard

2 teaspoons ground cinnamon

2 teaspoons ground mace

2 teaspoons ground dried chipotle chile peppers (see Notes, page 6)

½ teaspoon ground allspice

½ teaspoon cayenne

½ teaspoon black pepper

½ teaspoon white pepper

¼ teaspoon ground mustard

✳

1 pound dried white beans, picked over and rinsed

1 cup yellow cornmeal

2 tablespoons vegetable oil plus 2 cups for frying

2 cups chopped onions

1 cup chopped green bell peppers

1 tablespoon minced fresh garlic

3 cups chicken stock, in all (see Notes, page 10)

1 cup rice wine (see Glossary, page 297)

4 large eggs

2 tablespoons baking powder

1½ cups raisins

Day 1: Add enough water to the beans to cover them by 3 to 4 inches and soak overnight in the refrigerator.

Day 2: Toast the cornmeal in a small skillet over high heat, stirring constantly, until the cornmeal begins to brown and give off a rich, nutty aroma, about 4 minutes. Remove from the skillet to stop the toasting.

Combine the seasoning mix ingredients in a small bowl.

Drain but do not rinse the beans.

Heat 2 tablespoons of the oil in a 4-quart pot over high heat just until the oil begins to smoke, about 4 minutes. Add the onions, bell peppers, garlic, and seasoning mix. Cook until the vegetables are browned and wilted, about 12 minutes. Add 1 cup of the stock and stir and scrape the bottom, then add the beans and continue to cook and stir for 4 minutes. Add the rice wine and the remaining stock, bring to a boil, then reduce the heat to low. Cover and simmer, stirring occasionally, until the beans are tender, the liquid becomes thick and is almost completely evaporated, and the mixture is sticking hard (see Notes, page 10) to the bottom of the pot, about 45 minutes. Scrape the pot bottom thoroughly, then remove from the heat and cool.

Place three-quarters of the bean mixture, the eggs, baking powder, and cornmeal in a food processor or blender and purée until the mixture forms a very soft dough, about 2 minutes. Remove from the blender and stir in the remaining bean mixture and the raisins. Refrigerate until very cold, preferably overnight.

Heat the remaining 2 cups of oil in a large skillet over high heat to 350°. Shape the batter into 1/2 × 2-inch fritters and fry, turning often, until golden brown, about 2 minutes in all. Be careful not to overcook the fritters, as they darken very quickly. Drain on paper towels before serving.

This 'n' That

T. J.'s Spring Rolls

T.J. is the son of Thu (Thu's Wonderful Soup) and Jerry (Jerry's Lemon Grass Chicken), and what an offspring he is! Even at his tender age (he's just three years old), he knows and loves good food, and his very favorite snack is a plate of these crunchy spring rolls. You're gonna love 'em too.

My Spring Roll Dipping Sauce (page 114) adds the perfect finishing touch to this tubular feast.

Seasoning Mix

1 teaspoon cayenne

1 teaspoon garlic powder

1 teaspoon onion powder

1 teaspoon salt

1 teaspoon sugar

¾ teaspoon black pepper

¾ teaspoon ground árbol chile peppers (see Notes, page 6)

½ teaspoon ground allspice

½ teaspoon white pepper

✳

½ pound peeled shrimp

7 tablespoons Thu's Fish Sauce (page 115), in all

½ pound ground pork

4 ounces dried bean thread (see Glossary, page 292)

3 cups shrimp stock (see Notes, page 10)

2 cups julienne onions (see Notes, page 9)

2 cups julienne carrots

1 package (of at least 24) Vietnamese spring roll wrappers (see Glossary, page 298)

1 quart hot water

2 cups vegetable oil

Combine the seasoning mix ingredients in a small bowl.

Peel the shrimp, then cut them in half lengthwise and remove the vein. Cut each shrimp half into ½- to ¾-inch pieces. Season with 2 teaspoons of the seasoning mix and 1 tablespoon Thu's Fish Sauce, working the seasonings in with your hands.

Season the ground pork with 1 tablespoon plus 1 teaspoon of the seasoning mix and 2 tablespoons of Thu's Fish Sauce.

Cut the bean thread in half with a very sharp knife.

Bring the stock to a boil in a covered 12-inch skillet, turn off the heat, and cook the bean thread in the stock until soft. There will appear to be a lot of bean thread in the stock, but be patient and keep turning—it will soften. Drain the bean thread and season with the remaining seasoning mix. Return the stock to the skillet and reheat.

Season the vegetables with 1 teaspoon of the seasoning mix and 2 tablespoons of Thu's Fish Sauce.

To assemble, immerse 1 spring roll wrapper in water. Place the wrapper on your work surface and fill with 1 tablespoon of the meat mixture, about 15 strands each of the carrots and onions, and about 1 loose tablespoon bean thread. Moisten the edges of the wrapper with water, then fold 1 side of the wrapper over the filling and tuck it into a cylindrical shape. Fold in the sides, then roll up the wrapper. Repeat with the remaining wrappers and filling.

Heat the oil to 350° and fry the rolls, turning frequently, until golden brown, about 5 minutes. Drain on paper towels and serve with Spring Roll Dipping Sauce.

Beef and Peanut Wrap

MAKES 20 SPRING ROLLS

No matter where you've tried these Asian wraps, called spring rolls or egg rolls, it'd be very hard to find one with this particular non-Asian taste, but with these spectacular flavors and textures.

Meat filling

Seasoning Mix

2 teaspoons dried basil leaves

2 teaspoons cayenne

2 teaspoons onion powder

2 teaspoons dry mustard

2 teaspoons ground dried ancho chile peppers (see Notes, page 6)

2 teaspoons ground dried guajillo chile peppers (see Notes, page 6)

1¾ teaspoons ground fenugreek (see Glossary, page 294)

1½ teaspoons ground coriander (see Glossary, page 293)

1½ teaspoons ground cumin

1½ teaspoons salt

1 teaspoon garlic powder

1 teaspoon ground ginger

1 teaspoon black pepper

¾ teaspoon white pepper

✳

2 tablespoons vegetable oil

1½ cups chopped onions

1½ cups chopped green bell peppers

¼ cup finely chopped capers

1 tablespoon minced fresh garlic

1 cup beef stock, preferred, or chicken stock, in all (see Notes, page 10)

1 pound lean ground beef

1½ cups raisins

2 finely chopped fresh serrano or jalapeño chile peppers (see Notes, page 6)

Assembly and cooking

1 package (of at least 24) spring roll wrappers (see Glossary, page 298) or Vietnamese rice paper wrappers

1 quart hot water

1 cup loosely packed whole fresh cilantro leaves (see Notes, page 7, Glossary, page 293)

1¼ cups shelled fresh-roasted peanuts

3½ to 4 cups carrots, cut in fine julienne strips, about 2 inches long

3½ to 4 cups daikon, cut in fine julienne strips, about 2 inches long

3½ to 4 cups onion, cut in fine julienne strips, about 2 inches long (see Notes, page 9)

2 cups vegetable oil

MEAT FILLING: Combine the seasoning mix ingredients in a small bowl.

Heat the oil in a 12-inch skillet over high heat just until the oil begins to smoke, about 4 minutes. Add the onions, bell peppers, capers, and garlic and cook, stirring frequently, for 3 minutes. Add the seasoning mix and cook, scraping the pan constantly, until the seasoning mix begins to stick hard (see Notes, page 10). Add ½ cup of the stock and scrape vigorously to loosen the brown crust on the pan bottom. Remove from the heat and stir in the remaining stock.

Purée the mixture and refrigerate until cold. (If you want to chill the mixture quickly, spread it on a cookie sheet before refrigerating.) Combine the chilled purée with the meat, raisins, and chile peppers.

ASSEMBLY AND COOKING: To assemble, immerse 1 spring roll wrapper in the hot water until soft, about 1 minute. Place the wrapper on your work surface and place about 2 tablespoons of the meat filling across the center of the wrapper. Place 4 to 8 cilantro leaves (depending on size) in 1 layer on top of the meat filling, then 7 to 8 peanuts, about 20 strands of carrot julienne, about 20 strands of daikon julienne, and about 20 strands of onion julienne. Moisten the edges of the wrapper with water, then fold 1 side of the wrapper over the filling and tuck it into a cylindrical shape. Fold in the sides, then roll up the wrapper. Repeat with the remaining wrappers and filling.

Heat the oil to 350° and fry the rolls, turning frequently until golden brown, about 5 minutes. Drain on paper towels.

Serve with one of our dipping sauces (pages 114–116).

Fried Eggplant

MAKES 25 TO 30 PIECES

I was raised eating eggplant fixed many ways, and one of my favorites was fried. Just recently I discovered that putting sesame seeds in the final coating makes a huge difference in the taste and gives it extra crispness. The allspice, coriander, dill, and basil also make it different. Try a little powdered sugar on top right after you take the eggplant out of the skillet, or make one of our dipping sauces. I especially like the Spring Roll Dipping Sauce (page 114) and the Tamari Ginger Dipping Sauce (page 116) with this.

Seasoning Mix

1 tablespoon lightly packed light
    brown sugar

2 teaspoons salt

1 teaspoon ground allspice

1 teaspoon dried basil leaves

1 teaspoon cayenne

1 teaspoon ground coriander

1 teaspoon dill weed

1 teaspoon dried thyme leaves

¾ teaspoon onion powder

½ teaspoon garlic powder

½ teaspoon black pepper

½ teaspoon white pepper

Coating

1½ cups masa harina (see Glossary,
    page 294) or fine corn flour

½ cup sesame seeds

Egg wash

2 eggs

1 cup milk

✳

2 cups vegetable oil

1 large unpeeled eggplant, stem end
    trimmed

To make the coating, combine the seasoning mix ingredients, the masa harina, and sesame seeds in a large shallow bowl or flat pan.

To make the egg wash, whip the eggs with the milk in a bowl.

Heat the oil to 350° in a large skillet.

Slice the eggplant lengthwise into pieces about ½ inch thick and cut each slice into strips about 1 inch wide and 2 to 3 inches long. Dip the strips in the egg wash and drain off the excess liquid. Dredge the slices in the coating, then fry until the sesame seeds are golden brown, about 1½ to 2 minutes per side. Drain on paper towels and serve at once.

Twice-Fried Plantain Chips

MAKES 35 TO 40 PIECES

You don't have to like bananas to go ape over these snacks! They're very delicious, a little exotic, and the ladies say they look pretty on a serving plate. Serve them as an accompaniment to drinks or as a side dish with a tropical-style meal. Or sprinkle them with powdered sugar for an unusual dessert. Be sure to use very green plantains because the greener they are, the starchier they are, which gives them a better taste when fried.

Seasoning Mix

2 teaspoons sugar

1½ teaspoons salt

1 teaspoon ground turmeric

½ teaspoon ground cinnamon

½ teaspoon ground nutmeg

½ teaspoon ground dried chipotle chile peppers (see Notes, page 6)

✳

1 cup vegetable oil

4 very green plantains, peeled and sliced diagonally about ¾ inch thick (see Glossary, page 297)

Combine the seasoning mix ingredients in a small bowl.

Heat the oil in a large electric skillet (or use a regular skillet and a cooking thermometer and adjust the heat as necessary) over high heat to 350°, about 4 minutes.

Add just enough plantain slices to fill the skillet without crowding—it is important that the flat surfaces of the plantain slices remain in full contact with the bottom of the skillet at all times—and fry until golden brown, about 4 to 5 minutes per side. Keep the oil temperature as close to 350° as possible. Remove the browned slices and drain on paper towels, then repeat with the remaining slices.

With a meat mallet or similar object, mash each plantain slice to about ¼ inch thick—four good whacks should do it! Return the flattened slices to the oil and fry again until they are browned and crisp. Drain on paper towels and sprinkle each slice with a pinch of the seasoning mix. Serve immediately.

Chickpea Spread

MAKES ABOUT 3½ CUPS

Chickpea spreads and dips appear in a lot of cultures, but this particular recipe is one that I think is special. Serve it with your favorite raw vegetables, crackers, or chips, or as they do in Middle Eastern restaurants, with pita bread. You can also use it as you would a good mayonnaise—on sandwiches or with cold meats to add a wonderful flavor. I think it's good with anything in sight! Don't forget to soak the chickpeas overnight.

Seasoning Mix

2 teaspoons salt

1 teaspoon cayenne

1 teaspoon ground coriander
(see Glossary, page 293)

1 teaspoon ground fennel seeds

1 teaspoon garlic powder

1 teaspoon onion powder

1 teaspoon ground turmeric

½ teaspoon ground cumin

½ teaspoon black pepper

½ teaspoon white pepper

✳

½ pound dried chickpeas

2 whole heads garlic, yielding about
40 cloves

⅓ cup toasted sesame seeds
(instructions follow)

1 cup olive oil

2 tablespoons tamari (see Glossary,
page 299)

3 tablespoons white balsamic vinegar
(see Glossary, page 299)

½ cup honey

Juice of 2 lemons (about ¼ cup)

Day 1: Add enough water to the chickpeas to cover them by 3 or 4 inches and soak overnight.

Day 2: Drain but do not rinse the chickpeas.

Combine the seasoning mix ingredients in a small bowl.

To give the garlic a unique flavor essential to the outcome of this recipe, roast the whole heads. First remove the loose papery outer skins. If you have a gas range, simply place the heads right on the burner, in a high flame, and roast, turning with tongs, until the garlic is well charred on all sides. If your range is electric, you can roast in a preheated 500° oven. Plunge the roasted garlic into ice water to stop the cooking, then gently remove the cloves by pulling off the burned outer husk, which will be fairly hard and can be removed like a shell. The cloves will be a rich brown color and fairly soft inside. Removing the cloves is easy if you work from the bottom of the garlic head, gently prying the head open with your fingers, and removing the cloves one at a time.

Toast the sesame seeds to enhance their natural sweetness. Place them in a skillet over high heat and stir constantly as they brown, being careful to mix them completely so all brown evenly. As the seeds begin to heat up, they will start to pop— if the popping gets too active, reduce the heat slightly. Once the desired shade of brown is achieved, immediately remove from the hot skillet to stop the toasting action.

Purée the chickpeas with the seasoning mix, roasted garlic cloves, toasted sesame seeds, olive oil, tamari, vinegar, honey, and lemon juice. That's it!

Fresh Pickles

MAKES 15 CUPS

An unusual condiment, these vegetables are flavored but not actually preserved by the vinegars and spices, so you'll need to store them in the refrigerator. They make a wonderful addition to a salad plate, really jazz up cold meats, and are a great relish for the dinner table.

Seasoning Mix

6 tablespoons lightly packed light brown sugar

1 tablespoon plus 1 teaspoon onion powder

2 teaspoons ground allspice

2 teaspoons ground coriander (see Glossary, page 293)

2 teaspoons ground cumin

2 teaspoons garlic powder

2 teaspoons ground ginger

2 teaspoons dry mustard

2 teaspoons salt

2 teaspoons ground turmeric

1 teaspoon ground fenugreek (see Glossary, page 294)

1 teaspoon ground mace

※

2 cups rice wine (see Glossary, page 297)

1 cup balsamic vinegar (see Glossary, page 299)

1 cup cane vinegar (see Glossary, page 299)

1½ cups cane syrup (see Glossary, page 298)

3 cups water

1 large or 2 medium onions, medium diced

1 kohlrabi root, peeled and medium diced (see Glossary, page 295)

½ cup thinly sliced fresh ginger

1 head garlic, peeled and cut into ¼-inch slices (about 20 cloves)

1 mirliton, cut in half, seed removed, then peeled and diced (see Glossary, page 296)

4 medium carrots, cut into bite-sized pieces

4 ribs celery, sliced into ½-inch pieces

3 parsnips, peeled and diced into bite-sized pieces

1 large turnip, peeled and diced into bite-sized pieces

Combine the seasoning mix ingredients with the wine, vinegars, syrup, and water in a 3-quart pot. Bring to a boil, which will take about 20 minutes, and pour over the vegetables. Allow the vegetables to marinate for at least 2 hours, preferably overnight, and serve at room temperature. Remember to refrigerate any leftovers.

Marinated Roasted Peppers

MAKES 7 CUPS

Roasting the peppers gives them a delicious flavor that you can't get any other way. The fragrance reminds many people of rural Mexico, where the method is very popular. These peppers go well with just about any grilled or roasted meat, poultry, or fish, especially those that are lightly seasoned.

Seasoning Mix

2 tablespoons lightly packed dark brown sugar

2 teaspoons white sugar

1 teaspoon brown mustard seeds

1 teaspoon yellow mustard seeds

1 teaspoon salt

$1/2$ teaspoon garlic powder

$1/2$ teaspoon onion powder

40 black peppercorns

10 allspice berries

10 whole cloves

 ✳

$1/2$ cup balsamic vinegar (see Glossary, page 299)

$1/4$ cup rice vinegar (see Glossary, page 297)

$1/4$ cup tamari (see Glossary, page 299)

$1/2$ cup water

3 roasted green bell peppers (instructions follow)

3 roasted red bell peppers (instructions follow)

3 roasted yellow bell peppers (instructions follow)

Combine the seasoning mix ingredients with the vinegars, tamari, and water in a bowl.

To roast the peppers, if you have a gas range, simply place the peppers right on the burner, in a high flame, and roast, turning with tongs, until the outer skin is charred all the way around. If your range is electric, you can roast in a preheated 500° oven. Plunge the roasted peppers into ice water to stop the cooking, then rub off the black, charred skin under running water. It should slip right off, but if there are stubborn spots, just remove them with a sharp knife.

Cut the peppers into 1-inch squares and add them to the marinade. Marinate for at least 4 hours, preferably overnight, before serving. Store in the refrigerator.

Spiced Apples

If you like this recipe as much as I do, I'll bet you'll serve it with everything from scrambled eggs to pork chops to sandwiches! Have it always available so you can use it as often as you use pepper sauce, mustard, or any other relish or condiment. It perks up bland foods, and a small amount will bring much happiness.

Seasoning Mix

2 teaspoons onion powder

1 teaspoon ground allspice

1 teaspoon ground coriander
    (see Glossary, page 293)

1 teaspoon ground cumin

1 teaspoon garlic powder

1 teaspoon ground ginger

1 teaspoon dry mustard

1 teaspoon salt

1 teaspoon ground turmeric

½ teaspoon ground fenugreek
    (see Glossary, page 294)

½ teaspoon ground mace

✳

3 tablespoons olive oil

2 cups chopped onions

¼ cup sesame seeds

1 cup white vinegar

1½ cups white grape juice

3 cups finely diced unpeeled crisp
    red apples

3 cups finely diced unpeeled crisp
    green apples

2 cups raisins

1 tablespoon grated lemon peel

1 tablespoon grated lime peel

Combine the seasoning mix ingredients in a small bowl.

Heat the oil in a 3-quart pot over high heat just until it starts to smoke, about 3 to 4 minutes. Add the onions and cook, stirring frequently, for 8 minutes, reducing the heat to medium if necessary to prevent burning. Add the sesame seeds and cook for 2 minutes. Stir in the vinegar, grape juice, apples, raisins, lemon and lime peels, and seasoning mix. Bring to a boil, then reduce the heat to low, cover, and simmer for 1 hour. Refrigerate, covered, for at least 1 day, preferably longer, before serving.

Beet and Daikon Salad

MAKES 6 SERVINGS

Lots of people think they don't like beets, but then most people have tasted only canned ones. Fresh beets have a unique, earthy taste and a great texture. They also stain like indelible ink, so keep your good clothes and valuable papers far away when preparing this dish.

Seasoning Mix

2 teaspoons salt

1 teaspoon dried rosemary leaves

3/4 teaspoon ground cumin

1/2 teaspoon cayenne

1/2 teaspoon garlic powder

1/2 teaspoon onion powder

1/2 teaspoon white pepper

✳

1 daikon, about 9 inches long
(see Glossary, page 294)

1 quart water

5 medium beets, scrubbed but not
peeled, and the ends trimmed

2 tablespoons unsalted butter

2 cups diced onions

1/2 teaspoon brown mustard seeds

1/2 teaspoon yellow mustard seeds

3 bay leaves

1/4 cup rice vinegar (see Glossary,
page 299)

1/4 cup balsamic vinegar (see Glossary,
page 299)

1/2 cup white vinegar

1/4 cup dry sherry

1/2 cup medium packed light brown
sugar

2 tablespoons tamari (see Glossary,
page 299)

Combine the seasoning mix ingredients in a small bowl.

Peel the daikon and slice it into thin rounds.

Bring the water to a boil, add the beets, and boil until a fork penetrates slightly, about 20 minutes. Remove the beets, reserving the water in which they were cooked, and let them cool. When cool enough to handle, slice the beets into thin rounds.

Melt the butter in a 4-quart pot. When it begins to sizzle, add the onions, mustard seeds, bay leaves, and the seasoning mix and cook, stirring occasionally, until the onions begin to brown, about 12 minutes. Add the vinegars, sherry, brown sugar, and tamari and cook, stirring occasionally for 3 minutes, then add the daikon and cook for 5 minutes.

Add the beets and 2 cups of the reserved water in which they were cooked, bring just to a boil, and remove from the heat. Cool to room temperature and refrigerate. Allow the salad to marinate for at least 4 hours, preferably overnight, before serving.

Cucumber Salad with Yogurt Dressing

MAKES 9 CUPS OF SALAD AND DRESSING

When we say "matchstick size," we mean to cut the vegetables into strips about 3 inches long and only about ⅛ inch wide—about the size of old-fashioned kitchen matches. Slicing vegetables like this takes a little practice. The important thing is to get the first cut right because if you make it too big, then you'll have to go back and cut that piece once or twice more. After you get the hang of it, you'll be proud of how attractive your salad is. Try this versatile dressing with other fresh vegetable salads or as a dip for crudités.

Dressing

3 tablespoons sugar

1 teaspoon ground dried ancho chile peppers (see Notes, page 6)

1 teaspoon salt

¾ teaspoon caraway seeds

¾ teaspoon dill weed

1 (16-ounce) container lemon yogurt

½ teaspoon crushed red pepper flakes

¼ cup cane vinegar (see Glossary, page 299)

✳

½ medium onion, cut into matchstick strips

2 cucumbers, scraped lengthwise with the tines of a fork, or peeled, then sliced into rounds ⅛ inch thick

1 small green bell pepper, sliced into matchstick size

1 small red bell pepper, sliced into matchstick size

Process the dressing ingredients in a blender, and refrigerate for at least 4 hours. Combine the vegetables with the dressing in a large bowl just before serving.

Jicama Salad

Don't worry if you can't find rice vinegar and cane vinegar—you can use whatever varieties are available where you shop. You'll use only half the daikon, but that's OK, because you can grate or thinly slice the other half and add it to a green salad for a nice crunch.

Seasoning Mix

½ teaspoon salt

¼ teaspoon ground cinnamon

¼ teaspoon dry mustard

¼ teaspoon ground nutmeg

¼ teaspoon white pepper

¼ teaspoon ground dried ancho chile peppers (see Notes, page 6)

¼ teaspoon ground dried guajillo chile peppers (see Notes, page 6)

⅛ teaspoon ground allspice

⅛ teaspoon ground cloves

✳

½ cup orange juice

¼ cup water

¼ cup cane syrup, preferred, or light molasses (see Glossary, page 298)

2 tablespoons cane vinegar (see Glossary, page 299)

2 tablespoons rice vinegar (see Glossary, page 299)

1 small apple

1 small jicama (see Glossary, page 295)

1 small onion

1 small turnip

1 small cucumber

½ small daikon (see Glossary, page 294)

Combine the seasoning mix and liquid ingredients in a large bowl. Stir thoroughly until well blended.

Peel the apple and vegetables, core the apple, and cut them all into julienne strips (see Notes, page 9). Add the vegetables to the liquid mixture, stir well, cover, and marinate for at least 4 hours, preferably overnight. Stir gently and occasionally while it's marinating. Just before serving, stir again and drain each portion.

Homemade Noodles

MAKES ABOUT 3 POUNDS COOKED NOODLES

You don't have to be a kid to play with dough, and you don't have to own an expensive machine to make noodles. Working with this dough is very satisfying—there's something about really getting your hands into food that fills some kind of need to create, to make a useful product. When the product is a platter full of delicious homemade noodles, your pleasure expands to please a lot of other people.

Seasoning Mix

2 tablespoons medium packed light brown sugar

2 teaspoons ground dried California Beauty chile peppers (see Notes, page 6)

2 teaspoons ground dried guajillo chile peppers (see Notes, page 6)

2 teaspoons salt

1½ teaspoons cayenne

1¼ teaspoons onion powder

1½ teaspoons white pepper

1 teaspoon garlic powder

✳

1½ cups unsalted peanuts

3 tablespoons olive oil

2 cups chopped onions

1 tablespoon minced fresh garlic

2 cups all-purpose flour

6 ounces finely grated Parmesan cheese

6 large eggs

1 quart chicken or vegetable stock for cooking noodles (see Notes, page 10)

Combine the seasoning mix ingredients in a small bowl.

Grind the peanuts. The simplest way is to use a small coffee grinder, and the only difficult thing is to stop before you make peanut butter! Put a few peanuts in, turn the grinder on for no more than 1 or 2 seconds, and check to see if the peanuts are ground. If not, turn it on for a split second longer and check again. An alternative method is to chop the peanuts very fine, but this is more difficult and time-consuming.

Heat the oil in a medium-sized skillet over high heat just until the oil begins to smoke, about 4 minutes. Add the onions and cook, stirring frequently, until they are nicely browned, about 6 minutes. Add the seasoning mix and garlic, cook for 2 minutes, then remove from the heat.

continued

In a food processor or mixer, blend the flour, ground peanuts, cheese, eggs, and onion mixture until a soft, sticky dough forms, about 2 minutes. Turn out the dough onto a floured surface and fold it over several times, flouring each time until the dough is no longer sticky. Refrigerate for at least 4 hours.

Heat the stock to a brisk simmer.

Roll out the dough on a well-floured surface, then cut into strips. You may want to try different thicknesses and widths, but we found that rolling the dough to about 1/8 inch thick and cutting strips about 1/2 inch wide and no more than about 6 inches long worked well for us. This procedure makes flat noodles; if you want round ones, put a strip of dough on a floured surface, pinch it to a rounded shape, and roll with your floured hands until the noodle is round and smooth. The dough is fairly tender, so handle it with care to keep it from tearing.

Boil in the stock without crowding until tender, about 4 to 6 minutes, and drain on paper towels or in a colander before serving.

For a tasty snack, you can also deep-fry these noodles in 350° oil just until they start to brown; drain on paper towels before serving.

Sauces

Greens Sauce

MAKES ABOUT 5¾ CUPS

This combination of vegetables, herbs, and spices is the result of the kind of luck that sometimes happens while developing recipes. Use this sauce as a relish—it's tasty on its own, plus it enhances anything you put it on, from a piece of bread or a sandwich to a steak, boiled seafood, or cold chicken. It can be served cool or at room temperature.

Seasoning Mix

2 teaspoons dill weed

2 teaspoons salt

2 teaspoons dried tarragon leaves

1 teaspoon dried basil leaves

1 teaspoon cayenne

1 teaspoon dried chervil leaves

1 teaspoon garlic powder

1 teaspoon onion powder

1 teaspoon lightly packed dark brown sugar

1 teaspoon dried thyme leaves

½ teaspoon black pepper

½ teaspoon white pepper

✳

3 green bell peppers, roasted (instructions follow)

2 tablespoons vegetable oil

2 cups chopped onions

2 tablespoons chopped fresh ginger

2 cups chopped bok choy, white parts only (see Glossary, page 292)

4 cups chopped bok choy, green parts only

8 cups medium packed chopped spinach

1 cup chopped celery

2 teaspoons chopped fresh garlic

3 tablespoons balsamic vinegar (see Glossary, page 299)

1 tablespoon tamari (see Glossary, page 299)

2 tablespoons red wine vinegar

2 tablespoons rice wine (see Glossary, page 297)

½ cup medium packed chopped fresh cilantro (see Notes, page 7, Glossary, page 293)

½ cup chicken stock, preferred, or vegetable stock (see Notes, page 10)

Combine the seasoning mix ingredients in a small bowl.

continued

To roast the peppers, if you have a gas range, simply place the peppers right on the burner, in a high flame, and roast, turning with tongs, until the outer skin is charred all the way around. If your range is electric, you can roast in a preheated 500° oven. Plunge the roasted peppers into ice water to stop the cooking, then rub off the black, charred skin under running water. It should slip right off, but if there are stubborn spots, just remove them with a sharp knife.

Heat the vegetable oil in a 4-quart pot over high heat just until the oil begins to smoke, about 4 minutes. Add the onions and cook, stirring occasionally, until they begin to brown, about 8 minutes. Add the ginger and cook, stirring occasionally, until it is slightly browned, 1 to 2 minutes. Add all the bok choy and 3 tablespoons of the seasoning mix and stir very well, then add the spinach, celery, roasted bell peppers, and garlic. Cook, stirring occasionally, for 5 minutes, then add the remaining seasoning mix, balsamic vinegar, tamari, red wine vinegar, rice wine, cilantro, and stock. Stir briefly, then remove from the heat and cool.

Purée the mixture in a blender or food processor before serving. This sauce will last for weeks in the refrigerator.

Spring Roll Dipping Sauce

MAKES ABOUT 3 CUPS

Besides spring rolls, this dip is great with egg rolls, pot stickers (Chinese dumplings), or as a substitute for soy sauce.

2 cups water

6 tablespoons cane vinegar
(see Glossary, page 299)

2 tablespoons Magic Pepper
Sauce®

2 tablespoons sugar

2 tablespoons tamari (see Glossary,
page 299)

Combine all the ingredients, stir until blended, and serve at room temperature.

Thu's Fish Sauce

MAKES ABOUT 1¼ CUPS

After reading recipes sent from Hawaii by our friend Thu, I thought I'd like to make a fish sauce from scratch, instead of the prepared sauce called for. My sauce (version 1) is great, and so is Thu's (version 2), so here are both for you to take your choice.

Version 1

2 garlic cloves, smashed

1 chopped small fresh serrano or other variety chile pepper

1 tablespoon sugar

Juice of 1 lime

1 cup shrimp stock (see Notes, page 10)

½ teaspoon soy sauce

½ teaspoon Worcestershire sauce

1 tablespoon chopped dried shrimp

Version 2

2 garlic cloves, smashed

1 chopped small fresh serrano or other variety chile pepper (see Notes, page 6)

1 tablespoon sugar

Juice of 1 lime

1 cup water

3 tablespoons purchased Thai fish sauce

Combine all the ingredients and refrigerate for at least 1 hour, preferably 4, and serve at room temperature. Refrigerate any leftover sauce.

Herbal Brown Sugar Dipping Sauce

MAKES ABOUT 1¼ CUPS

Use this sauce as a zesty dip with fresh vegetables or as an accompaniment to our fried fish. It's hard to believe something so tasty can be so easy to make!

1 large egg

1 tablespoon balsamic vinegar

1 teaspoon lightly packed dark brown sugar

½ teaspoon dried basil leaves

1 tablespoon lime juice

1 teaspoon garlic powder

1 cup vegetable oil

Place all the ingredients except the oil in a blender and process at medium speed until smooth. With the blender still running, slowly add the oil in a thin trickle, making a mayonnaise-like mixture. Serve at room temperature and refrigerate any leftover sauce.

Tamari Ginger Dipping Sauce

MAKES ABOUT 1¼ CUPS

A flavorful sauce like this one has many uses—as a dip with crudités, as an unusual cocktail sauce for boiled seafood (shrimp comes to mind, but try other favorites), or as a condiment with broiled fish or poultry. I like it on a wedge of lettuce, and I'm sure you can come up with original ways to serve it.

1 large egg

Juice of 1 lemon

1 tablespoon tamari (see Glossary, page 299)

2 teaspoons Magic Pepper Sauce®

2 tablespoons ketchup

1 teaspoon ground ginger

½ teaspoon onion powder

1 cup vegetable oil

Place all the ingredients except the oil in a blender and process at medium speed until smooth. With the blender still running, slowly add the oil in a thin trickle, making a mayonnaise-like mixture to serve 101 different ways. Refrigerate any leftover sauce.

End of
the Line

Scallops and Eggplant

Curried Shrimp

Hot and Sour Shrimp

Pepper Tomato Shrimp

Shrimp and Okra

Shrimp in Mango Cream

Shrimp in a Salad Sauce

Shrimp and Sugar Snap Peas

Shrimp-Stuffed Poblanos

Sweet Shrimp in a Portabello Cream

Crawfish Pie

Crawfish in Tomato-Sugar Snap Pea Gravy

Fried Catfish

Fried Orange Roughy

Fried Tilapia

Broiled Catfish

Broiled Orange Roughy

Broiled Tuna Steaks

Scallops and Eggplant

MAKES 4 SERVINGS

Admittedly a very different way to serve scallops, this recipe is interesting for its herbal tomato sauce. And instead of serving the scallops and sauce on pasta, we present them on fried eggplant slices—a sweet change of pace.

Seasoning Mix

2 teaspoons dried oregano leaves

2 teaspoons salt

1½ teaspoons ground fenugreek (see Glossary, page 294)

1¼ teaspoons dried basil leaves

1¼ teaspoons onion powder

1¼ teaspoons black pepper

1 teaspoon cayenne

1 teaspoon ground fennel seeds

1 teaspoon garlic powder

1 teaspoon dried savory leaves

1 teaspoon dried thyme leaves

¾ teaspoon white pepper

✳

2 tablespoons olive oil

1 cup chopped onions

1 cup chopped green bell peppers

½ cup chopped celery

2 teaspoons minced fresh garlic

2 teaspoons minced fresh ginger

2 cups tomato sauce

½ cup chicken stock (see Notes, page 10)

1 pound bay scallops

2 cups vegetable oil

2 large eggs

1 cup corn flour (see Glossary, page 293)

1 large eggplant (at least 4 to 5 inches in diameter), cut crosswise into 8 slices

Combine the seasoning mix ingredients in a small bowl.

Heat the olive oil in a 4-quart pot over high heat just until the oil begins to smoke, about 4 minutes. Add the onions, bell peppers, celery, garlic, ginger, and 2 tablespoons of the seasoning mix. Cook, stirring and scraping the pan bottom frequently, until the vegetables are wilted and beginning to brown, about 10 to 12 minutes. Add the tomato sauce and the stock, reduce the heat to very low and cook, stirring frequently, until the sauce is thick and slightly reduced, up to but no more than 20 minutes. Add the scallops to the pot, return the sauce to a full boil, and remove from the heat.

continued

End of the Line **119**

Meanwhile, heat the vegetable oil in a large skillet over high heat just until the oil begins to smoke, about 4 minutes.

Whisk the eggs with 1 tablespoon of the seasoning mix in a shallow pan. Combine the corn flour with the remaining seasoning mix in another shallow pan. Dip the eggplant rounds into the egg mixture, then into the corn flour mixture, coating both sides. Fry in the oil until golden brown, about 2 to 3 minutes per side. Drain on paper towels.

Serve 2 eggplant rounds per person, and divide the scallops and sauce among the portions.

Curried Shrimp

MAKES 6 CUPS

The fresh chile peppers are important to this dish, but it doesn't matter greatly what kind you use, although red ones are best. Select whatever variety is freshest and firmest, but not too hot, at your market; some examples are Anaheim, California Beauty, New Mexico Red, Big Jim, and jalapeño.

Seasoning Mix

2 teaspoons ground cumin

1½ teaspoons ground cardamom

1½ teaspoons garlic powder

1½ teaspoons ground ginger

1 teaspoon ground allspice

1 teaspoon cayenne

1 teaspoon ground coriander
(see Glossary, page 293)

1 teaspoon onion powder

1 teaspoon ground dried ancho chile
peppers (see Notes, page 6)

1 teaspoon salt

1 teaspoon ground turmeric

¾ teaspoon black pepper

½ teaspoon white pepper

✳

2 tablespoons unsalted butter

2 cups chopped onions

2 finely diced very ripe bananas

¼ cup finely diced ripe chile peppers
(see Notes, page 6)

1 cup chopped yellow or red bell peppers

¾ cup raisins

¾ cup chopped hazelnuts

1 cup shrimp stock (see Notes, page 10)

1 (13½-ounce) can unsweetened
coconut milk (see Glossary,
page 293)

1 (8-ounce) container plain or vanilla
yogurt

1 pound peeled shrimp

Combine the seasoning mix ingredients in a small bowl.

Preheat a heavy 5-quart pot over high heat for 4 minutes. Add the butter, onions, and bananas. Stir thoroughly to coat the onions and bananas with butter, then add the chile peppers, bell peppers, raisins, hazelnuts, and seasoning mix. Reduce the heat to medium and cook, stirring and scraping the bottom of the pan frequently to pre-vent burning, until the mixture becomes very dry and sticks hard to the pot bottom (see Notes, page 10), about 15 minutes. Add the stock and continue to stir and scrape frequently until the mixture again becomes very dry and pasty and sticks hard to the pot bottom, about 10 minutes. Stir in the coconut milk and yogurt, return to a boil, then add the shrimp. Stir vigorously, reduce the heat to low, and cook just until the shrimp are opaque and plump, about 3 to 4 minutes. Serve hot over rice.

Hot and Sour Shrimp

MAKES ABOUT 10 CUPS

Mrs. Podunk told Chef Paul that this is way too hot! Chef Paul told Mrs. Podunk to go dunk!
He says this one jumps—and that's the way he likes it.

Seasoning Mix

1 teaspoon dill weed

1 teaspoon ground dried ancho
   chile peppers (see Notes,
   page 6)

1 teaspoon ground dried chipotle
   chile peppers (see Notes,
   page 6)

1 teaspoon ground dried guajillo
   chile peppers (see Notes,
   page 6)

1 teaspoon salt

$\frac{3}{4}$ teaspoon cayenne

$\frac{3}{4}$ teaspoon onion powder

$\frac{3}{4}$ teaspoon black pepper

$\frac{1}{2}$ teaspoon garlic powder

$\frac{1}{2}$ teaspoon ground ginger

$\frac{1}{2}$ teaspoon white pepper

✳

4 tablespoons sifted browned flour
   (instructions follow)

4 tablespoons unsalted butter

3 cups chopped onions

1 tablespoon minced fresh garlic

1 tablespoon minced fresh ginger

$4\frac{1}{2}$ cups shrimp stock, in all (see Notes,
   page 10)

3 cups chopped daikon (see Glossary,
   page 294)

3 cups chopped jicama (see Glossary,
   page 295)

Juice of 1 lime (about 3 tablespoons)

2 tablespoons firmly packed dark
   brown sugar

2 tablespoons white balsamic vinegar
   (see Glossary, page 299)

1 pound peeled shrimp

Combine the seasoning mix ingredients in a small bowl.

Brown the flour by heating over high heat in a small skillet, stirring constantly, just until it turns the color of milk chocolate. Immediately transfer it from the hot skillet to a bowl to stop the browning. Sift and set aside.

continued

Preheat a heavy 5-quart pot over high heat for 4 minutes. Add the butter, onions, garlic, ginger, and seasoning mix. Cook, stirring frequently, until the mixture begins to stick hard (see Notes, page 10), about 7 to 9 minutes. Stir in 1/2 cup of the stock and scrape the pot bottom vigorously to loosen the brown bits. Add the flour and stir until it is completely absorbed. Stir in the remaining stock, then add the daikon, jicama, lime juice, brown sugar, and vinegar. Cover and bring to a boil, then reduce the heat to low and simmer, stirring occasionally, for 15 minutes. Stir in the shrimp, return just to a boil, then lower the heat to medium and simmer just until the shrimp are opaque and plump, about 3 to 5 minutes. Serve immediately over rice.

Pepper Tomato Shrimp

MAKES ABOUT 8½ CUPS

This dish is sooooo good that I want to serve it almost every time I see beautiful fresh shrimp at the market! With the three colors of bell peppers, it's pretty too and makes a fine dish to set before company. It goes really well over pasta, but in the coastal states we generally serve food like this with rice.

Seasoning Mix

1½ teaspoons garlic powder

1½ teaspoons dried oregano leaves

1 teaspoon dried basil leaves

1 teaspoon cayenne

1 teaspoon ground coriander (see Glossary, page 293)

1 teaspoon ground fennel seeds

1 teaspoon onion powder

1 teaspoon ground dried árbol chile peppers (see Notes, page 6)

1 teaspoon salt

1 teaspoon dried thyme leaves

¾ teaspoon black pepper

½ teaspoon white pepper

∗

4 tablespoons unsalted butter

1 cup chopped green bell peppers

1 cup chopped red bell peppers

1 cup chopped yellow bell peppers

2 cups chopped onions

1 cup chopped celery

1 tablespoon minced fresh garlic

1 tablespoon minced fresh ginger

3 finely diced medium fresh jalapeño chile peppers (about 5 tablespoons) (see Notes, page 6)

1 (6-ounce) can tomato paste

1 cup shrimp stock (see Notes, page 10)

2 (14½-ounce) cans diced tomatoes (see Notes, page 7)

1 pound peeled shrimp

Combine the seasoning mix ingredients in a small bowl.

Preheat a heavy 5-quart pot over high heat for 4 minutes. Add the butter, bell peppers, onions, celery, garlic, ginger, jalapeño peppers, and seasoning mix. Cook, stirring and scraping the bottom of the pot frequently, until the vegetables are wilted and browned, and the mixture is sticking to the bottom, about 8 to 10 minutes. Add the tomato paste and stir constantly until the tomato paste begins to stick hard (see Notes, page 10), about 5 minutes, then immediately stir in the stock. Scrape the pan bottom to loosen any brown bits, and add the tomatoes. Cook, stirring frequently, for 10 minutes, then add the shrimp. Bring just to a boil, reduce the heat to medium, and simmer just until the shrimp are opaque and plump, about 3 to 5 minutes. Serve hot.

Shrimp and Okra

Here's an example of a really different seasoning combination—tarragon, cumin, dill weed, savory, filé, sage, and fresh ginger—that enhances the major ingredients. Okra, tomatoes, and shrimp go well together, and they are popular throughout the world wherever they are found.

Seasoning Mix

1½ teaspoons dried tarragon leaves

1 teaspoon ground cumin

1 teaspoon onion powder

1 teaspoon dill weed

1 teaspoon salt

1 teaspoon dried savory leaves

¾ teaspoon filé powder (see Glossary, page 294)

¾ teaspoon garlic powder

¾ teaspoon white pepper

½ teaspoon cayenne

½ teaspoon black pepper

½ teaspoon ground sage

✳

4 tablespoons unsalted butter

3 cups okra (no longer than 5 inches), sliced into rounds ¼ inch thick, in all

2 cups chopped onions

1 cup chopped celery

1 (14½-ounce) can diced tomatoes (see Notes, page 7)

2 teaspoons minced fresh garlic

2 teaspoons minced fresh ginger

1 (6-ounce) can tomato paste

2 cups shrimp stock (see Notes, page 10)

1 pound peeled shrimp

Combine the seasoning mix ingredients in a small bowl.

Preheat a heavy 5-quart pot over high heat for 4 minutes. Add the butter, 1 cup of the okra, the onions, celery, and seasoning mix. Cook, stirring and scraping the pan bottom frequently, until the mixture sticks hard (see Notes, page 10), about 6 to 8 minutes. Stir in the tomatoes, garlic, and ginger and cook, scraping the pan bottom frequently, for 10 minutes—it will stick hard again, so be careful! Stir in the tomato paste, scrape the pan bottom, and cook for 5 minutes. Add the remaining okra and the stock. Return to a boil, reduce the heat to low, and simmer, stirring occasionally, for 30 minutes. Stir in the shrimp and cook just until they are plump and opaque, about 3 to 5 minutes. Serve over rice.

Shrimp in Mango Cream

MAKES ABOUT 6 CUPS

Beautiful to look at, this smooth and creamy shrimp dish is great over rice or pasta. The use of fresh mangoes with shrimp may remind you of the Caribbean, and I think you'll enjoy the unusual and romantic combination of flavors.

Seasoning Mix

1 teaspoon ground coriander
(see Glossary, page 293)

1 teaspoon onion powder

1 teaspoon black pepper

1 teaspoon ground dried ancho chile
peppers (see Notes, page 6)

1 teaspoon salt

¾ teaspoon cayenne

¾ teaspoon ground cinnamon

¾ teaspoon garlic powder

¾ teaspoon white pepper

½ teaspoon ground cloves

½ teaspoon ground nutmeg

✳

2 medium-sized ripe mangoes, peeled
and pitted (see Glossary, page 295)

8 tablespoons (1 stick) unsalted butter

3 cups heavy cream

1 pound peeled shrimp

Combine the seasoning mix ingredients in a small bowl.

Purée the mangoes in a blender and set aside.

Heat the butter in a 4- or 5-quart pot over high heat, add the seasoning mix, and stir until the butter melts. Stir in the cream and cook, whisking constantly (which will help incorporate air into the sauce, making it light and fluffy), until the mixture just begins to boil. Stir in the shrimp, and as soon as they begin to turn opaque and plump and bubbles appear around the edges of the pot, add the mango purée. Stir constantly and bring the mixture to a full boil. Remove from the heat and serve immediately.

Shrimp in a Salad Sauce

We've jazzed up this shrimp and tomato dish with the addition of fresh ginger and sprouts. We used alfalfa sprouts, but you can use any variety of bean sprouts, radish sprouts, or whatever kind is available when you shop. They're all good, and you'll find each will give the dish a slightly different taste. Serve this over rice or pasta.

Seasoning Mix

2 teaspoons dried basil leaves

1 teaspoon garlic powder

1 teaspoon dry mustard

1 teaspoon salt

1 teaspoon dried thyme leaves

¾ teaspoon onion powder

½ teaspoon cayenne

¼ teaspoon black pepper

¼ teaspoon white pepper

✳

2 tablespoons olive oil

2 cups chopped onions

4 ounces tasso or your favorite smoked ham, cut into small julienne strips (see Notes, page 9)

1 cup chopped sprouts, in all

3 (14½-ounce) cans diced tomatoes (see Notes, page 7)

2 teaspoons minced fresh garlic

2 teaspoons minced fresh ginger

3 tablespoons finely diced fresh jalapeño chile peppers (see Notes, page 6)

1 pound peeled shrimp

½ cup packed chopped fresh cilantro (see Notes, page 7, Glossary, page 293)

Combine the seasoning mix ingredients in a small bowl.

Heat the oil in a 5-quart pot over high heat just until it begins to smoke, about 3 to 4 minutes. Add the onions, tasso or ham, ½ cup of the sprouts, and the seasoning mix. Cook, stirring frequently, for 10 minutes, then stir in the tomatoes, garlic, ginger, and jalapeño peppers. Continue to cook, stirring occasionally, for 10 minutes, then add the shrimp, the remaining sprouts, and the cilantro. Bring to a boil and cook just until the shrimp are plump and opaque, about 3 to 5 minutes. Serve immediately.

Shrimp and Sugar Snap Peas

This piquant dish shows its Asian heritage in its inclusion of fenugreek and sugar snap peas. Serve it over rice, either plain white or King Midas Rice (page 233), for a beautiful and healthful main dish. I must warn you, though, that it's a bit spicy, so if you prefer less heat, reduce the cayenne to 1 or ¹/₂ teaspoon. With all the other herbs and spices, it will still be well seasoned.

Seasoning Mix

2 teaspoons lightly packed dark
    brown sugar

1¹/₂ teaspoons cayenne

1 teaspoon ground fennel seed

1 teaspoon garlic powder

1 teaspoon onion powder

1 teaspoon black pepper

1 teaspoon salt

1 teaspoon dried savory leaves

1 teaspoon dried thyme leaves

³/₄ teaspoon white pepper

¹/₂ teaspoon ground fenugreek
    (see Glossary, page 294)

¹/₂ teaspoon ground ginger

✳

1 cup chopped onions

1 cup chopped celery

1 cup chopped green bell peppers

1 cup chopped carrots

4 tablespoons unsalted butter

2 tablespoons chopped fresh garlic

3¹/₂ cups shrimp stock, in all (see Notes,
    page 10)

3 tablespoons all-purpose flour

1 pound sugar snap peas, ends
    snipped and strings removed
    (see Glossary, page 298)

1 pound peeled shrimp

Combine the seasoning mix ingredients in a small bowl.

Preheat a heavy 5-quart pot over high heat for 4 minutes. Add the onions, celery, bell peppers, carrots, butter, and seasoning mix and cook, stirring frequently, for 10 minutes. Add the garlic, $1/2$ cup of the stock, and the flour and cook, stirring and scraping the pot bottom, until the mixture becomes pasty, about 1 to 2 minutes. Add the remaining stock and scrape the pot bottom thoroughly to loosen any brown bits. Bring the mixture to a boil, then add the sugar snap peas. Return the mixture to a full boil and add the shrimp. Reduce the heat to medium and cook just until the shrimp are plump and opaque, about 3 to 5 minutes. Serve immediately.

Shrimp-Stuffed Poblanos

MAKES 8 SERVINGS

This recipe reminds one of my assistants of a chorus—she says it's like a group of very different kinds of people all contributing their varied voices to create a unified piece of music. At first glance you might not think anyone can make a dish out of plantains, chile peppers, ground beef, shrimp, and tortillas. But you can and it will be absolutely fantastic! It will be beautiful to look at too. A note on poblano chiles: they're very irregular in shape, often twisted or bent. When choosing chiles for stuffing, try to find enough that are even and roundish.

Seasoning Mix

1³⁄₄ teaspoons ground cumin

1¹⁄₂ teaspoons cayenne

1¹⁄₂ teaspoons dried oregano leaves

1 teaspoon garlic powder

1 teaspoon onion powder

1 teaspoon white pepper

1 teaspoon ground dried ancho chile peppers (see Notes, page 6)

1 teaspoon ground dried chipotle chile peppers (see Notes, page 6)

1 teaspoon ground dried guajillo chile peppers (see Notes, page 6)

1 teaspoon salt

³⁄₄ teaspoon black pepper

*

8 fresh poblano chile peppers (see Notes, page 6)

2 tablespoons olive oil

¹⁄₂ pound lean ground beef

1 cup chopped onions

1 cup chopped green bell peppers

1 cup chopped red bell peppers

1 cup chopped yellow bell peppers

1 tablespoon minced fresh garlic

2 teaspoons minced fresh ginger

2 very ripe plantains, peeled and sliced into very thin rounds (see Glossary, page 297)

2 cups shrimp stock, in all (see Notes, page 10)

4 corn tortillas (the thick variety if possible), cut into ¹⁄₂-inch pieces

1 pound peeled shrimp

7 ounces grated Muenster cheese

10 ounces grated Monterey Jack cheese, in all

Combine the seasoning mix ingredients in a small bowl.

Prepare the chile peppers for stuffing by carefully cutting them in half and cutting out the seed pod with a sharp knife. Be careful not to pierce the skin within the cavity to be stuffed. If the peppers do not sit flat, and if their skins are thick enough to do so, make a small slice in the bottoms of the peppers to help keep them upright. Set them aside while you prepare the stuffing.

Heat the oil in a 4-quart pot over high heat just until it smokes, about 4 minutes. Add the ground beef and cook, stirring constantly, until the meat is nicely browned, about 3 to 4 minutes. Add the onions, all the bell peppers, and the seasoning mix and cook, stirring frequently, for 10 minutes. Add the garlic, ginger, and plantains and cook, stirring and scraping the pan bottom frequently and mashing the plantains with your spoon, for 10 minutes. When the mixture sticks hard (see Notes, page 10) to the pan bottom and turns brown in places, add 1 cup of the stock and scrape the pan bottom thoroughly to loosen any brown bits. Then add the remaining stock and the tortilla pieces, shrimp, Muenster cheese, and half of the Monterey Jack cheese. Cook, stirring occasionally, for 5 minutes or until the cheeses melt. Remove from the heat.

Preheat the oven to 350°.

Stuff each pepper half with ½ cup of the mixture. Top with the remaining Monterey Jack cheese. Bake until the tops are bubbly and beginning to brown, about 8 to 10 minutes. Serve hot.

Sweet Shrimp in a Portobello Cream

MAKES 4 SERVINGS

*If you've never cooked with portobello mushrooms, you're in for a treat. Our unusual season-
ing mix, with its combination of sweet and hot spices, really sets off the mushrooms' distinctive
flavor. Because the dish is a little hot, I think it is just perfect over a mound of basmati rice.*

Seasoning Mix

1½ teaspoons ground coriander
(see Glossary, page 293)

1 teaspoon black pepper

1 teaspoon ground dried ancho chile
peppers (see Notes, page 6)

1 teaspoon salt

¾ teaspoon ground allspice

¾ teaspoon ground cinnamon

¾ teaspoon garlic powder

¾ teaspoon onion powder

½ teaspoon cayenne

½ teaspoon ground mace

½ teaspoon ground nutmeg

½ teaspoon ground dried árbol chile
peppers (see Notes, page 6)

✳

3 tablespoons unsalted butter

1 cup chopped onions

½ cup chopped red bell peppers

½ cup chopped yellow bell peppers

12 ounces portobello mushrooms, cut
into pieces ½ × ½ × 2 inches
(see Glossary, page 296)

1 tablespoon minced fresh garlic

1 tablespoon minced fresh ginger

1 cup shrimp stock (see Notes, page 10)

1½ cups heavy cream

¼ cup cane syrup (see Glossary,
page 298) or your favorite syrup
(but please, not flavored
pancake syrup!) or honey

1 pound peeled shrimp

Combine the seasoning mix ingredients in a small bowl.

Heat a heavy 5-quart pot over high heat for 4 minutes. Add the butter, onions,
bell peppers, portobello mushrooms, garlic, ginger, and seasoning mix. Cook, stirring
frequently, until the mixture is sticking hard (see Notes, page 10) to the bottom of

the pot, about 5 to 6 minutes. Add the stock and scrape the bottom of the pot thoroughly to loosen the brown bits. Cook, stirring frequently, for 7 minutes, then add the cream and cane syrup (or your favorite syrup or honey). Bring just to a boil, then reduce the heat to low and simmer for 10 minutes. Stir in the shrimp, return the heat to high, and bring to a boil. Cook just until the shrimp are plump and opaque, about 4 minutes, then remove from the heat and serve.

Crawfish Pie

MAKES 2 9-INCH PIES

I've cooked many different kinds of crawfish pies in my life, starting when I was 10 years old! This one is unique, not only because of the seasonings we chose for the crawfish, but because of the unusual pie crust made with corn flour and seasoned with dry mustard and basil. Adding the mashed potatoes ties all the tastes together.

Pie Crusts

Seasoning Mix

1 tablespoon sugar

2 teaspoons dried basil leaves

2 teaspoons salt

1 teaspoon dry mustard

✳

2 cups all-purpose flour

1¼ cups yellow corn flour
(see Glossary, page 293)

1¼ cups very cold vegetable
shortening

¾ cup very cold water

Mashed Potatoes

1 cup heavy cream

4 tablespoons unsalted
butter, in all

4 cups mashed cooked white
potatoes

1 teaspoon salt

½ teaspoon black pepper

Vegetable mixture

Seasoning Mix

2 teaspoons cayenne

2 teaspoons ground coriander
(see Glossary, page 293)

2 teaspoons garlic powder

2 teaspoons dry mustard

2 teaspoons onion powder

2 teaspoons paprika

1½ teaspoons dried basil leaves

1½ teaspoons salt

1¼ teaspoons white pepper

✳

4 tablespoons unsalted butter

1 cup chopped celery

2 cups chopped onions

1½ cups chopped green bell peppers

✳

2 pounds peeled crawfish tails with fat

PIE CRUSTS: Combine the seasoning mix ingredients in a small bowl.

Combine the all-purpose flour, corn flour, and seasoning mix in an electric mixer equipped with a dough hook. Add the cold shortening and blend at low speed, scraping the sides and bottom of the bowl, until the ingredients just come together and resemble very coarse meal or dried split peas. Gradually add the very cold water and continue to process at low speed just until the water is absorbed, being careful not to overmix. As soon as the liquid is absorbed, gather the dough into a ball and refrigerate until cold, at least 4 hours, preferably overnight.

To make the pie shells, divide the dough in half and form each half into a ball. Liberally flour your hands, the working surface, and the rolling pin. Place one of the dough balls on the floured surface and roll it out, keeping it as even and round as possible. Turn the dough as you roll, and dust with flour as necessary, until the circle is about 11 inches in diameter. Carefully fit the circle into a 9-inch pie tin and crimp the edges with your hands or with the tines of a fork. Repeat with the remaining ball of dough. Set aside while you prepare the filling.

MASHED POTATOES: Heat the cream and butter in a small, heavy pot over medium-low heat, stirring occasionally, until the butter melts. Stir to combine and keep hot (but don't let it boil) until ready to add to the potatoes.

Whip the potatoes by hand or in an electric mixer until they are smooth and free of lumps. Stir in the cream and butter mixture, the salt, and pepper, and mix until well combined. Set aside.

VEGETABLE MIXTURE: Combine the seasoning mix ingredients in a small bowl.

Melt the butter in a 10-inch skillet over high heat. When the butter begins to sizzle, stir in the celery, onions, bell peppers, and seasoning mix, and stir to combine. Cover the skillet and cook, stirring and scraping the skillet bottom frequently, especially toward the end of the cooking time, until the vegetables are very soft and well browned, about 20 minutes.

ASSEMBLY: Preheat the oven to 350°. Fold the crawfish and the vegetable mixture into the mashed potatoes and mix until the crawfish and seasonings are evenly distributed throughout the potatoes. Divide the filling between the prepared pie shells. Bake until the crust is browned and the filling is golden brown, about 30 minutes. Baking for this period of time will marry the flavors completely. Cut into wedges to serve and get out of the way! Yum!

Crawfish in Tomato–Sugar Snap Pea Gravy

MAKES 5 CUPS

We've found a perfect match for the taste of crawfish—sugar snap peas! Putting them together in a tomato sauce makes an absolutely wonderful dish.

Seasoning Mix

2 teaspoons salt

1 teaspoon dried basil leaves

1 teaspoon cayenne

1 teaspoon dry mustard

1 teaspoon dried thyme leaves

¾ teaspoon onion powder

½ teaspoon garlic powder

½ teaspoon white pepper

　　✻

2 cups chopped fresh tomatoes

½ cup finely diced yellow bell peppers

½ cup finely diced onions

4 tablespoons unsalted butter

2 tablespoons all-purpose flour

2 cups seafood stock, preferred, or chicken stock, in all (see Notes, page 10)

½ pound sugar snap peas (see Glossary, page 298)

½ cup lightly packed whole fresh cilantro leaves (see Notes, page 7, Glossary, page 293)

1 pound crawfish tails with fat

Combine the seasoning mix ingredients in a small bowl.

In a 12-inch skillet over high heat, combine the tomatoes, bell peppers, onions, butter, and seasoning mix. Cook, stirring occasionally, for 8 minutes, then stir in the flour. Stir and cook until it starts to stick hard (see Notes, page 10), then stir in $\frac{1}{2}$ cup of the stock and scrape the skillet bottom vigorously to loosen the brown bits. Continue to cook, constantly stirring and scraping up the brown crust from the skillet bottom, until the liquid is almost evaporated, about 8 minutes. Add the sugar snap peas and the remaining stock. Cook for 3 minutes, then add the cilantro and the crawfish tails and fat. Cook for 3 more minutes, then remove from the heat and serve.

Fried Catfish

MAKES 4 SERVINGS

Close to 100 percent of the catfish on the retail market in the '90s are farm raised. Even though farm-raised catfish have a different and "softer" taste than wild ones, their consistency and mellow flavor certainly make them one of the leading fish varieties available in our supermarkets today.

It's important when you're frying always to do the last flouring just before the fish goes in the pan. You can hold the fish for a while in the wet mixture, but always do the last flouring just before frying. Remember to shake off the excess flour.

Seasoning Mix

2 teaspoons salt

1 teaspoon dried basil leaves

1 teaspoon ground bay leaves

1 teaspoon cayenne

1 teaspoon garlic powder

1 teaspoon dried marjoram leaves

1 teaspoon ground nutmeg

1 teaspoon onion powder

1 teaspoon ground dried árbol chile peppers (see Notes, page 6)

1 teaspoon dried rosemary leaves

1 teaspoon dried thyme leaves

½ teaspoon black pepper

½ teaspoon white pepper

✳

4 (6- to 8-ounce) catfish fillets, at room temperature

1 cup buttermilk

1 large egg

2 cups all-purpose flour

2 tablespoons sugar

1 tablespoon plus 2 teaspoons baking powder

2 cups vegetable oil

Combine the seasoning mix ingredients in a small bowl.

Remove any skin remaining on the fillets, then scrape them lightly with a kitchen knife to remove any excess surface oil (this oil is what makes some catfish taste "muddy"). Sprinkle the fillets evenly with ¾ teaspoon of the seasoning mix per side, gently rubbing it in.

Whisk the buttermilk and egg and 1 tablespoon of the seasoning mix in a large bowl until well blended.

Combine the flour, sugar, baking powder, and remaining seasoning mix in a large flat pan.

Heat the oil in a large skillet to 350°.

Dredge the seasoned fish fillets in the flour mixture, then in the egg-milk mixture, then back in the flour mixture, being sure to coat them completely and evenly. Immediately transfer the fish to the hot oil and cook, turning often with a spatula, until golden brown, about 3 to 4 minutes. Drain on paper towels and serve immediately.

Fried Orange Roughy

MAKES 4 SERVINGS

Here is a great way to make your life easier when frying fish. Always work with one hand wet and one hand dry. If you do all the wet battering with one hand, your flouring hand will not get covered with a sticky mess of flour and batter. We batter a lot of fish at my restaurant, and I can promise you that this method really saves time and aggravation. And the combination of herbs and spices will make this fish a totally new experience!

Seasoning Mix

$1\frac{1}{2}$ teaspoons cayenne

$1\frac{1}{2}$ teaspoons salt

$\frac{1}{2}$ teaspoon ground coriander
(see Glossary, page 293)

$\frac{1}{2}$ teaspoon ground cumin

$\frac{1}{2}$ teaspoon ground fenugreek
(see Glossary, page 294)

$\frac{1}{2}$ teaspoon garlic powder

$\frac{1}{2}$ teaspoon ground ginger

$\frac{1}{2}$ teaspoon dry mustard

$\frac{1}{2}$ teaspoon onion powder

$\frac{1}{2}$ teaspoon white pepper

$\frac{1}{2}$ teaspoon ground dried ancho
chile peppers (see Notes, page 6)

$\frac{1}{2}$ teaspoon ground dried guajillo chile
peppers (see Notes, page 6)

$\frac{1}{2}$ teaspoon ground turmeric

$\frac{1}{4}$ teaspoon black pepper

✳

1 cup milk

1 large egg

1 cup all-purpose flour

2 tablespoons sugar

1 tablespoon plus 2 teaspoons baking
powder

4 orange roughy fillets, at room
temperature

2 cups vegetable oil

Combine the seasoning mix ingredients in a small bowl.

Whisk the milk and egg in a large bowl until well blended.

Combine the flour, sugar, baking powder, and 2 teaspoons of the seasoning mix in a large flat pan.

Sprinkle each fillet with $\frac{1}{2}$ to $\frac{3}{4}$ teaspoon of the seasoning mix per side, depending on the size of the fillet.

Heat the oil in a large skillet to 350°.

Dredge the seasoned fillets in the flour mixture, then in the egg-milk mixture, then back in the flour mixture, being sure to coat them completely and evenly. Immediately transfer the fish to the hot oil and cook, turning several times with a slotted spoon, until the fish is golden brown, about 3 to 4 minutes. Drain on paper towels and serve immediately.

Fried Tilapia

MAKES 4 SERVINGS

When seasoning fish, it's a good idea to start seasoning at the thickest part of the fillet. That way, more of the seasoning will be on the thick part, which keeps the flavor evenly distributed. The yogurt in the batter and the combination of cumin, fennel seeds, filé powder, and fenugreek give this fried tilapia a lingering, exciting taste!

Seasoning Mix

2½ teaspoons cayenne

2½ teaspoons salt

1¼ teaspoons ground coriander
   (see Glossary, page 293)

1¼ teaspoons garlic powder

1¼ teaspoons onion powder

¾ teaspoon ground cumin

¾ teaspoon ground fennel seeds

¾ teaspoon filé powder
   (see Glossary, page 294)

¾ teaspoon white pepper

¾ teaspoon black pepper

¾ teaspoon ground dried ancho
   chile peppers (see Notes,
   page 6)

½ teaspoon ground cardamom

½ teaspoon ground bay leaf

½ teaspoon ground cinnamon

½ teaspoon ground cloves

½ teaspoon ground fenugreek
   (see Glossary, page 294)

½ teaspoon dried tarragon leaves

＊

4 (6- to 8-ounce) tilapia fillets

1 (8-ounce) container plain yogurt

¾ cup milk

1 large egg

1 cup all-purpose flour

2 tablespoons sugar

1 tablespoon plus 2 teaspoons baking
   powder

2 cups vegetable oil

Combine the seasoning mix ingredients in a small bowl.

Sprinkle each fillet with ½ to ¾ teaspoon of the seasoning mix per side, depending on the size of the fillet.

Whisk the yogurt, milk, and egg in a large bowl until well blended.

Combine the flour, sugar, baking powder, and remaining seasoning mix in a large flat pan.

Heat the oil in a large skillet to 350°.

Dredge the seasoned fish fillets in the flour mixture, then in the yogurt-egg mixture, then back in the flour mixture, being sure to coat them completely and evenly. Immediately transfer the fish to the hot oil and cook, turning often with a spatula, until golden brown, about 3 to 4 minutes. Drain on paper towels and serve immediately.

Broiled Catfish

MAKES 6 SERVINGS

The ground dried chile peppers are what stand out in this seasoning blend, but the contrast with the cloves and mace is what makes it unique.

Seasoning Mix

1 tablespoon salt

2 teaspoons ground cumin

2 teaspoons onion powder

2 teaspoons ground dried chipotle chile peppers (see Notes, page 6)

1½ teaspoons cayenne

1½ teaspoons garlic powder

1 teaspoon ground bay leaf

1 teaspoon ground cinnamon

1 teaspoon ground coriander (see Glossary, page 293)

1 teaspoon black pepper

1 teaspoon ground dried ancho chile peppers (see Notes, page 6)

¾ teaspoon white pepper

½ teaspoon ground cloves

½ teaspoon ground mace

✳

6 (6- to 8-ounce) catfish fillets, at room temperature

4 tablespoons melted unsalted butter

Combine the seasoning mix ingredients in a small bowl.

Place the broiler rack in the middle position and preheat the broiler.

Dip each fillet in melted butter, coating both sides. Sprinkle one side of each fish with ¾ teaspoon of the seasoning mix and place all the fillets, seasoned side down, on a broiler-proof pan. Season the other side of each fillet with ¾ teaspoon seasoning mix. Broil until the tops are browned but not burned, about 4 minutes. In this method we do not turn the fish. The center of the fillets should be just cooked through—white and opaque. Serve immediately.

Broiled Orange Roughy

MAKES 6 SERVINGS

The tarragon, thyme, and savory are the flavor leaders here and make this seasoning blend really different. You can use this seasoning mix with any kind of fish.

Seasoning Mix

1 tablespoon salt

2½ teaspoons cayenne

2 teaspoons dried basil leaves

2 teaspoons ground cumin

1¾ teaspoons onion powder

1 teaspoon garlic powder

1 teaspoon dry mustard

1 teaspoon black pepper

1 teaspoon ground dried árbol chile peppers (see Notes, page 6)

1 teaspoon ground dried chipotle chile peppers (see Notes, page 6)

1 teaspoon ground tarragon

1 teaspoon ground thyme

1 teaspoon ground savory

½ teaspoon white pepper

✳

6 (6- to 8-ounce) orange roughy fillets, at room temperature

4 tablespoons melted unsalted butter

Combine the seasoning mix ingredients in a small bowl.

Place the broiler rack in the middle position and preheat the broiler.

Dip each fillet in melted butter, coating both sides. Sprinkle one side of each fillet with ¾ teaspoon of the seasoning mix and place them, seasoned side down, on a broiler-proof pan. Season the other side of each fillet with ¾ teaspoon seasoning mix. Broil until the tops are browned but not burned, about 4 minutes. In this method we do not turn the fish. The center of the fillets should be just cooked through—opaque. Serve immediately.

Broiled Tuna Steaks

The sweet spices—anise, cinnamon, cloves, and ginger—although not usually found in season-ings for fish, really bring out the flavor of the tuna. Tuna is very much like steak; if you cook all the moisture out, you cook all the flavor out, which is why we warn you not to overcook it.

Seasoning Mix

1 tablespoon cayenne

1 tablespoon salt

1½ teaspoons garlic powder

1½ teaspoons onion powder

1¼ teaspoons ground fennel seeds

1 teaspoon ground anise

1 teaspoon ground cinnamon

1 teaspoon ground cloves

1 teaspoon ground ginger

¾ teaspoon black pepper

½ teaspoon white pepper

*

6 (8- to 10-ounce) tuna steaks, cut 1 inch thick, at room temperature

4 tablespoons melted unsalted butter

Combine the seasoning mix ingredients in a small bowl.

Place the broiler rack in the middle position and preheat the broiler.

Dip each tuna steak in melted butter, coating both sides. Sprinkle one side of each steak with ¾ teaspoon of the seasoning mix and place them, seasoned side down, on a broiler-proof pan. Season the other side of each steak with ¾ teaspoon seasoning mix. Broil until the tops are browned but not burned, about 4 minutes. In this method we do not turn the fish. The centers of the steaks should still be pink. Serve imme-diately.

Well-Traveled Chicken

The Best Damned Grilled Chicken I Ever Ate!

Chicken with Cabbage

Chicken in a Fruit Sauce

Chicken Papaya

Chicken with Oyster Mushrooms

Coffee-Nut Chicken

Mango Chicken

Onion Gingered Chicken

Tomatillo and Mushroom Chicken

Red-Eye Chicken

Frontier Chicken

Chicken Dippin'

Jerry's Lemon Grass Chicken

Chicken in Tamari Cream

Coconut Chicken

Chicken Sean

Zucchini and Chicken Casserole

Tomato Cream Chicken

Chicken in Cauliflower Cream

Fenugreek Chicken

The Best Damned Grilled Chicken I Ever Ate!

MAKES 4 SERVINGS

The title says it all.

If a grill is not available, an alternative is to broil the pieces until a nice brown crust forms, then bake in a 300° oven until done. Or rub a whole chicken inside and out with the paste and roast in a 300° oven until done, about 3 hours.

Seasoning Paste

2 tablespoons salt

2 tablespoons sugar

1 tablespoon plus 1½ teaspoons soy sauce

1 tablespoon plus 1 teaspoon onion powder

1 tablespoon plus ¾ teaspoon ground ginger

1 tablespoon garlic powder

1 tablespoon grated lemon peel

1 tablespoon grated lime peel

1½ teaspoons white pepper

1¼ teaspoons ground cardamom

1¼ teaspoons ground cinnamon

1¼ teaspoons ground nutmeg

1¼ teaspoons ground savory

¾ teaspoon ground allspice

¾ teaspoon black pepper

¾ teaspoon ground dried habañero chile peppers (see Notes, page 6)

4 bay leaves

*

1 (3- to 4-pound) chicken, cut into 8 pieces

4 tablespoons unsalted butter

Combine the seasoning paste ingredients in a large bowl or 1-gallon zipper plastic bag. Place the chicken pieces in the bowl or bag and rub the pieces evenly with the seasoning paste. Cover the bowl tightly with plastic wrap, or zip the bag, and refrigerate for 6 to 8 hours.

When ready to cook, light the coals or prepare the grill according to directions. While waiting for the coals to reach the white-ash stage or for the grill to reach the cooking stage, bring the chicken to room temperature. Melt the butter. With a spoon, gently scrape as much of the seasoning paste as possible off the chicken, combine it with any paste remaining in the bowl or zipper bag, and stir it into the butter.

continued

Place the large pieces of chicken over the hottest coals or hottest section of the grill and the smaller pieces over the less-hot section, and cook, turning the pieces and basting several times with the butter-paste mixture, until done. Serve and enjoy!

Chicken with Cabbage

MAKES 4 SERVINGS

This very pretty chicken dish has a wonderfully fragrant sauce that's rich looking but not dark brown. And the bright green and red bell peppers contrast nicely in flavor, texture, and color with the light green cabbage. A delicious down-home dish like this one is a good choice when you or someone in your family needs a little comforting. I especially like it served with brown rice or browned white rice.

Seasoning Mix

1 tablespoon plus 1 teaspoon salt

1 tablespoon plus 1 teaspoon sugar

1 tablespoon onion powder

2½ teaspoons ground ginger

2 teaspoons garlic powder

2 teaspoons grated lemon peel

2 teaspoons grated lime peel

1 teaspoon white pepper

¾ teaspoon ground cardamom

¾ teaspoon ground cinnamon

¾ teaspoon ground nutmeg

¾ teaspoon ground savory

½ teaspoon ground allspice

½ teaspoon black pepper

½ teaspoon ground dried habañero chile peppers (see Notes, page 6)

3 bay leaves

*

2 tablespoons all-purpose flour

3 cups chicken stock, in all
(see Notes, page 10)

1 (3- to 4-pound) chicken, cut into
8 pieces

2 tablespoons vegetable oil

1 cup chopped onions

6 cups chopped cabbage (about
1 small head), in all

1½ cups chopped green bell peppers

1½ cups chopped red bell peppers

2 tablespoons chopped fresh cilantro
(see Notes, page 7, Glossary,
page 293)

¼ cup balsamic vinegar (see Glossary,
page 299)

1 tablespoon soy sauce

Combine the seasoning mix ingredients in a small bowl.

Dissolve the flour in ¼ cup of the stock and set aside.

Sprinkle the chicken evenly with half of the seasoning mix and rub it in well.

Heat the oil in a heavy 5-quart pot over high heat just until it begins to smoke, about 4 minutes. Add the seasoned chicken in batches, large pieces first and skin sides down first, and brown about 2 to 3 minutes per side. Remove the chicken from the pot and set it aside.

Add the onions and 3 cups of the cabbage to the pot and cook, stirring and scraping frequently, until the onions start to brown, about 4 minutes. Add all the bell peppers, the cilantro, vinegar, soy sauce, remaining seasoning mix, and flour stock mixture. Cook, stirring almost constantly, until the mixture comes to a boil, about 2 minutes, then add the remaining cabbage and the remaining stock. Return the chicken and the accumulated juices to the pot. Bring to a boil, reduce the heat to low, and simmer until the chicken is tender, about 30 minutes. Serve immediately.

Chicken in a Fruit Sauce

MAKES 4 SERVINGS

We don't often think of chicken and fruit together as a main dish, but such a combination is the kind of thing that makes the recipes in this book unique. Take advantage of the way the unusual and the unexpected come together to create flavors that reach deep down into your soul!

Seasoning Mix

2 teaspoons salt

1½ teaspoons cayenne

1 teaspoon dried basil leaves

1 teaspoon garlic powder

1 teaspoon dry mustard

1 teaspoon onion powder

1 teaspoon dried oregano leaves

1 teaspoon black pepper

1 teaspoon white pepper

1 teaspoon ground dried guajillo chile peppers (see Notes, page 6)

1 teaspoon ground dried pasilla chile peppers (see Notes, page 6)

1 teaspoon dried thyme leaves

❋

1 (3- to 4-pound) chicken, cut into 8 pieces

2 tablespoons vegetable oil

2 cups chopped onions

5 cups peeled, pitted, and sliced fresh plums

1 cup chopped green bell peppers

1 cup chopped red bell peppers

1 cup chopped yellow bell peppers

1 cup chicken stock (see Notes, page 10)

½ cup honey

Combine the seasoning mix ingredients in a small bowl.

Sprinkle the chicken pieces evenly with 1 tablespoon plus 2 teaspoons of the seasoning mix and rub it in well.

Heat the oil in a heavy 5-quart pot over high heat just until the oil begins to smoke, about 4 minutes. Lightly brown the seasoned chicken pieces, in batches if necessary, about 2 minutes per side. Remove the chicken pieces and add the onions and plums. Cover and cook, stirring occasionally, for 10 minutes, then add the remaining seasoning mix. Cover and cook for 4 minutes, then add the bell peppers and return the chicken to the pot. Cover and cook, stirring occasionally, for 10 minutes. Add the stock and honey, bring to a boil, reduce the heat to low, and simmer until the chicken is done, about 15 minutes. Serve with brown rice.

Chicken Papaya

MAKES 4 SERVINGS

My second favorite thing about this dish is the combination of textures—the crunch of the peanuts, the tender chicken, and the juicy chunks of papaya. My very favorite thing? The way the flavors contrast with one another, yet work together to form an exciting whole. Try serving this with boiled bulgur, barely blanched spinach, and lime wedges.

Seasoning Mix

2 teaspoons salt

1½ teaspoons onion powder

1 teaspoon whole anise seeds

1 teaspoon cayenne

1 teaspoon garlic powder

1 teaspoon ground ginger

1 teaspoon black pepper

1 teaspoon white pepper

¾ teaspoon ground cinnamon

½ teaspoon ground allspice

½ teaspoon ground nutmeg

✳

1 (3- to 4-pound) chicken, cut into 8 pieces

2 tablespoons vegetable oil

3 medium-size ripe papayas, peeled, seeded, and diced into 1-inch cubes (see Glossary, page 297)

2 cups chopped onions

2 cups medium packed chopped fresh parsley

1 cup chopped roasted unsalted peanuts

1½ cups chicken stock (see Notes, page 10)

1 (12-fluid-ounce) can natural papaya nectar

Combine the seasoning mix ingredients in a small bowl.

Sprinkle 2 tablespoons of the seasoning mix evenly over the chicken and rub it in well.

Heat the oil in a heavy 5-quart pot over high heat just until the oil begins to smoke, about 4 minutes. Add the seasoned chicken in batches, large pieces first and skin sides down first, and brown about 2 to 3 minutes per side. Remove the chicken from the pot and set it aside.

Add the papayas, onions, parsley, and peanuts to the pot, mix well, and cover and cook, stirring once or twice, for 5 minutes. Stir in the remaining seasoning mix and cook for 3 minutes. Add the stock, scrape the bottom of the pot to loosen any brown bits, and cook for 10 minutes. Stir in the papaya nectar, then return the chicken and the accumulated juices to the pot. Cover and bring to a boil, then reduce the heat to low and simmer, covered, until the chicken is done, about 10 minutes. Serve immediately.

Chicken with Oyster Mushrooms

MAKES 4 SERVINGS

This savory chicken is cooked in a beautiful, creamy, golden sauce that is spicy but not too hot for my friend Mrs. Podunk. I like to serve it with perfectly plain white rice, maybe garnished with thin slices of green onions and a dollop of pungent chutney. Be careful not to overcook the chicken—you don't want it to get tough—so you might remove the smaller pieces before the cooking time is up. Check the larger pieces by cutting into the center part; if the meat is firm and opaque, without a trace of red, it's done.

Seasoning Mix

1 tablespoon lightly packed light
   brown sugar

2 teaspoons salt

2 teaspoons garlic powder

2 teaspoons ground turmeric

1½ teaspoons onion powder

1½ teaspoons dry mustard

1½ teaspoons ground dried guajillo
   chile peppers (see Notes, page 6)

1 teaspoon ground dried ancho chile
   peppers (see Notes, page 6)

¾ teaspoon black pepper

¾ teaspoon white pepper

¾ teaspoon ground coriander
   (see Glossary, page 293)

¾ teaspoon ground dried chipotle
   chile peppers (see Notes, page 6)

¾ teaspoon dill weed

¾ teaspoon ground nutmeg

   ✳

1 tablespoon all-purpose flour

1 cup chicken stock, in all (see Notes,
   page 10)

1 (3- to 4-pound) chicken, cut into
   8 pieces

2 tablespoons vegetable oil

2 cups chopped onions

¾ cup chopped fresh oyster mushrooms (see Glossary, page 296)

1½ tablespoons minced fresh ginger

1 tablespoon minced fresh garlic

1 cup raisins

3 cups canned unsweetened coconut
   milk (see Glossary, page 293)

Combine the seasoning mix ingredients in a small bowl.

Dissolve the flour in 2 tablespoons of the stock and set aside.

Sprinkle the chicken evenly with 4 tablespoons of the seasoning mix and rub it in well.

Heat the oil in a heavy 5-quart pot over high heat just until the oil begins to smoke, about 4 minutes. Add the seasoned chicken in batches, large pieces first and skin sides down first, and brown about 2 to 3 minutes per side. Remove the chicken from the pot and set it aside.

Add the onions and the mushrooms to the pot and cook, scraping as necessary to keep from sticking, until the onions begin to brown, about 2 to 3 minutes. Add the ginger and garlic, reduce the heat to medium, and stir in the raisins, the remaining stock, and the remaining seasoning mix. Scrape the bottom of the pot to loosen any brown bits, then stir in the coconut milk and the flour-stock mixture. Bring just to a boil and stir again to make sure the flour is evenly distributed throughout the mixture. Return the chicken and the accumulated juices to the pot, cover, and return just to a boil. Reduce the heat to low and simmer, stirring occasionally, until the chicken is done, about 25 to 30 minutes. Serve hot.

Coffee-Nut Chicken

MAKES 4 SERVINGS

This is the kind of unusual recipe that can make your reputation for innovation! Practice your Mona Lisa smile and be very mysterious about what secret ingredients give this dish its unique flavor. If you can't find instant coffee with chicory where you shop, don't panic; just use the darkest, best-quality instant coffee available.

Seasoning Mix

2 tablespoons lightly packed light brown sugar

2 teaspoons ground dried guajillo chile peppers (see Notes, page 6)

2 teaspoons ground dried ancho chile peppers (see Notes, page 6)

2 teaspoons salt

1½ teaspoons ground cumin

1½ teaspoons garlic powder

1¼ teaspoons onion powder

1¼ teaspoons dried oregano leaves

1 teaspoon dried basil leaves

½ teaspoon ground cloves

Coffee-nut purée

½ cup pumpkin seeds, toasted (instructions follow)

½ cup chopped pecans, toasted (instructions follow)

2 tablespoons poppy seeds, toasted (instructions follow)

2 tablespoons sesame seeds, toasted (instructions follow)

1 cup chicken stock (see Notes, page 10)

2 tablespoons lightly packed light brown sugar

3 tablespoons instant coffee with chicory

✳

1 (3- to 4-pound) chicken, cut into 8 pieces

2 tablespoons vegetable oil

1 cup chopped onions

2½ cups chicken stock, in all

Combine the seasoning mix ingredients in a small bowl.

Toast the pumpkin seeds, pecans, poppy seeds, and sesame seeds, one type at a time, in a small skillet over medium heat, stirring and shaking the pan constantly to avoid scorching, until they start to darken. The pumpkin seeds and pecans will take 4 to 6 minutes, and the poppy and sesame seeds will take 1 to 2 minutes.

To make the coffee-nut purée, process the seeds and pecans with the stock in a blender until smooth. Add the brown sugar and instant coffee and process at high speed for 1 minute.

Sprinkle the chicken evenly with 2 tablespoons of the seasoning mix and rub it in well.

Heat the oil in a heavy 5-quart pot over high heat just until the oil begins to smoke, about 4 minutes. Brown the seasoned chicken in batches, large pieces first and skin sides down first, about 2 to 3 minutes per side. Remove the chicken from the pot and set it aside.

Add the onions and 1 tablespoon seasoning mix to the pot. Cook for 5 minutes or until the onions are wilted and turning a rich golden brown. Stir in 1 cup of the stock and scrape the bottom of the pot to loosen the brown bits. Stir in the coffee-nut purée, the remaining seasoning mix, and the remaining stock. Bring to a boil, then return the chicken and the accumulated juices to the pot. Reduce the heat to low and simmer until the chicken is tender, about 30 minutes. Remove from the heat and serve.

Mango Chicken

MAKES 4 SERVINGS

In the United States, if we eat mangoes at all, we generally have them uncooked, splashed with a bit of lime juice. But throughout the tropics, wherever they grow, good cooks use mangoes in a variety of ways—cooked and raw. In this dish they add sweetness and, along with the eggplant, an interesting texture contrast to the chicken.

Seasoning Mix

2 tablespoons lightly packed dark brown sugar

2 teaspoons salt

1½ teaspoons onion powder

1½ teaspoons ground dried chipotle chile peppers (see Notes, page 6)

1 teaspoon ground cumin

1 teaspoon dry mustard

1 teaspoon white pepper

1 teaspoon ground dried guajillo chile peppers (see Notes, page 6)

½ teaspoon cayenne

½ teaspoon garlic powder

½ teaspoon ground mace

✳

1 (3- to 4-pound) chicken, cut into 8 pieces

2 tablespoons vegetable oil

1½ cups chopped onions, in all

1½ cups finely diced red bell peppers, in all

2 bay leaves

8 finely diced fresh serrano chile peppers (see Notes, page 6)

3½ cups chopped unpeeled eggplant

1½ cups chicken stock, in all (see Notes, page 10)

2 tablespoons tamari (see Glossary, page 299)

2 large or 3 small ripe mangoes, peeled and diced into ½-inch cubes (see Glossary, page 295)

2 cups heavy cream

Combine the seasoning mix ingredients in a small bowl.

Sprinkle 2 tablespoons of the seasoning mix evenly over the chicken and rub it in well.

Heat the oil in a heavy 5-quart pot over high heat just until the oil begins to smoke, about 4 minutes. Brown the seasoned chicken in batches, large pieces first and skin sides down first, about 2 to 3 minutes per side. Remove the chicken from the pot and set it aside.

Add 1 cup of the onions, 1 cup of the bell peppers, the bay leaves, and the chile peppers to the pot. Cook, stirring occasionally, for 4 minutes and add the eggplant. Cook, stirring occasionally, for 2 minutes, then add 1 cup of the stock, the tamari, the mangoes, and the remaining onions, bell peppers, and seasoning mix. Stir well, then return the chicken and the accumulated juices to the pot. Reduce the heat to low, cover, and simmer, stirring and scraping the bottom of the pot occasionally, for 12 minutes. Stir in the remaining stock and simmer, covered, for 15 minutes more. Stir in the heavy cream and cook for 4 minutes. Serve immediately.

Onion Gingered Chicken

MAKES 4 SERVINGS

While this dish is cooking, its spicy-sweet aroma is going to make it hard to keep your family or friends from sneaking tastes. Tell them it's OK to have some of the sauce—it would be great to dunk French bread into it—but they have to wait until it's done before they can have any chicken. Give them a really stern look if you have to! One of the things I like best about this recipe is that it looks very impressive, but it's incredibly easy to put together. Serve with rice or pasta, a green vegetable cooked just until it's tender-crisp, and a bit of salsa, and you have a beautiful, well-balanced meal.

Seasoning Mix

1 tablespoon salt

1 tablespoon sugar

2 teaspoons dried basil leaves

2 teaspoons garlic powder

2 teaspoons ground ginger

1 teaspoon ground cumin

1 teaspoon onion powder

1 teaspoon dried thyme leaves

3/4 teaspoon cayenne

3/4 teaspoon ground cinnamon

3/4 teaspoon white pepper

1/2 teaspoon ground allspice

1/2 teaspoon ground cardamom

1/2 teaspoon ground dill seed

1/2 teaspoon ground nutmeg

1/2 teaspoon black pepper

1/4 teaspoon ground cloves

1/4 teaspoon ground sage

✳

3 tablespoons all-purpose flour

1 (3- to 4-pound) chicken, cut into 8 pieces

2 tablespoons vegetable oil

4 cups chopped onions, in all

3 tablespoons minced fresh ginger

4 cups chicken stock, in all (see Notes, page 10)

Combine the seasoning mix ingredients in a small bowl. Mix 2 tablespoons of the seasoning mix with the flour and set aside for use later in the recipe. Sprinkle 4 tablespoons of the seasoning mix evenly over the chicken and rub it in well.

Heat the oil in a heavy 6-quart pot over high heat just until the oil begins to smoke, about 4 minutes. Brown the seasoned chicken in batches, large pieces first and skin sides down first, about 2 to 3 minutes per side. Remove the chicken from the pot and set it aside. *Caution: Because this seasoning mixture contains so many dark spices plus sugar, it will brown very quickly, so watch the process carefully. If necessary, reduce the heat to medium-high.* Be sure to brown the chicken well, though, because this step will affect the color and taste of the finished dish.

Add the onions to the pot and scrape the bottom of the pot to loosen the brown bits. Cook, stirring and scraping frequently, until the onions are brown, about 4 minutes. Add the ginger, seasoned flour, and 1/2 cup of the stock and stir until the flour is completely incorporated into the mixture. Continue to cook, stirring occasionally, until the flour begins to stick, about 2 to 3 minutes. Stir in the remaining stock and the remaining seasoning mix and scrape the pot bottom well. Return the chicken and the accumulated juices to the pot, then bring the mixture to a boil, reduce the heat to low, and simmer until the chicken is tender and the sauce has reduced to about 4 cups, about 30 minutes. Remove from the heat and serve.

Tomatillo and Mushroom Chicken

MAKES 4 SERVINGS

Browning the chicken is a very important step in this recipe because it affects the final color and taste of the dish—you want the pieces to be well browned, but you don't want the seasoning to burn, so watch carefully and lower the heat if necessary. As you peel off the papery husks from the tomatillos, you'll notice that they feel sticky, but that sensation disappears once they're cooked.

Seasoning Mix

2 tablespoons ground dried guajillo chile peppers (see Notes, page 6)

1 tablespoon plus 1 teaspoon ground dried ancho chile peppers (see Notes, page 6)

1 tablespoon sugar

2 teaspoons garlic powder

2 teaspoons onion powder

2 teaspoons salt

2 teaspoons dried thyme leaves

1 teaspoon ground cinnamon

1 teaspoon ground nutmeg

1 teaspoon ground dried chipotle chile peppers (see Notes, page 6)

　✳

30 tomatillos (see Glossary, page 299)

1 (3- to 4-pound) chicken, cut into 8 pieces

1 tablespoon vegetable oil

3 cups sliced fresh mushrooms

3 cups chopped onions

2 cups chicken stock (see Notes, page 10)

Combine the seasoning mix ingredients in a small bowl.

Peel, then parboil the tomatillos: drop them into 1½ quarts of boiling water, and when the water boils again, reduce the heat to low and simmer for 10 minutes. Drain the tomatillos and set them aside.

Sprinkle the chicken evenly with 2 tablespoons of the seasoning mix and rub it in well.

Heat the oil in a heavy 5-quart pot over high heat just until the oil begins to smoke, about 4 minutes. Brown the seasoned chicken in batches, large pieces first and skin sides down first, about 2 to 3 minutes per side. Remove the chicken from the pot and set it aside.

Add the mushrooms, onions, and remaining seasoning mix to the pot, cook and stir for 3 minutes, then add the tomatillos. Reduce the heat to medium, cover the pot, and cook for 5 minutes, then mash the tomatillos with a spatula or spoon. Stir in the stock, return the chicken and the accumulated juices to the pot, and bring to a boil. Reduce the heat to low, re-cover the pot, and simmer until the chicken is tender, about 30 to 35 minutes. Remove from the heat and serve.

Red-Eye Chicken

MAKES 6 SERVINGS

The paprika for this chicken may be Hungarian in ancestry, but the chile pepper is 100 percent New World, for a taste combination that's truly world-class! When you're browning the chicken, the seasoning mix on its surface absorbs most of the oil, so you're really working with a dry pot when you add the onions and remaining seasoning mix. The result is that you're toasting the paprika, which changes its flavor and ultimately gives the dish a wonderful slightly smoky taste. Serve Red-Eye Chicken over broad noodles or with small boiled potatoes. If you buy a 16-ounce net weight container of sour cream, as we often do, you'll have just enough left over to crown a couple of baked potatoes or enjoy with chips and salsa another time.

Seasoning Mix

3 tablespoons paprika

2 1/2 teaspoons salt

2 teaspoons ground dried California Beauty chile peppers (see Notes, page 6)

1 1/2 teaspoons onion powder

1 1/2 teaspoons dried basil leaves

1 teaspoon cayenne

1 teaspoon garlic powder

1 teaspoon black pepper

1/2 teaspoon white pepper

✳

6 (4- to 6-ounce) boneless, skinless chicken breast halves

3 tablespoons all-purpose flour

4 cups chicken stock, in all (see Notes, page 10)

2 tablespoons vegetable oil

2 cups chopped onions

1 1/2 cups sour cream

Combine the seasoning mix ingredients in a small bowl.

Sprinkle the chicken breasts evenly with 2 tablespoons of the seasoning mix and rub it in well.

Make a paste by combining the flour with 3 tablespoons of the stock.

Heat the oil in a 4-quart pot over high heat just until the oil begins to smoke, about 4 minutes. Brown the seasoned chicken breasts in batches about 2 to 3 minutes per side. Remove the chicken from the pot and set it aside.

Add the onions and remaining seasoning mix to the pot and cook, stirring constantly, until the paprika begins to darken and smell wonderful, about 3 minutes. Stir in 1 cup of the stock and scrape the bottom of the pot to loosen the brown bits. Add the flour paste and whisk until the mixture is smooth, thick, and pasty, about 2 or 3 minutes.

Add the remaining stock and whisk vigorously. Continue to whisk constantly to distribute the flour evenly throughout the sauce, and bring to a boil over high heat, about 5 minutes. Return the chicken and the accumulated juices to the pot, reduce the heat to medium, and cook for 4 minutes. Remove the chicken and whisk in the sour cream until thoroughly blended. Return the chicken to the pot, stir gently, and serve immediately.

Frontier Chicken

MAKES 4 SERVINGS

This chicken is so beautiful while it's cooking that you may want to show off and prepare it while your company watches. Serve it with hot white rice and something crunchy, like sesame breadsticks or our Skillet Breads (page 48).

Seasoning Mix

2 teaspoons salt

1 teaspoon ground cardamom

1 teaspoon cayenne

1 teaspoon ground coriander
(see Glossary, page 293)

1 teaspoon ground cumin

1 teaspoon ground fenugreek
(see Glossary, page 294)

1 teaspoon garlic powder

1 teaspoon ground ginger

1 teaspoon dry mustard

1 teaspoon onion powder

1 teaspoon black pepper

1 teaspoon white pepper

1 teaspoon ground dried pasilla
chile peppers
(see Notes, page 6)

1 teaspoon ground turmeric

✳

6 (4- to 6-ounce) boneless, skinless
chicken breast halves

3 tablespoons olive oil

1½ cups chopped onions, in all

1 cup chopped green bell
peppers, in all

1 cup chopped red bell peppers,
in all

1 cup chopped yellow bell
peppers, in all

1 large ripe banana, peeled and sliced

2 cups chicken stock, in all (see Notes,
page 10)

1 tablespoon minced fresh garlic

2 tablespoons minced fresh ginger

2 tablespoons plus 2 teaspoons
all-purpose flour

¼ cup chopped fresh cilantro (see
Notes, page 7, Glossary, page 293)

2 tablespoons seeded and finely diced
fresh jalapeño chile peppers (see
Notes, page 6)

1 (14½-ounce) can diced tomatoes
(see Notes, page 7)

Combine the seasoning mix ingredients in a small bowl.

Sprinkle each side of each chicken breast with $1/2$ teaspoon of the seasoning mix and rub it in well with your hands.

Heat the oil in a large skillet or 5-quart pot over high heat just until the oil begins to smoke, about 4 minutes. Brown the seasoned chicken breasts (in batches if necessary) about 2 to 3 minutes per side, then remove them from the pan. The oil and turmeric give the chicken a gorgeous yellow-gold color that is really dramatic.

To the same skillet (or pot) add 1 cup of the onions, $1/2$ cup of each color bell pepper, the banana, and the remaining seasoning mix. Cook, stirring and scraping occasionally, for 10 minutes. If necessary to prevent burning, add $1/4$ cup stock and deglaze the pot (use it as you scrape to loosen any brown bits); you may also have to lower the heat to medium. Add the garlic, ginger, and flour and stir until the flour is thoroughly absorbed. Add the remaining bell peppers and onions, the cilantro, and the jalapeño peppers. Cook for 5 minutes, then add the tomatoes and remaining stock and return the chicken and the accumulated juices to the pan. Bring to a boil, reduce the heat to low, and simmer until the chicken is done, about 10 minutes. Serve hot.

Chicken Dippin'

MAKES 6 SERVINGS

This extra-rich dish, incredibly easy to prepare, is the kind of recipe that guarantees you can impress your guests without spending hours and hours in the kitchen! It's great served with rice, and some of my staff members say they like to serve it with spaghetti. Add steamed fresh broccoli and you have a beautiful dinner.

Seasoning Mix

2 teaspoons salt

2 teaspoons dry mustard

2 teaspoons ground turmeric

2 teaspoons paprika

2 teaspoons ground dried ancho chile peppers (see Notes, page 6)

1½ teaspoons ground cumin

1½ teaspoons garlic powder

1½ teaspoons ground ginger

1 teaspoon ground allspice

¾ teaspoon onion powder

¾ teaspoon white pepper

½ teaspoon cayenne

½ teaspoon black pepper

✳

6 (4- to 6-ounce) boneless, skinless chicken breast halves

2 tablespoons vegetable oil

2½ cups chopped onions

½ cup cane syrup (see Glossary, page 298)

¼ cup finely diced fresh jalapeño chile peppers (see Notes, page 6)

2 cups heavy cream

Combine the seasoning mix ingredients in a small bowl.

Sprinkle the chicken evenly with 2 tablespoons of the seasoning mix and rub it in well. The turmeric in the seasoning mix turns the chicken a pretty golden color.

Heat the oil in a heavy 5-quart pot over high heat just until the oil begins to smoke, about 4 minutes. Brown the chicken in batches about 3 minutes on each side, then remove from the pot. Add the onions to the pot and cook, stirring and scraping the pot frequently, for 8 minutes. Stir in the syrup, jalapeño peppers, heavy cream, and remaining seasoning mix and scrape the pot bottom thoroughly to loosen all the brown bits. Return the chicken and the accumulated juices to the pot and push it into the sauce. Bring just to a boil, reduce the heat to low, then cover and cook, stirring occasionally, until the chicken is done, about 15 minutes. Serve hot.

Jerry's Lemon Grass Chicken

MAKES 4 SERVINGS

On every trip to Hawaii I get to eat wonderful home cooking at the home of Jerry and Thu Kringel—Jerry is a cousin of Shawn McBride, president of my company, Magic Seasoning Blends. Jerry's cooking is direct from Wisconsin, with a Vietnamese influence, thanks to Thu. I look forward to this dish on each trip—it's great!

Seasoning Mix

1 tablespoon medium packed dark brown sugar

1½ teaspoons salt

1 teaspoon cayenne

1 teaspoon ground dried ancho chile peppers (see Notes, page 6)

1 teaspoon ground dried guajillo chile peppers (see Notes, page 6)

½ teaspoon garlic powder

½ teaspoon onion powder

½ teaspoon black pepper

¼ teaspoon white pepper

4 (4- to 6-ounce) boneless, skinless chicken breast halves

1 tablespoon vegetable oil

1 large or 2 medium stalks lemon grass, cut into diagonal slices about ½ inch long, then mashed (see Glossary, page 295)

3 tablespoons Thu's Fish Sauce (page 115)

2 cloves garlic, thinly sliced

1½ cups chicken stock (see Notes, page 10)

1 tablespoon lightly packed chopped fresh parsley

✳

Combine the seasoning mix ingredients in a small bowl.

Slice each chicken breast in half crosswise, then cut each half into diagonal strips 1½ to 2 inches long. Sprinkle the seasoning mix evenly over the chicken and rub it in well.

Heat the oil and lemon grass in a 12-inch skillet over high heat, and as soon as the lemon grass begins to brown, about 1 minute, add the seasoned chicken. Cook, stirring constantly, making sure that the lemon grass does not burn, until the chicken starts to brown, about 2 minutes. Stir in the fish sauce, garlic, and stock and cook for 8 minutes. Remove the lemon grass from the sauce, stir in the parsley, and remove the dish from the heat. Serve hot with rice or noodles.

Chicken in Tamari Cream

MAKES 6 SERVINGS

This is a subtle little recipe that sneaks up on you. It's easy to prepare, and at first bite its flavor seems simple, but the complex seasonings get your attention in just a few minutes. When planning side dishes, one good choice would be a mixture of julienne vegetables cooked quickly, drained, and very lightly buttered.

Seasoning Mix

1½ teaspoons onion powder

1 teaspoon cayenne

1 teaspoon ground cumin

1 teaspoon garlic powder

1 teaspoon ground dried ancho chile peppers (see Notes, page 6)

1 teaspoon dry mustard

1 teaspoon salt

½ teaspoon ground dried guajillo chile peppers (see Notes, page 6)

½ teaspoon black pepper

½ teaspoon white pepper

✳

6 (4- to 6-ounce) boneless, skinless chicken breast halves

1 tablespoon vegetable oil

½ cup chopped onions

1 tablespoon all-purpose flour

½ cup rice wine (see Glossary, page 297)

2 tablespoons plus 2 teaspoons tamari (see Glossary, page 299)

1 cup chicken stock (see Notes, page 10)

3 cups heavy cream

Combine the seasoning mix ingredients in a small bowl.

Sprinkle the chicken evenly with the seasoning mix and rub it in well.

Heat the oil in a large, heavy skillet over high heat just until the oil begins to smoke, about 4 minutes. Add the onions and stir to coat them with the oil. Move the onions to one side of the skillet and add the chicken to the other side. Brown the chicken breasts on both sides, about 3 minutes per side, remove them from the skillet, and set them aside. Stir in the flour, rice wine, and tamari—the mixture will look very dark and pasty. Whisk in the stock and heavy cream, blend thoroughly, and scrape the skillet. Return the chicken and the accumulated juices to the skillet, bring the sauce just to a boil, reduce the heat to low, and simmer until the chicken is done, about 5 to 7 minutes. Serve hot.

Coconut Chicken

MAKES 4 SERVINGS

You can practically hear the whitecaps breaking on the beach when you prepare this chicken dish with its coconut milk, fresh pineapple, rum, and lime juice. Start the meal with cool drinks and Twice-Fried Plantain Chips (page 101), serve King Midas Rice (page 233) as a side dish and cinnamon cookies for dessert, and you'll have your guests thinking they're in the tropics!

Seasoning Mix

1¾ teaspoons onion powder

1½ teaspoons garlic powder

1 teaspoon cayenne

1 teaspoon dried oregano leaves

1 teaspoon ground sage

1 teaspoon salt

½ teaspoon ground nutmeg

½ teaspoon white pepper

½ teaspoon black pepper

＊

2 tablespoons all-purpose flour

¾ to 1 cup chicken stock, in all (see Notes, page 10)

4 (4- to 6-ounce) boneless, skinless chicken breast halves

2 tablespoons vegetable oil

¼ cup white rum

Juice of 1 lime

1 cup raisins

1 whole pineapple, peeled, cored, sliced, and each slice cut into bite-sized wedges

1 cup unsweetened coconut milk (see Glossary, page 293)

Combine the seasoning mix ingredients in a small bowl.

Dissolve the flour in $1/4$ cup of the stock.

Sprinkle the chicken evenly with the seasoning mix and rub it in well.

Heat the oil in a heavy 5-quart pot over high heat just until the oil begins to smoke, about 4 minutes. Brown the chicken breasts in batches about 2 to 3 minutes per side. Remove the chicken from the pot and set it aside.

Add the rum to the pot and cook until it evaporates, about 2 minutes. Stir in the lime juice, the flour-stock mixture, and $1/2$ cup of the stock. Bring to a boil, whisking vigorously to distribute the flour evenly. If the mixture appears to be getting too pasty, add the remaining $1/4$ cup stock. Add the raisins and pineapple, and return the chicken and the accumulated juices to the pot. Bring just to a boil, reduce the heat to low, then cover and simmer for 5 minutes. Stir in the coconut milk, raise the heat to high, and, stirring frequently, bring just to a boil. Reduce the heat to low, cover, and simmer until the chicken is done, about 5 minutes. Serve and accept the compliments graciously.

Chicken Sean

MAKES 4 SERVINGS

In spite of its name, this dish is not Irish. Sean O'Meara, a computer expert who has been involved with several of my projects, assisted me in the test kitchen during the creation of recipes for this book. He liked this one so much that I had to name it for him. Coconut milk comes in different size cans; one popular brand is 15 fluid ounces, which is less than the 2 cups called for in this recipe. We tested it once with the 15-ounce can, and even I couldn't tell the difference. Don't stress about 1 ounce out of 2 cups.

Seasoning Paste

1 cup chopped onions

1/2 cup raisins

4 yellow, green, or red fresh jalapeño chile peppers, seeds and tops removed (see Notes, page 6)

1/4 cup pine nuts (see Glossary, page 297)

1/4 cup fresh garlic cloves

1/4 cup lightly packed dark brown sugar

Juice of 1/2 lemon

Juice of 1/2 lime

1 teaspoon onion powder

1 teaspoon dried oregano leaves

1 teaspoon salt

1/2 teaspoon ground cinnamon

1/2 teaspoon ground coriander (see Glossary, page 293)

1/2 teaspoon garlic powder

1/2 teaspoon black pepper

1/4 teaspoon ground nutmeg

1/4 cup chicken stock (see Notes, page 10)

✳

1 large or 2 small stalk(s) lemon grass (see Glossary, page 295), outer leaves discarded, inner stalk cut diagonally 1 1/2 inches long

Seasoning Mix

2 teaspoons dried basil leaves

2 teaspoons garlic powder

2 teaspoons onion powder

1 teaspoon cayenne

1 teaspoon black pepper

1 teaspoon white pepper

1 teaspoon salt

1 teaspoon dried thyme leaves

✳

8 (4- to 6-ounce) boneless, skinless chicken breast halves, sliced into strips 2 inches long and ½ inch wide

2 cups canned unsweetened coconut milk (see Glossary, page 293)

1 cup chicken stock

2 tablespoons vegetable oil

Combine the seasoning paste ingredients in a blender and purée until smooth, about 1 minute. It looks sort of like thin guacamole. Transfer to a 5-quart pot, add the lemon grass, and cook over low heat, stirring frequently (especially toward the end of the cooking time), until the liquid evaporates and the mixture forms a thick paste, about 1 hour.

Combine the seasoning mix ingredients in a small bowl.

Sprinkle the seasoning mix evenly over the chicken strips and rub in well.

When the seasoning paste has finished cooking, stir the coconut milk and the stock into the pot and raise the heat to high. Bring just to a boil, reduce the heat to medium, and simmer, stirring occasionally, for 5 minutes.

Meanwhile, heat the vegetable oil in a 12-inch nonstick skillet over high heat just until the oil begins to smoke, about 4 minutes. Add the chicken strips and cook, stirring constantly, until the chicken is well browned, about 4 minutes. Transfer the chicken to the sauce in the pot, bring just to a boil, reduce the heat to medium, and simmer for 3 minutes. Remove the lemon grass before serving. Serve hot and invite Sean for dinner!

Zucchini and Chicken Casserole

MAKES 6 SERVINGS

This is the kind of dish that's perfect for covered-dish suppers or for ladies' club meetings, and it's so hearty and filling that men love it too.

Seasoning Mix

1 tablespoon salt

2 teaspoons dried basil leaves

2 teaspoons cayenne

2 teaspoons dried marjoram leaves

2 teaspoons onion powder

2 teaspoons white pepper

2 teaspoons dried savory leaves

2 teaspoons dried tarragon leaves

1½ teaspoons black pepper

1 teaspoon garlic powder

✳

5 tablespoons unsalted butter

3 tablespoons olive oil

2 cups chopped onions

1 cup chopped green bell peppers

1 cup chopped red bell peppers

1 cup chopped yellow bell peppers

1 tablespoon minced fresh garlic

1 tablespoon minced fresh ginger

3 tablespoons finely diced fresh jalapeño chile peppers (see Notes, page 6)

3 tablespoons all-purpose flour

2 large zucchini, scrubbed but not peeled, diced into ¾-inch cubes

6 (4- to 6-ounce) boneless, skinless chicken breast halves, sliced into ½-inch strips

1 (14½-ounce) can diced tomatoes (see Notes, page 7)

1 (16-ounce) container sour cream

3½ ounces freshly grated Parmesan cheese

1 cup toasted unseasoned bread crumbs

Combine the seasoning mix ingredients in a small bowl.

Preheat the oven to 350°.

Melt the butter with the oil in a 5-quart pot over high heat. As soon as the butter sizzles, add the onions, bell peppers, garlic, ginger, jalapeño peppers, and 3 tablespoons of the seasoning mix. Cook, stirring frequently, for 8 minutes, then stir in the flour and mix well to distribute it evenly. Add the zucchini and cook, stirring occasionally, until a golden brown crust develops on the bottom of the pot, about 4 minutes. Scrape the bottom of the pot until the crust is completely removed. Spread the vegetables evenly over the bottom of the pot and allow the crust to form again, being careful not to let the mixture burn. Add the chicken, the remaining seasoning mix, and the tomatoes. Stir and scrape vigorously, then remove from the heat and gently fold in the sour cream.

Transfer the mixture to a 9 × 12-inch baking pan and sprinkle the Parmesan cheese and the bread crumbs evenly on top of the casserole. Bake until the cheese is golden brown and bubbly, about 20 to 25 minutes. Serve piping hot.

Tomato Cream Chicken

MAKES 4 SERVINGS

This is a recipe that really grows on you. The first bite is good, the second very good, and by the third you realize you love it! I think you're going to like trying out some of the less common ingredients, like the lemon grass and pine nuts. Along with the combination of seasonings, they are what give the dish its complex flavor.

Seasoning Paste

1 cup chopped onions

1/2 cup raisins

4 green, yellow, or red fresh jalapeño chile peppers, seeds and tops removed (see Notes, page 6)

1/4 cup pine nuts (see Glossary, page 297)

1/4 cup fresh garlic cloves

1/4 cup lightly packed dark brown sugar

Juice of 1/2 lemon

Juice of 1/2 lime

1 teaspoon onion powder

1 teaspoon dried oregano leaves

1/2 teaspoon ground cinnamon

1/2 teaspoon ground coriander (see Glossary, page 293)

1/2 teaspoon garlic powder

1/2 teaspoon black pepper

1/4 teaspoon ground nutmeg

1/4 cup chicken stock (see Notes, page 10)

✳

1 large or 2 small stalk(s) lemon grass (see Glossary, page 295) outer leaves discarded, inner stalk cut diagonally 1 1/2 inches long

Seasoning Mix

2 teaspoons dried basil leaves

2 teaspoons salt

2 teaspoons onion powder

2 teaspoons paprika

1 teaspoon ground coriander

1 teaspoon garlic powder

1 teaspoon black pepper

1/2 teaspoon cayenne

✳

8 (4- to 6-ounce) boneless, skinless chicken breast halves

2 tablespoons vegetable oil

2 cups chopped onions

2 (14 1/2-ounce) cans diced tomatoes (see Notes, page 7)

2 cups heavy cream

1 cup chicken stock

Combine the seasoning paste ingredients in a blender and purée until smooth, about 1 minute. It looks sort of like thin guacamole. Transfer to a large nonstick skillet, stir in the lemon grass, and cook over low heat, stirring frequently (especially toward the end of the cooking time), until the liquid evaporates and the mixture forms a thick paste, about 1 hour.

Combine the seasoning mix ingredients in a small bowl.

Sprinkle the chicken evenly with 2 tablespoons of the seasoning mix and rub it in well.

Heat the oil in a heavy 5-quart pot over high heat just until the oil begins to smoke, about 4 minutes. Brown the seasoned chicken in batches about 2 to 3 minutes per side. Remove the chicken from the pot and set it aside.

Add the onions to the pot and cook, stirring frequently, until they reach a brown, sweet, caramelized state, about 5 to 7 minutes. Add 1 tablespoon of the seasoning mix and stir constantly for 30 seconds, then add the tomatoes, seasoning paste, and remaining seasoning mix. Cook for 5 minutes, then whisk in the heavy cream and stock. Return the chicken and the accumulated juices to the pot, bring just to a boil, reduce the heat to low, and simmer, stirring occasionally, until the chicken is done, about 8 minutes. Remove the lemon grass before serving.

Chicken in Cauliflower Cream

MAKES 4 SERVINGS

Having grown up on a farm, I love vegetables, but I know there are people out there who don't care for them, even knowing how nutritious they are. If you have anyone in your family like that, try this recipe on them. Because the cauliflower is surrounded by chicken in a rich and creamy cheese sauce—a sauce that is really brightened by the unusual seasonings—you may be surprised at how quickly those florets disappear!

Seasoning Mix

2 teaspoons salt

1½ teaspoons onion powder

1 teaspoon cayenne

1 teaspoon dill weed

1 teaspoon white pepper

1 teaspoon ground dried California Beauty chile peppers (see Notes, page 6)

1 teaspoon ground dried guajillo chile peppers (see Notes, page 6)

¾ teaspoon garlic powder

¾ teaspoon black pepper

½ teaspoon ground cinnamon

½ teaspoon ground nutmeg

✳

6 (4- to 6-ounce) boneless, skinless chicken breast halves

2 tablespoons vegetable oil

8 ounces finely diced bacon

1 head cauliflower, cut into very small florets

1 cup chicken stock (see Notes, page 10)

3 cups heavy cream

8 ounces freshly grated mozzarella cheese

Combine the seasoning mix ingredients in a small bowl.

Sprinkle each side of each chicken breast evenly with ½ teaspoon of the seasoning mix.

Heat the oil in a large skillet or 5-quart pot over high heat just until the oil begins to smoke, about 4 minutes. Brown the chicken in batches for 3 to 4 minutes per side, then remove the chicken and set it aside.

In the same skillet or pot, render the bacon until it's crisp and brown, about 6 to 8 minutes. Add the cauliflower florets and the remaining seasoning mix, and toss and cook for 2 minutes. Add the stock, cream, and cheese and stir thoroughly until the cheese is melted and incorporated. When the cheese starts to melt, it gloms up into a big stringy mess, which can be kind of scary if you're not expecting it. Keep cool, though, for in a couple of minutes more the mess will melt completely. Return the chicken and the accumulated juices to the sauce. Reduce the heat to very low and simmer, scraping the bottom of the skillet or pot occasionally, until the chicken is done, about 25 minutes.

Fenugreek Chicken

MAKES 4 SERVINGS

My favorite thing about this dish is the contrast between the warm seasonings of the chicken and the smooth, creamy, nutty sauce. They're very different, but they work together very well.

Seasoning Mix

1 tablespoon lightly packed light brown sugar

1½ teaspoons ground dried pasilla chile peppers (see Notes, page 6)

1 teaspoon ground fenugreek (see Glossary, page 294)

1 teaspoon paprika

1 teaspoon salt

¾ teaspoon cayenne

¾ teaspoon garlic powder

½ teaspoon ground allspice

½ teaspoon ground coriander (see Glossary, page 293)

½ teaspoon ground cumin

½ teaspoon ground dill seed

½ teaspoon ground ginger

½ teaspoon onion powder

¼ teaspoon black pepper

¼ teaspoon white pepper

✳

1 (3- to 4-pound) whole chicken

1 (4.4-ounce) package slivered almonds

1 cup whole Brazil nuts

3 cups chopped onions

1 cup chopped green bell peppers

1 cup chopped red bell peppers

2 cups chicken stock (see Notes, page 10)

2 cups heavy cream

Combine the seasoning mix ingredients in a small bowl.

Preheat the oven to 350°.

Rub the chicken, inside and out, with 3 tablespoons of the seasoning mix. Place the chicken in a roasting pan—no rack is necessary—and bake for 20 minutes. Lower the heat to 200° and bake for 20 minutes, then add the almonds and Brazil nuts to the juices in the bottom of the pan and bake 20 minutes longer. Remove the chicken from the pan, set it aside, and keep it warm. Add the onions and bell peppers to the pan and place it on top of the stove over high heat. Cook, stirring occasionally, for 5 minutes. Purée half of the mixture in a food processor, then return the purée mixture to the pan and stir it into the mixture remaining in the pan.

Add the remaining seasoning mix to the roasting pan. Stir to mix well, then stir in the stock. Cook for 5 minutes, then stir in the cream. Cook, stirring frequently, just until the sauce comes to a simmer and remove from the heat. Cut the chicken into quarters and serve drizzled with some of the sauce. Pass the remaining sauce separately.

Let's Meat for Dinner

Hot and Sour Beef

Flank Steak with Black Mushrooms

Flank, Cabbage, and Beets

Flank and Broccoli

Beef in Coconut Cream

Brisket of Beef

Spinach, Arugula, and Meat Pie

Mirliton and Ground Beef Pie

Enchilada Casserole

Cabbage Casserole

Sweet Beef and Fresh Chiles

Spicy Beef Stew

Pork Patties

Chickpea and Pork Pie

Smothered Potatoes, Cabbage, and Andouille

Sausage and Millet Stew

Italian Sausage and Tomato Custard Pie

Patricia's Pork Roast

Lamb with Spinach

Sweet Spiced Lamb Patties

Hot and Sour Beef

MAKES 6 SERVINGS

This dish will make you want to get out your saddle and throw it across the steering wheel of a Bronco, and head out to the cactus and tumbleweed. It has a great sour taste and it's hot enough to light a campfire with, so put your spurs on and enjoy!

Seasoning Mix

1 tablespoon salt

2 teaspoons grated lemon peel

2 teaspoons grated lime peel

1½ teaspoons onion powder

1½ teaspoons ground dried ancho chile peppers (see Notes, page 6)

1½ teaspoons ground dried chipotle chile peppers (see Notes, page 6)

1 teaspoon cayenne

1 teaspoon garlic powder

1 teaspoon black pepper

1 teaspoon white pepper

1 teaspoon ground dried guajillo chile peppers (see Notes, page 6)

✳

2 pounds flank steak, scalloped (see Notes, page 9)

3 tablespoons olive oil

1½ cups chopped onions

Juice of 1 lemon

Juice of 1 lime

3 tablespoons all-purpose flour

1 tablespoon minced fresh garlic

1 tablespoon white vinegar

2 cups beef stock, in all (see Notes, page 10)

½ cup lightly packed whole fresh cilantro leaves (see Notes, page 7, Glossary, page 293)

Combine the seasoning mix ingredients in a small bowl.

Sprinkle the scalloped meat evenly with 3 tablespoons of the seasoning mix and rub it in well.

Heat the oil in a heavy 5-quart pot over high heat just until the oil begins to smoke, about 4 minutes. Add the steak and cook, stirring frequently, for 7 minutes. Add the onions and cook, stirring frequently, for 4 minutes, then add the lemon juice, lime juice, flour, garlic, vinegar, and remaining seasoning mix. Scrape the bottom of the pot well and cook, stirring occasionally, for 4 minutes. Add 1 cup of the stock, scrape up the brown bits, and continue to cook, stirring occasionally, for 6 minutes. Add the remaining stock and scrape the bottom of the pot to loosen all the brown bits. Add the cilantro, cover, reduce the heat to low, and simmer, stirring occasionally, for 20 minutes. Serve hot, with plenty of sauce, to the toughest hombres you know.

Flank Steak with Black Mushrooms

MAKES ABOUT 10 CUPS

This recipe probably has the most unusual mix of ingredients of all the recipes in the book. The combination—Jerusalem artichokes, burdock root, cracked wheat, and especially the unusual black mushrooms, plus five different peppers and cream—produces one of the most astounding tastes I've ever experienced.

Seasoning Mix

2 teaspoons salt

1½ teaspoons garlic powder

1½ teaspoons onion powder

1½ teaspoons dried oregano leaves

1½ teaspoons dried ground chipotle chile peppers (see Notes, page 6)

1 teaspoon dry mustard

1 teaspoon ground dried ancho chile peppers (see Notes, page 6)

1 teaspoon dried thyme leaves

½ teaspoon black pepper

½ teaspoon white pepper

¼ teaspoon cayenne

✳

2 pounds flank steak, scalloped (see Notes, page 9)

3 tablespoons vegetable oil

2 cups chopped onions

2 cups peeled and diced Jerusalem artichokes (see Glossary, page 298)

3 cups peeled and cubed (½-inch pieces) burdock root (see Glossary, page 292)

2 cups diced red cabbage

3 cups beef stock, in all (see Notes, page 10)

½ cup finely chopped fresh cilantro (see Notes, page 7, Glossary, page 293)

½ cup cracked wheat cereal (see Glossary, page 294)

1½ cups dried black mushrooms, soaked, drained, and chopped (see Glossary, page 296)

2 cups heavy cream

continued

Combine the seasoning mix ingredients in a small bowl.

Sprinkle the seasoning mix evenly over the meat and rub it in well.

Heat the oil in a heavy 5-quart pot just until the oil begins to smoke, about 4 minutes. Add the seasoned meat, onions, Jerusalem artichokes, and burdock root. Cover and cook for 4 minutes, then add the cabbage. Cook, uncovering to stir frequently, for 15 minutes. Add 1 cup of the stock, the cilantro, cracked wheat cereal, and black mushrooms. Cook, covered, stirring frequently, until the liquid evaporates and the mixture becomes dry and begins to stick to the bottom of the pot, about 8 minutes. Add the remaining stock and stir vigorously, scraping the bottom of the pot to loosen any brown bits. Stir in the cream, reduce the heat to low, and simmer, uncovered, for 10 minutes. Serve and enjoy.

Flank, Cabbage, and Beets

MAKES 4 TO 6 SERVINGS

Cabbage and beets are great cooked together, and the rich flavor of beef combines with the all-spice, basil, caraway, and cumin to bring an unusual, rich, pungent flavor to the dish. Because the beets will stain a wooden chopping board, use a plastic board if you have one.

Seasoning Mix

1½ teaspoons salt

1 teaspoon dried basil leaves

1 teaspoon caraway seeds

1 teaspoon cayenne

1 teaspoon dry mustard

¾ teaspoon ground cumin

¾ teaspoon garlic powder

¾ teaspoon onion powder

¾ teaspoon black pepper

½ teaspoon ground allspice

½ teaspoon white pepper

✳

1 pound flank steak, scalloped (see Notes, page 9)

2 tablespoons vegetable oil

2 cups chopped onions

3 cups beef stock, in all (see Notes, page 10)

2 cups medium-diced peeled fresh beets

4 cups medium diced cabbage

2 teaspoons minced fresh garlic

2 teaspoons minced fresh ginger

1 tablespoon minced fresh serrano chile peppers (see Notes, page 6)

2 tablespoons all-purpose flour

Combine the seasoning mix ingredients in a small bowl.

Sprinkle the steak scallops evenly with 1 tablespoon plus 1 teaspoon of the seasoning mix and rub it in well.

Heat the oil in a 4-quart pot over high heat just until the oil begins to smoke, about 4 minutes. Add the seasoned steak and cook, stirring frequently, until the steak is browned, about 4 minutes. Stir in the onions, cover, and cook, stirring occasionally, for 6 minutes. Uncover and cook, scraping up the brown bits on the pot bottom, until the juices almost completely evaporate and the onions brown and begin to stick to the pot, about 6 minutes. Add ½ cup of the stock and use it to loosen and dissolve the brown bits. Add the beets, cabbage, garlic, ginger, serrano chile peppers, and remaining seasoning mix. Stir until the seasoning mix is evenly distributed throughout the mixture. Cover and cook, stirring and scraping the pan bottom to make sure the mixture does not stick, for 8 minutes. Add ½ cup stock, stir thoroughly, and scrape up any remaining brown bits, then add the flour and stir until the flour is no longer visible.

Cover and cook for 2 minutes. Add the remaining stock and scrape up the brown bits once more. Bring to a boil and scrape the pot bottom again. Reduce the heat to low, cover, simmer for 15 minutes, and serve.

Flank and Broccoli

MAKES ABOUT 7 CUPS

Both the flank steak and the broccoli seem to come alive with flavor thanks to the herb and spice blend and the special taste of buckwheat mixed with coconut milk. Adding the broccoli in the last 5 minutes keeps it crunchy but tender, and the green broccoli and white coconut milk make an attractive color combination on your plate.

Seasoning Mix

2 teaspoons salt

1½ teaspoons dried basil leaves

1½ teaspoons ground cumin

1½ teaspoons dry mustard

1 teaspoon cayenne

1 teaspoon ground coriander
(see Glossary, page 293)

1 teaspoon ground fenugreek
(see Glossary, page 294)

1 teaspoon garlic powder

1 teaspoon onion powder

1 teaspoon ground dried árbol
chile peppers (see Notes,
page 6)

¾ teaspoon white pepper

½ teaspoon black pepper

✳

1½ pounds flank steak, scalloped
(see Notes, page 9)

2 tablespoons vegetable oil

2 cups chopped onions

1 cup chopped green bell peppers

2 tablespoons tamari (see Glossary,
page 299)

2 cups sliced fresh mushrooms

1 cup medium-diced carrots

1 tablespoon minced fresh garlic

2 tablespoons minced fresh ginger

3 tablespoons buckwheat flour,
preferred, or all-purpose flour

2 cups beef stock (see Notes, page 10)

2 (13½-ounce) cans unsweetened
coconut milk (see Glossary,
page 293)

4 cups broccoli florets

Combine the seasoning mix ingredients in a small bowl.

Sprinkle the scalloped steak evenly with 1 tablespoon plus 2 teaspoons of the seasoning mix and rub it in well.

continued

Heat the oil in a 4-quart pot over high heat just until the oil begins to smoke, about 4 minutes. Add the seasoned steak and cook, stirring frequently, for 4 minutes. Add the onions and bell peppers and cook, stirring frequently, for 12 minutes. Add the tamari, mushrooms, carrots, garlic, ginger, and remaining seasoning mix. Cover and cook, stirring occasionally, for 12 minutes, then stir in the flour. Stir constantly until the flour is absorbed, then add the stock. Scrape all the brown bits from the pot bottom and stir in the coconut milk. Cover, bring to a boil, reduce the heat to low, and simmer for 10 minutes. Add the broccoli florets, return to a boil, reduce the heat to low, and simmer for 5 minutes more. Remove from the heat and serve.

Beef in Coconut Cream

MAKES ABOUT 6 CUPS

I think this exotic beef dish goes really well with roasted sweet potatoes and turnips, plus a salad made of tropical fruits and topped with a tangy, almost sour dressing. If you've never bought daikon before, it looks like a huge, smooth, white carrot. Another name for it is Japanese radish, so you'd be correct if you guessed that its taste and texture are a little like the small red and white radishes you're used to. If you have some left over, slice or grate it raw for salads.

Seasoning Mix

2 teaspoons ground dried guajillo
   chile peppers (see Notes,
   page 6)

2 teaspoons salt

1½ teaspoons onion powder

1 teaspoon ground allspice

1 teaspoon dried basil leaves

1 teaspoon garlic powder

1 teaspoon ground mace

1 teaspoon dry mustard

1 teaspoon ground nutmeg

1 teaspoon white pepper

½ teaspoon cayenne

½ teaspoon black pepper

1 cup pine nuts (see Glossary,
   page 297)

1 cup canned unsweetened coconut
   milk (see Glossary, page 293)

2 pounds flank steak, scalloped
   (see Notes, page 9)

3 tablespoons vegetable oil

1 cup chopped onions

1 tablespoon chopped fresh ginger

1 tablespoon chopped fresh jalapeño
   chile peppers (see Notes, page 6)

1 cup beef stock (see Notes, page 10)

2 cups daikon, diced into ½-inch pieces
   (see Glossary, page 294)

½ cup chopped fresh cilantro (see
   Notes, page 7, Glossary, page 293)

✳

Combine the seasoning mix ingredients in a small bowl.

Process the pine nuts and coconut milk in a blender until smooth.

Sprinkle the seasoning mix evenly over the meat and rub it in well.

Heat the oil in a 5-quart pot over high heat just until it begins to smoke, about 4 minutes. Add the seasoned meat and cook, stirring frequently, until it begins to brown, about 4 minutes. Add the onions, ginger, and jalapeño peppers. Cover

...d cook, stirring and scraping the pot bottom occasionally, for 15 minutes. Add the stock, daikon, cilantro, and the pine nut–coconut milk mixture. Cover and cook, stirring occasionally, until the meat is tender, about 15 minutes. Serve piping hot.

Brisket of Beef

MAKES 6 SERVINGS OF BEEF, WITH SLIGHTLY MORE THAN 4 CUPS SAUCE

Not only is this an unusual method for cooking a brisket but you probably haven't seen these seasonings together before. It's not a big deal to grind the fenugreek seeds yourself if you can't find this spice already ground. A small coffee grinder works well, but be sure to clean it thoroughly after use.

Seasoning Mix

2 teaspoons salt

1½ teaspoons dried basil leaves

1½ teaspoons ground coriander (see Glossary, page 293)

1½ teaspoons ground cumin

1 teaspoon caraway seeds

1 teaspoon ground fenugreek (see Glossary, page 294)

1 teaspoon garlic powder

1 teaspoon dry mustard

1 teaspoon onion powder

1 teaspoon black pepper

¾ teaspoon cayenne

½ teaspoon white pepper

✳

1 (3-pound) beef brisket

8 ounces finely diced bacon

2 cups finely diced leeks (white part plus 1 inch of green, about 2 medium)

2 cups chopped celery

4 peeled and finely diced medium-sized unripe plantains (see Glossary, page 297)

2 cups sliced fresh mushrooms

1 tablespoon minced fresh garlic

2 tablespoons minced fresh ginger

2½ cups beef stock, in all (see Notes, page 10)

1 (16-ounce) container sour cream

Combine the seasoning mix ingredients in a small bowl.

Sprinkle the brisket evenly with 1 tablespoon plus 1 teaspoon of the seasoning mix and rub it in well.

To make the stuffing, render the bacon in a 4-quart pot over high heat, stirring frequently, until it is nicely browned, about 6 minutes. Add the leeks, celery, plantains, mushrooms, garlic, ginger, and remaining seasoning mix. Stir well, then cook, stirring and scraping the pan bottom frequently, for 5 minutes. Let cool slightly. Reserve 2 cups of the stuffing for the sauce. Set the pot aside without washing for later use.

Preheat the oven to 250°.

Place the stuffing in a roasting pan, place the brisket on top of the stuffing, cover tightly with a fitted lid or foil, and roast for 30 minutes. Add 1½ cups of the stock to the bottom of the pan and continue roasting, covered, until the brisket is done, about 4 hours. Remove the brisket from the oven and let it sit while you make the sauce.

Purée the reserved 2 cups of the stuffing with the remaining stock in a blender or food processor.

Pour the juices from the roasting pan into the pot in which the vegetables were cooked and add the puréed mixture and the sour cream. Cook over medium heat, stirring constantly, just until the sauce is warm. Do not let the sauce boil or the sour cream will "break" or separate. To serve, slice the roast and drizzle some of the sauce over each portion. Pass the remaining sauce separately.

Spinach, Arugula, and Meat Pie

MAKES 9 SERVINGS

There's nothing complicated or difficult about this recipe, but there are several steps, so you do have to give it your full attention. Your reward will be one of the most delicious, beautiful, unusual, and intriguing main-dish pies you've ever tasted! If for some reason you make the masa crust dough before you're ready to complete the dish, just store it in a plastic bag to keep it moist and fresh. By the way, when buying ricotta cheese, choose the solid kind, not the variety that looks like cottage cheese, then grate it.

Masa crust

8 ounces finely diced bacon

3 cups corn masa (see Glossary, page 294)

¼ cup lightly packed light brown sugar

2 teaspoons ground dried guajillo chile peppers (see Notes, page 6)

1 teaspoon ground allspice

1 teaspoon ground cumin

½ teaspoon ground mace

1½ cups chicken stock (see Notes, page 10)

¼ pound (1 stick) unsalted butter, softened

Filling

Seasoning Mix

2 teaspoons paprika

1½ teaspoons onion powder

1½ teaspoons salt

1 teaspoon dill weed

1 teaspoon dry mustard

1 teaspoon ground dried New Mexico chile peppers (see Notes, page 6)

1 teaspoon ground dried pasilla chile peppers (see Notes, page 6)

¾ teaspoon garlic powder

¾ teaspoon black pepper

½ teaspoon white pepper

¼ teaspoon cayenne

✳

1½ tablespoons vegetable oil

1½ cups chopped onions

1 cup chopped green bell peppers

3 tablespoons minced capers

2 teaspoons minced fresh garlic

1 cup roasted unsalted peanuts

1 pound lean ground beef

1 cup raisins

1 tablespoon all-purpose flour dissolved in 2 tablespoons water

½ cup loosely packed whole fresh cilantro leaves (see Notes, page 7, Glossary, page 293)

2 cups loosely packed stemmed fresh arugula

1 (10-ounce) bag fresh spinach, stemmed and washed

1 cup beef stock

¼ cup cornmeal

8 ounces solid imported ricotta cheese, grated

8 ounces grated Monterey Jack cheese

MASA CRUST: Preheat the oven to 500°.

Render the bacon in a skillet but don't let it brown. Set it aside to cool slightly.

Combine the dry ingredients in the large bowl of a food mixer. Add the bacon and all the rendered drippings, the stock, and butter and mix until the dough has the consistency of a soft pie dough, approximately 3 minutes.

Spread the masa dough with your hands as evenly as possible over the bottom and sides of a 9 × 13-inch baking dish. Pierce the bottom of the dough at regular intervals with the tines of a fork to make several small air holes. Bake for 10 to 12 minutes, or until the edges of the dough just start to brown. Remove the crust from the oven—it will have a wonderful aroma and should still be a beautiful terra-cotta orange color—and reduce the temperature to 350°.

FILLING: Combine the seasoning mix ingredients in a small bowl.

Heat the oil in a 5-quart pot over high heat just until the oil begins to smoke, about 4 minutes. Add the onions and cook, stirring frequently, until they begin to brown, about 4 minutes. Add the bell peppers, capers, garlic, peanuts, and 3 tablespoons of the seasoning mix. Stir thoroughly and cook for 2 minutes, then add the ground beef and cook, stirring constantly and breaking up the clumps of meat, for 2 minutes. Add the remaining seasoning mix and the raisins and cook until the beef is nicely browned, about 2 minutes more. Mix in the flour-water mixture and cook for 1 additional minute. Add the cilantro, arugula, spinach, and stock. Cook, stirring occasionally, until the greens are wilted, about 8 minutes. Stir in the cornmeal and cook for 3 minutes. Remove from the heat and blend in the ricotta cheese.

Pour the filling into the crust and top with the Monterey Jack cheese. Bake until the cheese is golden brown, about 20 minutes. Cut into squares to serve.

Mirliton and Ground Beef Pie

MAKES 2 (9-INCH) PIES

I've been cooking mirlitons since I was tall enough to reach the kitchen counter, and I've noticed mirlitons never fail to produce amazing results. I think you'll agree that this pie, with its topping of sour cream, cream cheese, and dill weed, is one of the best ways to use this vegetable.

The secret of making good pie crusts is to refrigerate the dough before baking. It's also very important not to overmix—little flecks of the shortening should be visible in the dough. When working with dough, liberally flour all the working surfaces—table, hands, and rolling pin.

Whole wheat pie crusts

Seasoning Mix

2 teaspoons ground dried guajillo chile peppers (see Notes, page 6)

1 teaspoon ground cumin

1 teaspoon ground coriander (see Glossary, page 293)

✳

2 cups all-purpose flour

1½ cups whole wheat flour

1 tablespoon sugar

2 teaspoons salt

1¼ cups very cold vegetable shortening

½ cup plus 1 tablespoon very cold water

Ground beef filling

Seasoning Mix

1 tablespoon paprika

1 tablespoon salt

2 teaspoons dried basil leaves

2 teaspoons dry mustard

2 teaspoons dried oregano leaves

1¾ teaspoons black pepper

1½ teaspoons cayenne

1½ teaspoons garlic powder

1½ teaspoons onion powder

1½ teaspoons dried thyme leaves

1 teaspoon white pepper

✳

4 tablespoons unsalted butter

1 pound lean ground beef

1 cup chopped onions

1 cup chopped green bell peppers

1 cup chopped celery

2 teaspoons minced fresh garlic

4 mirlitons (see Glossary, page 296), parboiled and diced into 1-inch cubes

Topping

1 (8-ounce) package cream cheese

1 (8-ounce) container sour cream

½ teaspoon dill weed

CRUSTS: Combine the seasoning mix ingredients in a small bowl.

Combine the all-purpose flour, whole wheat flour, sugar, salt, and seasoning mix in an electric mixer equipped with a dough hook and process until well blended. Add the cold shortening and blend at low speed, scraping the sides and bottom of the bowl, until the ingredients just come together and resemble very coarse meal or dried split peas. Gradually add the water and continue to process at low speed just until the water is absorbed, being careful not to overmix. As soon as the liquid is absorbed, gather the dough into a ball and refrigerate until cold, at least 4 hours, preferably overnight.

To make the crusts, divide the dough in half and form each half into a ball. Liberally flour your hands, the working surface, and the rolling pin. Place one of the dough balls on the floured surface and roll it out, keeping it as even and round as possible. Turn the dough as you roll, and dust with flour as necessary, until the circle is about 11 inches in diameter. Carefully fit the circle into a 9-inch pie tin and crimp the edges with your hands or with the tines of a fork. Repeat with the remaining ball of dough. Set the shells aside while you prepare the filling.

FILLING: Combine the seasoning mix ingredients in a small bowl.

Melt the butter in a 4-quart pot over high heat. As soon as it begins to sizzle, add the meat, onions, bell peppers, celery, garlic, and seasoning mix. Cook, stirring frequently, until the meat and vegetables are browned, about 10 minutes. Add the mirlitons and cook, stirring frequently and scraping the bottom of the pot, for 5 minutes. Remove from the heat and cool to room temperature. Divide the filling between the prepared pie crusts.

Preheat the oven to 350°.

TOPPING: Combine the cream cheese, sour cream, and dill weed and divide the topping between the pies.

Bake until the filling is cooked through, the top is light golden, and the crust edges are browned, about 40 minutes. Cut into wedges to serve.

Enchilada Casserole

MAKES 10 ENCHILADAS

This is a great dish to serve when you entertain because you can prepare it completely, up to the point of baking, well ahead of time, and slip it into the oven 15 minutes before you plan to serve. If you've refrigerated it, let it come to room temperature before baking. Using a combination of several chile peppers gives the casserole the authentic aroma and complex flavor that'll make you think you're in the middle of the Southwest.

Seasoning Mix

2 teaspoons salt

1½ teaspoons ground cumin

1½ teaspoons garlic powder

1½ teaspoons onion powder

1 teaspoon dry mustard

1 teaspoon dried oregano leaves

1 teaspoon ground dried árbol chile peppers (see Notes, page 6)

1 teaspoon ground dried guajillo chile peppers (see Notes, page 6)

1 teaspoon ground dried pasilla chile peppers (see Notes, page 6)

½ teaspoon cayenne

½ teaspoon black pepper

✳

7 tablespoons all-purpose flour, in all

3½ cups beef stock, in all (see Notes, page 10)

2 tablespoons plus ¼ cup vegetable oil, in all

2 cups chopped onions, in all

2 cups chopped green bell peppers

1 tablespoon minced fresh garlic

2 tablespoons minced fresh ginger

1 pound lean ground beef

4 tablespoons ground dried California Beauty chile peppers (see Notes, page 6)

10 large (9- to 10-inch diameter) corn tortillas

1 pound grated sharp Cheddar cheese

1 cup finely diced onions, soaked for 30 minutes in white vinegar to cover, then drained (discard the vinegar)

Combine the seasoning mix ingredients in a small bowl.

Dissolve 2 tablespoons of the flour in ¾ cup of the stock and set aside.

FILLING: Heat 2 tablespoons of the vegetable oil in a 12-inch skillet over high heat just until the oil begins to smoke, about 4 minutes. Add 1 cup of the onions and all of the bell peppers and cook, stirring occasionally, until the vegetables begin to brown, about 8 to 10 minutes. Stir in the garlic, ginger, and 1 tablespoon of the seasoning mix. Add the meat and cook, stirring to break up the clumps, until it is nicely browned, about 8 minutes. Stir in the flour-stock mixture, cook for 1 minute, and remove from the heat.

SAUCE: Heat the remaining $1/4$ cup vegetable oil in a 10-inch skillet over high heat just until the oil begins to smoke, about 4 minutes. Add the remaining 5 tablespoons flour and whisk constantly until it turns light tan. Whisking constantly and vigorously to keep the peppers from burning, add the California Beauty chile peppers and the remaining 1 cup onions. Immediately remove from the heat and add the remaining seasoning mix. Add the remaining $2^{3}/4$ cups stock, place over medium heat, and cook, whisking frequently, until the sauce is a rich reddish-brown, about 15 minutes.

ASSEMBLY: Preheat the oven to 350°.

Dip a tortilla in the sauce and top it with a generous $1/4$ cup of the meat mixture, 1 tablespoon of the cheese, and 1 teaspoon of the drained onions. Roll up the filled tortilla and place it in a 9 × 13-inch casserole. Repeat the process with the remaining tortillas. Place the remaining sauce and cheese on top and bake for 15 minutes. Serve hot.

Cabbage Casserole

MAKES 9 VERY GENEROUS SERVINGS

Stuffed cabbage is a popular dish in several different cultures, but it's a lot of trouble to make. For those of you who love the taste but don't relish the prospect of blanching several dozen cabbage leaves, topping them with meat filling, then rolling them up, this recipe is for you! And it's the perfect choice for occasions when you have to produce something for a covered-dish supper.

Seasoning Mix

2 teaspoons salt

1½ teaspoons garlic powder

1 teaspoon dried basil leaves

1 teaspoon caraway seeds

1 teaspoon cayenne

1 teaspoon ground ginger

1 teaspoon brown mustard seeds

1 teaspoon onion powder

1 teaspoon dried oregano leaves

¾ teaspoon white pepper

½ teaspoon black pepper

*

1 cup pumpkin seeds, toasted
   (instructions follow)

Vegetable oil cooking spray

2 tablespoons vegetable oil

1 pound lean ground beef

1½ cups chopped onions

½ cup chopped green bell peppers

½ cup chopped red bell peppers

½ cup chopped yellow bell peppers

½ cup chopped celery

1 head cabbage, chopped

1 (14½-ounce) can diced tomatoes
   (see Notes, page 7)

1 (8-ounce) container sour cream

5 cups cooked rice

1½ cups beef stock (see Notes, page 10)

Combine the seasoning mix ingredients in a small bowl.

Toast the pumpkin seeds in a small skillet over high heat, stirring constantly, until they brown slightly and release their wonderful aroma. Immediately remove the seeds from the hot skillet to stop the toasting and set aside.

Coat a 9 × 13-inch casserole or baking pan with vegetable oil spray.

Preheat the oven to 400°.

Heat the oil in a heavy 5-quart pot over high heat just until the oil begins to smoke, about 4 minutes. Add the meat and 2 tablespoons of the seasoning mix and cook, stirring occasionally and breaking up the clumps, until the meat is nicely browned, about 4 to 6 minutes. Remove the meat from the pot and set it aside. Add the onions, bell peppers, celery, cabbage, and 2 more tablespoons of the seasoning mix. Cook, stirring frequently, until the onions are well browned, about 15 minutes. Return the meat and any accumulated juices to the pot and add the remaining seasoning mix, the tomatoes, sour cream, rice, pumpkin seeds, and stock. Stir to blend completely and transfer the mixture to the prepared casserole.

Bake until cooked through, about 40 minutes. Serve hot.

Sweet Beef and Fresh Chiles

MAKES 10 CUPS

Don't let the fact that the meat marinates overnight discourage you from trying this recipe. The preparation is not hard to do, but it is going to take a little while. The remarkable flavor, with its combination of sweet and spicy, will inspire you to serve it again and again. I think it goes really well with the yellow King Midas Rice (page 233).

Seasoning Mix

1 tablespoon salt

2 teaspoons onion powder

1½ teaspoons garlic powder

1½ teaspoons ground ginger

1 teaspoon ground dried chipotle chile peppers (see Notes, page 6)

¾ teaspoon ground cumin

½ teaspoon cayenne

½ teaspoon ground coriander (see Glossary, page 293)

½ teaspoon black pepper

½ teaspoon white pepper

✷

2 tablespoons sugar

2 pounds sirloin steak

2 to 3 tablespoons olive oil

3 cups fresh green beans, sliced into ½-inch pieces

2 cups fresh corn kernels (about 4 ears)

1 julienne red bell pepper (see Notes, page 9)

1 julienne yellow bell pepper

2 fresh jalapeño chile peppers, seeded and sliced (see Notes, page 6)

4 fresh serrano chile peppers, sliced (see Notes, page 6)

1 cup lightly packed whole fresh cilantro leaves, all stems removed (see Notes, page 7, Glossary, page 293)

1 cup julienne onions (see Notes, page 9)

1 tablespoon minced fresh garlic

1 tablespoon minced fresh ginger

2 cups beef or chicken stock (see Notes, page 10)

1 (15-ounce) can unsweetened coconut milk (see Glossary, page 293)

Day 1: Combine the seasoning mix ingredients in a small bowl. In a separate bowl, combine the sugar with 1 tablespoon plus 1 teaspoon of the seasoning mix.

Cut the meat into strips about ½ inch thick by 2 inches long. Season the meat evenly with the sugar-seasoning mixture and refrigerate in a covered bowl or plastic zipper bag for as long as possible, but at least overnight.

Day 2: Heat 2 tablespoons of the oil in a 5-quart pot over high heat just until the oil begins to smoke, about 4 minutes. Add just enough of the meat strips to cover the pot bottom in a single layer. Cook the meat quickly, stirring constantly, until it is browned on all sides, and remove it from the pot immediately. Add the remaining oil if necessary, and cook the remaining meat.

Add the remaining seasoning mix and all the remaining ingredients except the coconut milk, then scrape the bottom of the pot vigorously until the brown bits are loosened. Cover and cook over high heat for 5 minutes. Return the meat to the pot and stir in the coconut milk. Bring to a rolling boil, then remove from the heat and serve.

Spicy Beef Stew

MAKES ALMOST 6 CUPS

This stew packs a wallop! If you need to reduce the amount of pepper in the seasoning mix, that's OK, or you can serve each portion with a dollop of sour cream, at room temperature, as a cooling topping. Delicious! I really appreciate recipes like this one, because once you've finished it, you've got the whole dinner ready, since meat, starch, and vegetable are all in one dish.

Seasoning Mix

2 tablespoons paprika

2 teaspoons salt

1 teaspoon garlic powder

1 teaspoon dry mustard

1 teaspoon onion powder

1 teaspoon dried oregano leaves

¾ teaspoon caraway seeds

¾ teaspoon cayenne

½ teaspoon ground cumin

½ teaspoon black pepper

½ teaspoon white pepper

✳

2 tablespoons unsalted butter

1½ pounds boneless chuck, cut into ½-inch cubes

1 large potato, peeled and medium diced, in all

2 large carrots, peeled and medium diced, in all

1 cup chopped green bell peppers, in all

2 cups beef stock, in all (see Notes, page 10)

Combine the seasoning mix ingredients in a small bowl.

Melt the butter in a heavy 5-quart pot over high heat. When it begins to sizzle, add the meat and brown it on all sides. Remove the meat from the pot and set it aside.

Add half of the potato, half of the carrots, and half of the bell peppers to the pot. Cover and cook, stirring occasionally, until the potato is tender, about 10 to 12 minutes. Stir in the seasoning mix and 1 cup of the stock and scrape the pot bottom thoroughly. Transfer to a blender, purée, and return to the pot. Return the meat and accumulated juices to the pot and bring the mixture to a boil. Cook, stirring occasionally, until the mixture just begins to stick, then stir in the remaining vegetables and stock and scrape the bottom of the pot. Bring to a boil and reduce the heat to low, then cover and simmer until the vegetables are tender, about 25 minutes.

Remove from the heat and serve.

Pork Patties

MAKES ABOUT 18 TO 20 PATTIES

When we were testing the recipes for this book, someone saw these patties and said, "Oh, I just love homemade sausage!" So call them sausages if you like and serve them with eggs for breakfast, or call them patties and have them for dinner with beans and salad. Either way, they're easy and delicious. They make great party food too—just reduce the size of each patty and make three dozen or so. Serve them with homemade mayonnaise to which you've added a bit of mustard or with one of our dipping sauces (pages 114–116).

Seasoning Mix

2 teaspoons salt

1½ teaspoons dried basil leaves

1 teaspoon ground allspice

1 teaspoon cayenne

1 teaspoon ground cumin

1 teaspoon ground fenugreek
(see Glossary, page 294)

1 teaspoon garlic powder

1 teaspoon onion powder

½ teaspoon black pepper

½ teaspoon white pepper

✳

8 ounces diced bacon

2 cups chopped onions

¼ cup finely diced fresh jalapeño
chile peppers (see Notes, page 6)

¼ cup sesame seeds

1½ pounds ground pork

Vegetable oil for frying

Combine the seasoning mix ingredients in a small bowl.

Cook the bacon in a skillet over high heat until it is rendered but not crisp. Stir in the onions, jalapeño peppers, and sesame seeds and cook, stirring occasionally, for 10 minutes. Add the seasoning mix, lower the heat to medium, and cook, scraping the bottom of the pan frequently, for 10 more minutes.

Grind the mixture in a food processor for about 1 minute, allow to cool, then combine with the pork. Shape into patties about 2½ inches across.

Pour enough vegetable oil into a large skillet to measure 1 inch deep and heat to 350° (use an electric appliance, or set a regular skillet over high heat for 4 minutes and use a cooking thermometer, adjusting the heat as necessary). Fry the patties in the hot oil, turning several times, until they're done, about 6 to 7 minutes in all. Drain on paper towels before serving.

Flank, Cabbage, and Beets

Flank and Broccoli

Brisket of Beef

Spinach, Arugula, and Meat Pie

Lamb with Spinach

Staggering Red Beans

Artichoke, Potato, and Cheese Casserole

Gingered Green Vegetables

Dinner Vegetables

Spinach and Cream Cheese Pie

Three-Squash Stew

Thu's Wonderful Soup

Peach Nectar Pie

Banana Poppy Seed Pie

Apple Raisin Custard

Pine Nut Custard

White Cheese Custard

Mango

Papaya

Plantain

Coconut

Merliton

Fennel

Shiitake

Jicama

Daikon

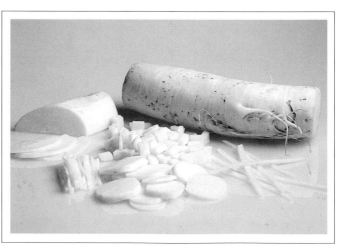

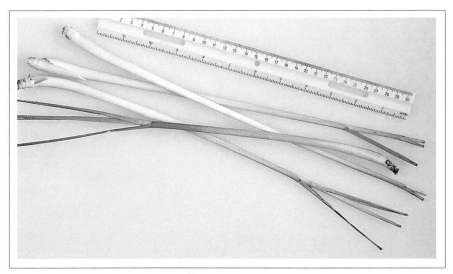

Lemon grass

Parsley

Sugar snap peas

Cilantro

Pasilla

Guajillo

Chipotle

Árbol

Ancho

Fenugreek

Curry mix

Paprika

Turmeric

Chickpea and Pork Pie

MAKES 2 (9-INCH) PIES

The day that we cooked this pie in our test kitchen, there was a full crew of carpenters, brick-layers, and painters working behind our kitchen building. They were so fascinated by the aroma of this pie cooking that I could not resist setting one out for them to try. They said it tasted great, and so will you. Because the chickpeas must be soaked overnight, you'll have to plan ahead. You're going to have some chickpeas left over—be inventive—boil them until tender and add to a salad, or sprinkle with seasonings and roast in a 350° oven for an hour for a crunchy snack.

1 pound dried chickpeas, soaked overnight (instructions follow)

✳

Sesame seed pie crust

Seasoning Mix

¼ cup sesame seeds

2 teaspoons dried oregano leaves

1 teaspoon cayenne

1 teaspoon garlic powder

1 teaspoon dried thyme leaves

✳

3¼ cups all-purpose flour

1 tablespoon sugar

2 teaspoons salt

1¼ cups very cold vegetable shortening

½ cup plus 1 tablespoon very cold water

Chickpea and pork filling

Seasoning Mix

1 tablespoon dried basil leaves

1 tablespoon ground fenugreek (see Glossary, page 294)

1 tablespoon salt

1 tablespoon dried thyme leaves

2 teaspoons caraway seeds

2 teaspoons ground dried árbol chile peppers (see Notes, page 6)

1½ teaspoons cayenne

1½ teaspoons garlic powder

1 teaspoon onion powder

1 teaspoon black pepper

¾ teaspoon white pepper

✳

3 cups pork or chicken stock, in all (see Notes, page 10)

2 tablespoons olive oil

2 pounds ground pork

2 cups chopped onions

2 cups chopped green bell peppers

1 tablespoon chopped fresh garlic

1 cup raisins

Yogurt topping

1 teaspoon dried basil leaves

1 (16-ounce) container plain yogurt

continued

Day 1: Add enough water to the chickpeas to cover them by 3 to 4 inches and soak overnight in the refrigerator.

PIE CRUSTS: Combine the seasoning mix ingredients in a small bowl.

Combine the flour, sugar, salt, and seasoning mix in an electric mixer equipped with a dough hook. Add the cold shortening and blend at low speed, scraping the sides and bottom of the bowl, just until the ingredients come together and resemble very coarse meal or dried split peas. Gradually add the very cold water and continue to process at low speed just until the water is absorbed, being careful not to overmix. As soon as the liquid is absorbed, gather the dough into a ball and refrigerate until cold, at least 4 hours, preferably overnight.

Day 2: To make the crusts, divide the dough in half and form each half into a ball. Liberally flour your hands, the working surface, and the rolling pin. Place one of the dough balls on the floured surface and roll it out, keeping it as even and round as possible. Turn the dough as you roll, and dust with flour as necessary, until the circle is about 11 inches in diameter. Carefully fit the circle into a 9-inch pie plate and crimp the edges with your hands or with the tines of a fork. Repeat with the remaining ball of dough. Set the shells aside while you prepare the filling.

CHICKPEA AND PORK FILLING: Combine the seasoning mix ingredients in a small bowl.

Drain but do not rinse the chickpeas, then purée $1\frac{1}{4}$ cups of them (set the whole chickpeas aside—you'll use most of them too), adding up to $\frac{1}{4}$ cup of stock if necessary. You should have about $1\frac{2}{3}$ cups of purée.

Heat the olive oil in a large skillet over high heat just until the oil begins to smoke, about 4 minutes. Add the pork, onions, bell peppers, garlic, and seasoning mix. Cover and cook, stirring occasionally, for 15 minutes. Stir and scrape the pan bottom thoroughly, then add 3 cups of the whole chickpeas. Cover and cook, stirring frequently, until the mixture begins to stick to the bottom of the pot, about 20 minutes. Add 1 cup stock, then stir and scrape thoroughly. Add 1 more cup stock, stir and scrape, and cook 10 minutes longer. Add the remaining stock and the chickpea purée,

cook for 3 minutes, then remove from the heat and add the raisins. Cool the mixture to room temperature.

Preheat the oven to 300°.

Divide the filling between the pie shells.

TOPPING: Combine the topping ingredients until blended, and divide the topping between the pies. Bake for 1 hour. Cool slightly before serving.

Smothered Potatoes, Cabbage, and Andouille

MAKES ABOUT 7 CUPS

If I were stranded on an island and had to eat the same food every day, this is one of the dishes I would wish for. It has the comfort of mashed potatoes, the down-home taste of cabbage, and the incredible flavor and spice of andouille.

Seasoning Mix

2 teaspoons salt

1½ teaspoons cayenne

1½ teaspoons onion powder

1½ teaspoons ground dried ancho chile peppers (see Notes, page 6)

1½ teaspoons ground dried guajillo chile peppers (see Notes, page 6)

1 teaspoon ground cumin

1 teaspoon garlic powder

1 teaspoon paprika

1 teaspoon white pepper

¾ teaspoon black pepper

✳

2 tablespoons vegetable oil

1 pound medium-diced andouille (see Glossary, page 292) or your favorite smoked pork sausage

2 pounds large-diced potatoes

6 cups large-diced cabbage

2 cups beef stock, in all (see Notes, page 10)

Combine the seasoning mix ingredients in a small bowl.

Heat the oil in a 4-quart pot over high heat just until the oil begins to smoke, about 4 minutes. Add the andouille and cook, stirring frequently, for 5 minutes. Add half of the potatoes, all of the cabbage, and 3 tablespoons of the seasoning mix and stir until all the ingredients are covered with the seasoning mix. Cover and cook, stirring frequently, for 4 minutes. Add ½ cup of the stock and cook for 5 minutes. Add the remaining potatoes and ½ cup stock and cook, stirring frequently, for 10 minutes. Add another ½ cup stock and cook for 10 more minutes. Reduce the heat to medium, add the remaining stock, and continue to cook, stirring and scraping frequently, especially toward the end of the cooking time when the starch from the potatoes will thicken the liquid and cause it to stick to the pot bottom. When the potatoes are cooked through, about 15 minutes, remove from the heat and serve.

Sausage and Millet Stew

MAKES ALMOST 4 QUARTS

This hearty one-dish meal offers a real change of pace because the combination of sausage, beans, millet, and seasonings is not exactly a traditional one in this country. Several weeks passed between developing the recipe in my test kitchen and the opportunity to taste the first re-cook brought in by one of my assistants, and to tell you the truth, I'd forgotten it. What a happy surprise!

Remember to plan ahead and soak the beans overnight. You don't want to get ready to cook and realize you forgot to soak the beans.

1 pound dried pinto beans, rinsed and picked over, soaked overnight (instructions follow)

＊

Seasoning Mix

2 teaspoons garlic powder

2 teaspoons salt

1 teaspoon ground allspice

1 teaspoon ground fennel seeds

1 teaspoon ground mace

1 teaspoon brown or yellow mustard seeds

1 teaspoon onion powder

1 teaspoon black pepper

³⁄₄ teaspoon cayenne

¹⁄₂ teaspoon ground cinnamon

¹⁄₂ teaspoon ground nutmeg

¹⁄₂ teaspoon white pepper

＊

3 tablespoons olive oil

3 cups chopped onions

2 cups chopped green bell peppers

2 cups chopped celery

1¹⁄₂ pounds sweet Italian sausage, casings removed

6 cups beef stock (see Notes, page 10)

1 cup millet (see Glossary, page 296)

¹⁄₂ cup dark molasses

Day 1: Add enough water to the beans to cover them by 3 to 4 inches and soak overnight in the refrigerator.

Day 2: Combine the seasoning mix ingredients in a small bowl.

Drain but do not rinse the beans.

Heat the olive oil in a 5-quart pot over high heat just until the oil begins to smoke, about 4 minutes. Add the onions, bell peppers, celery, and sausage and cook, stirring occasionally, for 10 minutes. Add the seasoning mix and cook, stirring and scraping the pot bottom frequently, for 15 minutes. Add the stock and drained beans, cover, and bring to a boil. Reduce the heat to low and simmer, stirring occasionally, until the beans are tender, about 1 hour. Add the millet and molasses, cover, and simmer until the millet is tender, about 15 minutes. Serve on a cold evening to a group of friends.

Italian Sausage and Tomato Custard Pie

MAKES 2 (9-INCH) PIES

Underneath the terra-cotta–colored topping is a gloriously rich pie filling. Be sure to use the most flavorful tomatoes you can find—they will make this dish sing!

Seasoned olive oil pie crusts

Seasoning Mix

1 teaspoon ground cardamom

1 teaspoon ground fenugreek (see Glossary, page 294)

1 teaspoon ground ginger

1 teaspoon ground dried ancho chile peppers (see Notes, page 6)

1 teaspoon ground turmeric

＊

3¼ cups all-purpose flour

1 tablespoon sugar

2 teaspoons salt

1 cup very cold vegetable shortening

¼ cup olive oil

½ cup plus 1 tablespoon very cold water

Tomato filling

Seasoning Mix

1 tablespoon dried basil leaves

1 tablespoon dried oregano leaves

2½ teaspoons cayenne

2 teaspoons dry mustard

2 teaspoons black pepper

2 teaspoons salt

1½ teaspoons ground coriander (see Glossary, page 293)

1 teaspoon ground allspice

1 teaspoon garlic powder

1 teaspoon onion powder

¾ teaspoon white pepper

＊

2 pounds sweet Italian sausage, casings removed

1½ cups chopped onions

1½ cups chopped green bell peppers

2 tablespoons chopped fresh garlic

5 cups chopped fresh tomatoes

3 tablespoons all-purpose flour

1 large egg

3 large egg yolks

1 cup heavy cream

¼ cup sugar

Ricotta topping

2 (15-ounce) packages soft curd ricotta cheese

2 tablespoons paprika

2 tablespoons grated Parmesan cheese

2 tablespoons grated Romano cheese

2 tablespoons sugar

PIE CRUSTS: Combine the seasoning mix ingredients in a small bowl.

Combine the flour, sugar, salt, and seasoning mix in an electric mixer equipped with a dough hook and process until well blended. Add the cold shortening and oil and blend at low speed, scraping the sides and bottom of the bowl, until the ingredients just come together and resemble very coarse meal or dried split peas. Gradually add the very cold water and continue to process at low speed just until the water is absorbed, being careful not to overmix. As soon as the liquid is absorbed, gather the dough into a ball and refrigerate until cold, at least 4 hours, preferably overnight.

To make the crusts, divide the dough in half and form each half into a ball. Liberally flour your hands, the working surface, and the rolling pin. Place one of the dough balls on the floured surface and roll it out, keeping it as even and round as possible. Turn the dough as you roll, and dust with flour as necessary, until the circle is about 11 inches in diameter. Carefully fit the circle into a 9-inch pie tin and crimp the edges with your hands or with the tines of a fork. Repeat with the remaining ball of dough. Set the shells aside while you prepare the filling.

FILLING: Combine the seasoning mix ingredients in a small bowl.

Combine the sausage, onions, bell peppers, garlic, and seasoning mix in a 4-quart pot. Cook over high heat, stirring frequently, for 15 minutes, then add the tomatoes and cook, stirring and scraping the bottom of the pot frequently, until the liquid falls below the level of the meat, about 20 minutes. Add the flour, stir until it is completely absorbed, and cook for 3 minutes. Remove from the heat and cool to room temperature.

Process the egg and egg yolk in a food processor or blender for 1 minute, then add the cream and sugar and process until combined, about 30 seconds. Fold the cream mixture into the meat mixture.

Preheat the oven to 300°.

TOPPING: Prepare the ricotta topping by processing all the ingredients in a blender or food processor until smooth.

Divide the filling between the pie shells and spread the ricotta topping over the filling. Bake until the tops are a rich red-brown, about 1 hour. Cut into wedges and serve hot.

Patricia's Pork Roast

MAKES 8 SERVINGS

The savory mixture that you cook, purée, and spread on the roast gives the meat a slightly crunchy coating and a flavor that is probably unlike any you've ever experienced. It gets very dark during roasting, but it's a sweet dark. In fact, the crust is so good that you'll want to be sure that each serving contains some of it. "Delicious" actually seems inadequate for this dish, so let me just say that among the many people who worked on this book and tasted recipes, this was the number-one favorite. Even people who say they don't like pork said this roast was "to die for." If you can't find unsalted peanuts, you can use salted ones and reduce the salt in the seasoning mix by ¹/₂ teaspoon. We have a great recipe for Sweet and Sour Kraut (page 269), which goes well with this.

Seasoning Mix

1 tablespoon salt

2 teaspoons ground dried ancho
   chile peppers (see Notes,
   page 6)

1 teaspoon ground cloves

1 teaspoon ground coriander
   (see Glossary, page 293)

1 teaspoon garlic powder

1 teaspoon dry mustard

1 teaspoon onion powder

1 teaspoon black pepper

³/₄ teaspoon cayenne

¹/₂ teaspoon white pepper

✳

¹/₂ cup unsalted pumpkin seeds,
   toasted (instructions follow)

¹/₂ cup unsalted peanuts, toasted
   (instructions follow)

1 tablespoon vegetable oil

2 cups chopped onions

1 ripe plantain, peeled and sliced
   (see Glossary, page 297)

1 large (or 2 medium or 3 small) apple,
   peeled, cored, and sliced

¹/₂ cup chopped pitted prunes
   (or raisins)

2 tablespoons chopped fresh garlic

¹/₄ cup chopped fresh ginger

4 cups chicken stock, in all (see Notes,
   page 10)

3 tablespoons dark molasses

1 (4-pound) bone-in pork loin roast

3 tablespoons all-purpose flour

2 cups heavy cream

Combine the seasoning mix ingredients in a small bowl.

Toast the pumpkin seeds and peanuts, separately, in a small skillet over high heat, stirring constantly, until they are lightly browned, then immediately remove from the hot skillet to stop the toasting.

Heat the oil in a 10-inch skillet over high heat just until the oil begins to smoke, about 4 minutes. Add the onions, plantain, apple, prunes (or raisins), garlic, ginger, pumpkin seeds, and peanuts. Cook, stirring frequently, until the onions begin to brown and the fruit becomes soft, about 10 minutes. Stir in 2 tablespoons of the seasoning mix, then spread the mixture over the bottom of the pan. Cook until the mixture begins to brown and stick, about 4 minutes. Stir in 1 cup of the stock and scrape the bottom of the pan to loosen any brown bits. Remove from the heat and add the molasses.

Purée the mixture in a food processor (preferred because it will keep the mixture thick, which is important since it's used as a stuffing) or a blender. If you use a blender, you may have to add some liquid.

Preheat the oven to 350°.

Make 15 to 20 pockets about 1 inch apart in the roast by inserting a small sharp knife into the top of the meat and straight down almost through the meat. Without enlarging the openings, move the knife back and forth slightly to increase the size of the pockets.

Sprinkle the roast evenly with the remaining seasoning mix and rub it on all surfaces of the meat and inside the cut pockets. (This works best if you use your hands—you can always wash them afterward. Or you may prefer to wear thin vinyl gloves to protect your skin from the chile pepper and cayenne in the seasoning mix.) Fill the pockets and coat the top and sides of the roast with half of the paste mixture, reserving the remaining paste for making the sauce.

Place the seasoned roast in a roasting pan without a rack, fat side up so that the meat rests on the bone side. Insert a meat thermometer so that it does not touch either bone or fat. Roast, uncovered, until the thermometer registers 165°, about 2 hours.

Remove the roast from the pan and keep it warm. The tantalizing aroma becomes even more intense once the roast is out of the oven. You're only human if you have a nibble at this point, but it gets even better, so continue. Pour off all the fat from the roasting pan except 3 tablespoons. Whisk the flour with the reserved fat in the pan and whisk in the remaining 3 cups of stock. Scrape thoroughly to loosen the brown particles in the bottom of the pan—they add even more flavor to the sauce. Place the pan over high heat on top of the stove and bring to a boil. Whisk in the heavy cream and the remaining paste, and continue to whisk vigorously until all the ingredients are combined. If the sauce seems to be too thick at this point, add more stock. Return just to a boil, whisking constantly, then remove from the heat.

To serve, slice the roast between the bones and drizzle with some of the sauce. Serve the remaining sauce separately. And bask in the compliments.

Lamb with Spinach

MAKES 4 SERVINGS

In this recipe the distinctive flavor of lamb is enhanced by the bell peppers, eggplant, tomatoes, and spinach. This is a hearty dish, and if you like to serve lamb in the spring, you will love having this alternative method of seasoning and cooking it.

Seasoning Mix

1 tablespoon salt

2 teaspoons garlic powder

2 teaspoons onion powder

1½ teaspoons ground turmeric

1 teaspoon dried basil leaves

1 teaspoon ground cloves

1 teaspoon ground coriander
(see Glossary, page 293)

1 teaspoon ground cumin

1 teaspoon black pepper

1 teaspoon dried tarragon leaves

½ teaspoon cayenne

½ teaspoon ground fenugreek
(see Glossary, page 294)

½ teaspoon ground mace

½ teaspoon white pepper

✳

1 tablespoon minced fresh garlic

1 tablespoon minced fresh ginger

4 (medium) lamb shanks

2 tablespoons vegetable oil

3 cups chopped onions

1 cup chopped green bell peppers

1 cup chopped red bell peppers

1 cup chopped yellow bell peppers

1 large eggplant, peeled, cut in half
lengthwise, and thinly sliced into
half-moon-shaped pieces (about
8 cups)

½ cup thinly sliced fresh ginger

2 (14½-ounce) cans diced tomatoes
(see Notes, page 7)

1 (10-ounce) bag fresh spinach, washed
and stemmed

¼ cup lightly packed dark
brown sugar

Combine the seasoning mix ingredients in a small bowl, then add the minced garlic and minced ginger.

Cut 4 or 5 pockets into each lamb shank by piercing the meat with a thin sharp knife and, without enlarging the point of entry, working the knife back and forth to form the pockets. Divide the seasoning mixture evenly among the pockets, and push these seasonings as far into the pockets as possible. Rub onto the surface of the meat any seasoning mixture that spills.

continued

Preheat the oven to 350°.

Heat the oil in a heavy 8-quart pot over high heat just until the oil begins to smoke, about 4 minutes. Brown the shanks in the hot oil, covered, about 8 or 9 minutes on each side. If you don't have such a large pot, a smaller one will work fine—just brown the shanks in batches. Transfer the lamb to a roasting pan.

Add the onions and all the bell peppers to the pot and scrape the bottom of the pot well. Add the eggplant, sliced ginger, and tomatoes, then cover and cook, stirring occasionally, for 25 minutes. Stir in the spinach and brown sugar and cook, covered, for 5 minutes. Remove from the heat and arrange the cooked vegetable mixture around the lamb in the roasting pan. Roast until you can easily pull the meat away from the bones with a fork, about 1 hour 50 minutes. To be sure the meat is completely done, test the biggest shank—if it's tender and the meat pulls away from the bone easily, the others will be done as well. Serve with the bones, or remove them first.

Sweet Spiced Lamb Patties

MAKES ABOUT 24 TO 28 PATTIES

These interesting little meat patties show their Middle Eastern origin in the chickpeas (called garbanzos in the Spanish-speaking world) and lamb. They're wonderful as an appetizer, go great with drinks (you could make them even smaller if you like), or can be the meat course of a lunch or light supper. Notice that you'll need to plan ahead—this recipe calls for you to soak the chickpeas overnight.

¾ cup dried chickpeas, soaked overnight (instructions follow)

✻

Seasoning Mix

2 tablespoons lightly packed light brown sugar

2 teaspoons ground coriander (see Glossary, page 293)

2 teaspoons ground dried ancho chile peppers (see Notes, page 6)

2 teaspoons salt

1 teaspoon cayenne

1 teaspoon ground cinnamon

1 teaspoon onion powder

1 teaspoon ground dried chipotle chile peppers (see Notes, page 6)

¾ teaspoon ground nutmeg

¾ teaspoon white pepper

½ teaspoon ground mace

½ teaspoon black pepper

✻

1½ tablespoons olive oil

1½ cups chopped onions

1 cup chopped celery

½ cup chicken stock (see Notes, page 10)

¼ cup all-purpose flour

1 pound ground lamb

Vegetable oil for frying

Day 1: Add enough water to the chickpeas to cover them by 3 or 4 inches and soak in the refrigerator overnight.

Day 2: Combine the seasoning mix ingredients in a small bowl.

Drain but do not rinse the chickpeas.

Heat the olive oil in a 10-inch skillet over high heat just until the oil begins to smoke, about 4 minutes. Add the onions, celery, and chickpeas and cook, stirring frequently, until the vegetables brown slightly, about 10 minutes. Add the seasoning mix and continue to stir and cook for 5 minutes more. Remove from the heat and process with the stock in a food processor or blender for 2 minutes.

Cool the mixture enough to handle comfortably and combine it with the flour and lamb in a mixing bowl. Cover the bowl and refrigerate for at least 4 hours, preferably overnight.

Pour enough vegetable oil into a large skillet to measure 1 inch deep and heat to 350° (use an electric appliance, or set a regular skillet over high heat for 4 minutes and use a cooking thermometer, adjusting the heat as necessary).

Remove the meat mixture from the refrigerator and, with a tablespoon, scoop up portions to form patties about 2^1/$_2$ inches across. Fry the patties in the hot oil, turning occasionally, until cooked through, about 8 minutes in all. These are tender patties and may crumble easily, so be careful when handling—the combination of a slotted spoon and a spatula seems to work pretty well. Drain on paper towels before serving.

General Beans
and
Major Rice

King Midas Rice

Spicy Black Rice

Gingered Cream Rice

Sweet Pepper Rice

Rice with Plantains

Rice with Split Peas

Rice Salad

Devilishly Delicious Black Beans

Refried Black Beans

Yo' Mama's Red Beans

Staggering Red Beans

Beans with Chorizo

Lentil Salad

King Midas Rice

MAKES 8 (1-CUP) SERVINGS

The gorgeous golden color of this rice comes from the saffron and turmeric, both used in several cultures for coloring as well as for flavor. Saffron is very expensive and sometimes hard to find. If it's unavailable (or you simply don't want to spend the money), you can still have a wonderful taste without it. Sometimes in India, when preparing for company, the cook will garnish a dish with very thin sheets of pure silver. Now, that's extravagant!

Any color bell peppers will taste fine, but use yellow peppers and substitute chopped bok choy stalks for the celery if you want to keep the dish completely gold.

Seasoning Mix

30 strands saffron (see Glossary, page 298)

2 teaspoons salt

2 teaspoons garlic powder

2 teaspoons onion powder

2 teaspoons ground turmeric

1 teaspoon cayenne

1 teaspoon dried thyme leaves

¾ teaspoon white pepper

½ teaspoon ground cardamom

½ teaspoon black pepper

✳

1 tablespoon unsalted butter

2 cups chopped onions, in all

1 cup chopped bell peppers

½ cup chopped celery

4 cups rich chicken stock (see Notes, page 10)

2 cups converted white rice

2 bay leaves

Combine the seasoning mix ingredients in a small bowl.

Melt the butter in a heavy 5-quart pot over high heat. When it sizzles, add 1 cup of the onions and cook until they begin to brown, about 4 minutes. Stir in the remaining onions, the bell peppers, celery, and seasoning mix. Cook, stirring and scraping the bottom of the pot frequently, for 2 minutes. Stir in the stock, rice, and bay leaves. Cover and bring to a boil, then reduce the heat to low and simmer until the rice is done, about 20 minutes. Fluff with a fork, cover, and let sit for 5 minutes before serving.

Spicy Black Rice

MAKES 7 (1-CUP) SERVINGS

Here is a rice dish with such an intense flavor that it will satisfy your emotional hunger. With the raisins, portobello mushroom cubes, and rice wine, it's somewhat exotic, yet it's hearty enough to satisfy a working man's appetite.

Seasoning Mix

1 tablespoon garlic powder

1 tablespoon onion powder

2 teaspoons salt

1½ teaspoons ground cumin

½ teaspoon cayenne

½ teaspoon ground cloves

½ teaspoon ground mace

½ teaspoon black pepper

½ teaspoon white pepper

✳

2 tablespoons vegetable oil

2 cups chopped onions

½ cup chopped celery

2 bay leaves

2 tablespoons chopped fresh ginger

1 large portobello mushroom, sliced 1 inch long and ½ inch wide (see Glossary, page 296)

¼ cup rice wine (see Glossary, page 297)

2 tablespoons tamari (see Glossary, page 299)

1 cup raisins

2 cups converted white rice

4 cups chicken stock (see Notes, page 10)

Combine the seasoning mix ingredients in a small bowl.

Heat the oil in a heavy 4-quart pot over high heat just until the oil begins to smoke, about 4 minutes. Stir in the onions, celery, bay leaves, ginger, mushroom, and 2 tablespoons of the seasoning mix. Cook, stirring frequently, until the mixture is a dark metallic color and sticks to the bottom of the pot, about 6 to 8 minutes. Add the rice wine and tamari and scrape the pot bottom to loosen the brown bits. Add the raisins and rice and continue to cook, stirring occasionally, until all the liquid is absorbed and the rice begins to stick to the bottom of the pot, about 5 to 6 minutes. Stir in the stock and scrape the pot bottom again. Stir in the remaining seasoning mix.

Cover and bring to a boil, then reduce the heat to low and simmer until the rice is tender, about 20 minutes. Remove from the heat, fluff with a fork, cover, and let sit for 5 minutes before serving.

Gingered Cream Rice

MAKES 10 (1-CUP) SERVINGS

Even people who've never been able to cook rice successfully will find this recipe a breeze! And who says you can't bake rice? This is one of the creamiest dishes I've ever come up with. It's perfect with broiled or grilled poultry or meat, and dynamite with Chicken in Tamari Cream (page 175). If you don't have an ovenproof skillet with a tight lid, improvise. One of my assistants tested this recipe using a pot that was the right size but had no lid, so she sealed it with two layers of foil. Worked just fine.

Seasoning Mix

1 tablespoon salt

1 teaspoon garlic powder

1 teaspoon ground ginger

1 teaspoon onion powder

1 teaspoon white pepper

½ teaspoon cayenne

✳

4 tablespoons unsalted butter

1 pound quartered fresh mushrooms

1 cup chopped onions

2 cups converted white rice

2 tablespoons chopped fresh ginger

2 cups chicken stock (see Notes, page 10)

2 to 3 cups heavy cream

½ cup freshly grated Parmesan cheese

Combine the seasoning mix ingredients in a small bowl.

Preheat the oven to 350°.

Heat the butter in a large ovenproof skillet, preferably one that has a tight-fitting lid. When the butter sizzles, add the mushrooms, onions, and seasoning mix. Cook, stirring frequently, for 6 minutes, then add the rice and ginger. Stir in the stock, 2 cups heavy cream, and the Parmesan cheese and mix thoroughly. Cover and bake for 45 minutes. Remove from the oven and check to see if there is still some liquid in the bottom of the pan. If not, add the remaining cup of cream. Let sit until the liquid is absorbed, about 10 minutes, before serving.

Sweet Pepper Rice

MAKES 7 (1-CUP) SERVINGS

If you have never used dried black mushrooms before, you're going to feel like a magician, because the way they expand in water is spellbinding! The real alchemy, though, is the subtle woodsy flavor they impart to the rice. The peppers add beautiful color and taste, and the peanuts add crunch and taste, giving this recipe a combination of textures as well as a complex, distinctive flavor.

Seasoning Mix

2 teaspoons salt

1½ teaspoons onion powder

1 teaspoon garlic powder

1 teaspoon black pepper

1 teaspoon cayenne

1 teaspoon dry mustard

1 teaspoon rubbed (or ground) sage

¾ teaspoon ground nutmeg

½ teaspoon white pepper

*

1 cup chopped unsalted peanuts, toasted (instructions follow)

1 cup dried black mushrooms (see Glossary, page 296)

½ cup vegetable oil

1 cup chopped green bell peppers, in all

1 cup chopped red bell peppers, in all

1 cup chopped yellow bell peppers, in all

½ cup medium-dry sherry

2 tablespoons minced fresh ginger

2 cups converted white rice

4 cups chicken stock (see Notes, page 10)

Combine the seasoning mix ingredients in a small bowl.

Toast the peanuts in a small skillet over high heat, stirring constantly, until they are lightly browned and produce a wonderful aroma. Immediately remove from the hot skillet and set aside.

Soak the mushrooms in enough warm water to cover them by 3 inches until they have fully expanded, about 10 minutes. Drain, chop, and set them aside.

Heat the oil in a heavy 2-quart pot over high heat just until the oil begins to smoke, about 4 minutes. Add the peanuts and ½ cup each of the green, red, and yellow bell peppers. Cook, stirring occasionally, until the peanuts start to brown, about

2 to 3 minutes. Add the sherry, ginger, seasoning mix, and mushrooms. Cook, stirring frequently, for 3 minutes. Stir in the remaining bell peppers, the rice, and the stock.

Cover and bring just to a boil, then reduce the heat to low and simmer until the rice is tender, about 20 minutes. Fluff with a fork, cover, and let stand for 5 minutes before serving.

Rice with Plantains

MAKES 12 (1-CUP) SERVINGS

This recipe doesn't claim to be authentically anything, but the use of plantains with rice flirts with ideas that come from the tropics. It goes really well with roast pork, grilled fish, and many other Caribbean-style main dishes. Be sure the plantains are really ripe; some recipes require green plantains, but in this case you want them soft, with a fully developed flavor. If you're an experienced rice cooker, you may wonder why I have you stir the rice before putting it into the oven. Normally you don't disturb rice once it starts to boil because stirring develops the starches in the rice and makes it sticky, but the ingredients in this dish might stick to the pot without that final scraping, so it's necessary. Just try to disturb the rice as little as possible, while giving the bottom of the pot a good scrape.

Seasoning Mix

1 tablespoon salt

1 tablespoon ground dried California Beauty chile peppers (see Notes, page 6)

2 teaspoons garlic powder

2 teaspoons onion powder

2 teaspoons ground dried ancho chile peppers (see Notes, page 6)

2 teaspoons paprika

1½ teaspoons ground cardamom

1 teaspoon white pepper

¾ teaspoon cayenne

½ teaspoon black pepper

＊

2 tablespoons vegetable oil

3 cups chopped onions

2 very ripe plantains, peeled and diced (see Glossary, page 297)

1 tablespoon minced fresh garlic

6 cups chicken stock, in all (see Notes, page 10)

3 cups converted white rice

Combine the seasoning mix ingredients in a small bowl.

Heat the oil in a heavy ovenproof 6-quart pot over high heat just until the oil begins to smoke, about 4 minutes. Add the onions and cook, stirring and scraping frequently, until they are brown, about 6 minutes. Add the plantains and cook, stirring and scraping frequently, for 6 minutes longer. Stir in 2 tablespoons of the seasoning mix and the garlic and cook until the mixture begins to stick to the bottom of the pot. Reduce the heat if necessary to prevent burning—different stoves put out different amounts of heat, and yours may be a dragon. Stir thoroughly and scrape the bottom of the pot to loosen any brown bits. Spread the mixture evenly over the bottom of the pot and cook until the moisture evaporates.

Preheat the oven to 350°.

When the mixture sticks hard (see Notes, page 10), add 1 cup of the stock and scrape the bottom of the pot thoroughly and completely. Add the remaining stock, the remaining seasoning mix, and the rice. Cover and bring to a boil. Stir once, scraping the bottom of the pot gently but completely, cover, and bake until the rice is tender and all the water is absorbed, about 25 minutes. Fluff with a fork before serving.

Rice with Split Peas

MAKES ABOUT 9 (1-CUP) SERVINGS

People all over the world cook rice with legumes—that is, peas and beans. What makes all these dishes different, besides the various legumes used, is the wide array of seasonings available in different places. And what makes these dishes of interest to us now is the fact that the proteins in rice and peas or beans combine in an especially nutritious way. Use vegetable stock instead of chicken stock to make the dish totally vegetarian.

Seasoning Mix

2 teaspoons salt

2 teaspoons lightly packed light brown sugar

1½ teaspoons dried basil leaves

1½ teaspoons garlic powder

1½ teaspoons onion powder

1½ teaspoons dried oregano leaves

1 teaspoon ground coriander (see Glossary, page 293)

½ teaspoon cayenne

½ teaspoon black pepper

½ teaspoon white pepper

*

2 tablespoons olive oil

2 cups chopped onions

1 cup chopped celery

7 cups chicken stock (see Notes, page 10)

1½ cups dried green or yellow split peas, rinsed and picked over

1 cup lightly packed whole fresh cilantro leaves (see Notes, page 7, Glossary, page 293)

1 cup converted white rice

Combine the seasoning mix ingredients in a small bowl.

Heat the oil in a 5-quart pot over high heat just until the oil begins to smoke, about 4 minutes. Add the onions and celery, cover, and cook, stirring occasionally, for 10 minutes. Add the stock and scrape the sides and bottom of the pot to loosen any brown bits. Stir in the split peas and seasoning mix and bring to a boil. Reduce the heat to low, cover, and simmer for 20 minutes. Add the cilantro and rice and bring to a boil, then reduce the heat to low and simmer, covered, for 15 minutes. Fluff the rice with a fork and let sit, covered, for 5 minutes before serving.

Rice Salad

MAKES ABOUT 12 (1-CUP) SERVINGS

Balsamic and red wine vinegars are easy to find, so don't worry if you can't find the cane vinegar or don't have time to order it. Just use any three vinegar varieties of your choice, then taste and adjust as necessary. This salad makes a nice surprise for people who are used to thinking of rice as only a side dish. In fact, I like it served as an appetizer on a bed of exotic greens.

Seasoning Mix

2 tablespoons sugar

2 teaspoons salt

2 teaspoons dried tarragon leaves

1 teaspoon dried basil leaves

1 teaspoon onion powder

1 teaspoon dried oregano leaves

1 teaspoon dried thyme leaves

¾ teaspoon garlic powder

½ teaspoon cayenne

½ teaspoon black pepper

½ teaspoon white pepper

6 cups cooked white rice, at room temperature

2 cups finely diced jicama (see Glossary, page 295)

2 cups finely diced bok choy, stems only (see Glossary, page 292)

3 tablespoons olive oil

1 cup chopped green bell peppers

1 cup chopped red bell peppers

2 cups chopped onions

1 (15-ounce) can tomato purée

¼ cup balsamic vinegar (see Glossary, page 299)

¼ cup cane vinegar (see Glossary, page 299)

¼ cup red wine vinegar

Combine the seasoning mix ingredients in a small bowl.

Mix the rice with the jicama and bok choy.

Heat the olive oil in a 4-quart pot over high heat just until the oil starts to smoke, about 4 minutes. Add all the bell peppers, onions, and seasoning mix and cook until the vegetables are wilted but still retain their color, about 4 minutes. Transfer the vegetables to a large bowl and stir in the tomato purée and all the vinegars. Add the rice mixture and toss until blended. Serve at room temperature and refrigerate any leftovers.

Devilishly Delicious Black Beans

MAKES 8 SERVINGS

I gotta be honest with you—these beans are hot as Hades—but goodness knows how I love 'em! If you absolutely must, you can reduce the amounts of the peppers, but if you serve the beans with rice, tortillas, sour cream, or big slabs of meat that are not too highly seasoned, even wimps will be able to handle the heat. You know how good for you beans of any kind are, and when combined with rice, their proteins work together especially well. I'm a chef and a lover, not a chemist, but I listen to nutritionists and wanted to pass that bit of information on to you. By the way, notice that the beans are soaked overnight, which shortens the cooking time.

1 pound dried black beans, rinsed and picked over, soaked overnight (instructions follow)

✳

Seasoning Mix

1 tablespoon plus 2 teaspoons ground dried ancho chile peppers (see Notes, page 6)

2 teaspoons salt

2 teaspoons garlic powder

2 teaspoons onion powder

2 teaspoons dried oregano leaves

2 teaspoons ground dried California Beauty chile peppers (see Notes, page 6)

1 teaspoon cayenne

1 teaspoon dried thyme leaves

¾ teaspoon black pepper

½ teaspoon white pepper

✳

5 cups chicken stock, in all (see Notes, page 10)

1 pound finely diced smoked sausage

2 cups chopped onions

2 cups chopped green bell peppers

3 bay leaves

Day 1: Add enough water to the beans to cover them by 3 to 4 inches and soak overnight in the refrigerator.

Day 2: Combine the seasoning mix ingredients in a small bowl.

Drain but do not rinse the beans and purée ½ cup of them with 1 cup of stock. Set aside.

Preheat a heavy 6-quart pot over high heat for 2 minutes, then add the sausage, onions, bell peppers, and bay leaves. Cook, stirring occasionally, for 10 minutes. At this point the fragrance is so wonderful that you may want to stop and eat the contents of the pot with crackers! Take a little bite if you must, but please keep going. Add the seasoning mix and the drained beans, and cook, stirring occasionally, for 45 minutes. Add the puréed bean-stock mixture and cook, stirring occasionally, for 15 minutes. Stir thoroughly, then add the remaining stock. Bring to a boil, then reduce the heat to low, cover, and simmer, stirring occasionally, until the beans are tender, about 1 hour. Have a fire extinguisher handy when you serve the beans.

Refried Black Beans

The art of cooking refried beans is in knowing when the perfect texture has been achieved. The refried beans should be soft and melt away very easily in your mouth. You should be able to take a spoonful of refried beans and place it on top of the remaining beans in the pan and it will hold its shape. The refried beans should taste wonderful and spread the aroma of each ingredient simultaneously and distinctly in your mouth with a feeling of pleasure.

1 recipe Devilishly Delicious Black
    Beans (page 244)

2¼ cups beef or chicken stock
    (see Notes, page 10)

12 tablespoons bacon drippings,
    in all

9 tablespoons unsalted butter, in all

Purée the black beans in a food processor, then add the stock. Stir the stock and beans until completely blended.

In a 10-inch skillet, heat 2 tablespoons of the bacon drippings over high heat for 2 minutes. Add a third of bean purée and cook, scraping the skillet bottom constantly, until the beans start to form a coating on the bottom of the skillet, about 8 minutes. Add 1 tablespoon butter and 1 tablespoon bacon drippings. Lower the heat to medium and continue to stir and scrape the skillet bottom. When beans start to get pasty, about 10 minutes, reduce the heat to very low and add 1 tablespoon unsalted butter and 1 tablespoon bacon drippings. Continue stirring and scraping the bottom and sides of the skillet until a soft paste has been achieved, about 6 minutes.

Repeat this process for the remaining beans. Serve as soon as all the beans are cooked.

Yo' Mama's Red Beans

MAKES 10 (1-CUP) SERVINGS

Except for our revved-up seasonings, this is a very traditional version of the Monday wash-day supper in New Orleans. Cooks usually didn't presoak beans, so they had to cook them for a long time, and while the pot simmered, they could tend to the laundry. If you don't have time to presoak your beans or if you forget, just cook them about an hour longer. If you like the liquid to have a little substance, as I do, when the beans are almost done, remove some of them— a cupful or so—mash or purée them, and return them to the pot. Red beans are just as good the next day and the day after that.

1 pound dried red (kidney) beans, rinsed and picked over, soaked overnight (instructions follow)

✳

Seasoning Mix

2 teaspoons dry mustard

2 teaspoons salt

1 teaspoon cayenne

1 teaspoon ground cumin

1 teaspoon garlic powder

1 teaspoon onion powder

1 teaspoon dried oregano leaves

1 teaspoon ground dried pasilla chile peppers (see Notes, page 6)

1 teaspoon black pepper

1 teaspoon dried thyme leaves

½ teaspoon white pepper

✳

2 tablespoons vegetable oil

2 cups chopped onions, in all

1 cup chopped green bell peppers

1 pound smoked sausage, sliced into rounds ¼ inch thick, then quartered

2 tablespoons minced fresh garlic

2 tablespoons minced fresh ginger

7 cups chicken stock (see Notes, page 10)

¼ cup lightly packed chopped fresh parsley

Day 1: Add enough water to cover the beans by 3 to 4 inches and soak them overnight in the refrigerator.

Day 2: Combine the seasoning mix ingredients in a small bowl.

Drain but do not wash the beans and set them aside.

continued

Heat the oil in a 5-quart pot over high heat just until the oil begins to smoke, about 4 minutes. Add 1 cup of the onions, the bell peppers, and smoked sausage. Cook, stirring frequently, for 6 minutes. Add the garlic, ginger, remaining onions, drained beans, and seasoning mix. Cook, stirring frequently, for 5 minutes, then add the stock, stir well, and cover. Bring to a boil, reduce the heat to low, and simmer until the beans are tender and starting to break, about 2 hours. Add the parsley, stir thoroughly, and remove from the heat. Serve over hot white rice.

Staggering Red Beans

MAKES ABOUT 11 (1-CUP) SERVINGS

Notice that the recipe calls for only the bok choy leaves, not the stems. Save them to add to a mixed green salad or to use in another recipe that calls for only the stems such as Rice Salad (page 243). Don't forget to soak the beans overnight to shorten the cooking time.

1 pound dried red (kidney) beans, rinsed and picked over, soaked overnight (instructions follow)

✳

Seasoning Mix

2 teaspoons dry mustard

2 teaspoons salt

1½ teaspoons cayenne

1 teaspoon garlic powder

1 teaspoon onion powder

1 teaspoon paprika

1 teaspoon black pepper

½ teaspoon white pepper

✳

2 tablespoons vegetable oil

1 cup chopped onions

1 pound smoked ham, diced into bite-sized pieces

1 cup lightly packed finely chopped fresh parsley

¼ cup tamari (see Glossary, page 299)

½ cup rice wine (see Glossary, page 297)

2 (12-ounce) bottles dark beer

6 cups vegetable or chicken stock, in all (see Notes, page 10)

4 cups chopped bok choy leaves (see Glossary, page 292)

4 cups chopped kale

Day 1: Add enough water to the red beans to cover them by 3 to 4 inches and soak overnight in the refrigerator.

Day 2: Drain but do not rinse the beans.

Combine the seasoning mix ingredients in a small bowl.

Heat the oil in a 5-quart pot over high heat just until the oil smokes, about 4 minutes. Add the onions, ham, parsley, tamari, and seasoning mix. Cook, stirring once or twice, for 4 minutes, then add the drained red beans. Cook, stirring occasionally, for 5 minutes, then add the rice wine and beer. Cook for 3 more minutes, then stir in 3 cups of the stock. Cover and bring to a boil, then reduce the heat to low and simmer for 20 minutes. Add the bok choy leaves and kale, stir, and simmer, covered, for 20 minutes. Stir in the remaining 3 cups of stock and simmer, covered, stirring occasionally, until the beans are tender, about 1½ to 2 hours. Serve over hot white rice.

Beans with Chorizo

MAKES ABOUT 10 (1-CUP) SERVINGS

Of Spanish origin, this hearty and easy-to-make recipe works as a one-dish meal because it contains meat, starch, and vegetables. What makes it work as a flavorful treat, however, is the combination of several kinds of chile peppers. Serve it with thick hunks of dark bread. Yum! Remember to soak the beans overnight to cut the cooking time.

1 pound dried pinto beans, rinsed and picked over, soaked overnight (instructions follow)

✳

Seasoning Mix

2 teaspoons ground dried chipotle chile peppers (see Notes, page 6)

2 teaspoons salt

1 teaspoon cayenne

1 teaspoon garlic powder

1 teaspoon onion powder

1 teaspoon white pepper

1 teaspoon ground dried ancho chile peppers (see Notes, page 6)

1 teaspoon ground dried guajillo chile peppers (see Notes, page 6)

1 teaspoon ground dried pasilla chile peppers (see Notes, page 6)

½ teaspoon black pepper

✳

8 ounces finely diced bacon

2 cups chopped onions

2 cups chopped green bell peppers

1 cup chopped celery

9 ounces diced chorizo (see Glossary, page 293)

1 tablespoon minced fresh garlic

½ cup lightly packed, finely chopped fresh cilantro (see Notes, page 7, Glossary, page 293)

¼ cup Magic Pepper Sauce®

9 cups chicken or beef stock, in all (see Notes, page 10)

Day 1: Add enough water to the pinto beans to cover them by about 3 to 4 inches and soak overnight in the refrigerator.

Day 2: Combine the seasoning mix ingredients in a small bowl.

Drain but do not rinse the beans.

Render the bacon in a 5-quart pot over high heat until the bits are crisp and browned. Add the onions, bell peppers, celery, chorizo, garlic, cilantro, Magic Pepper Sauce, drained beans, and seasoning mix. Cook until all the moisture is absorbed, about 20 minutes, then stir in 4 cups of the stock. Cook, stirring occasionally, for 20 minutes and stir in 2 cups more stock. Bring to a boil, reduce the heat to low, and simmer, stirring occasionally, for 1 hour. Stir in the remaining stock and cook until the sauce is thick and the beans are tender, about 45 minutes. Serve hot.

Lentil Salad

MAKES ABOUT 6½ CUPS

Tasty and nutritious, this salad makes a perfect accompaniment to a spicy main dish, or it can be served for a light lunch or supper. Lentils are quick and easy to use because they don't have to be soaked and don't take very long to cook.

Seasoning Mix

2 teaspoons dry mustard

2 teaspoons salt

1½ teaspoons cayenne

1 teaspoon garlic powder

1 teaspoon onion powder

1 teaspoon paprika

1 teaspoon black pepper

½ teaspoon white pepper

*

2 tablespoons vegetable oil

2 cups chopped onions, in all

1 pound lentils, rinsed and picked over

1 cup chopped green bell peppers

1 cup chopped red bell peppers

1 cup chopped yellow bell peppers

3 tablespoons tamari (see Glossary, page 299)

3 tablespoons dark molasses

2 cups vegetable or chicken stock (see Notes, page 10)

Combine the seasoning mix ingredients in a small bowl.

Heat the oil in a 5-quart pot over high heat just until the oil begins to smoke, about 4 minutes. Add 1 cup of the onions and cook, stirring occasionally, until they are browned, about 6 minutes. Add the remaining onions, the lentils, bell peppers, and seasoning mix. Stir and scrape the pan bottom thoroughly and add the tamari and molasses. Cook, stirring and scraping, for 3 minutes, then stir in the stock. Bring to a boil and reduce the heat to low, then cover and simmer for 12 minutes. Remove from the heat and allow to cool. Serve at room temperature or slightly chilled.

Radical
Roots
& Luscious
Leaves

Artichoke, Potato, and Cheese Casserole

Cauliflower Casserole

Gingered Green Vegetables

Dinner Vegetables

Hot Bittersweet Eggplant

Mirliton Casserole

Spinach and Cream Cheese Pie

Sweet and Sour Kraut

Three-Squash Stew

Artichoke, Potato, and Cheese Casserole

MAKES 12 SERVINGS

This dish is a little different—think of it as potatoes au gratin with artichokes added. It's hearty, rich, and very satisfying. And don't worry if you can't find serrano chile peppers; just use whatever variety of chile peppers looks fresh and good at your market.

Seasoning Mix

2 teaspoons salt

1½ teaspoons dried basil leaves

1½ teaspoons caraway seeds

1½ teaspoons paprika

1½ teaspoons ground dried California Beauty chile peppers (see Notes, page 6)

1½ teaspoons dried thyme leaves

1 teaspoon cayenne

1 teaspoon garlic powder

1 teaspoon dry mustard

1 teaspoon onion powder

1 teaspoon black pepper

½ teaspoon white pepper

∗

4 large artichokes

2 large potatoes

4 tablespoons unsalted butter

1½ cups chopped onions

1 tablespoon minced fresh ginger

2 tablespoons finely diced fresh serrano chile peppers (see Notes, page 6)

¼ cup tamari (see Glossary, page 299)

2 cups heavy cream

4 ounces grated mozzarella cheese

8 ounces grated Cheddar cheese

Combine the seasoning mix ingredients in a small bowl.

Place a large pot half filled with water over high heat. Add the artichokes and bring to a boil. Reduce the heat to low, cover, and simmer just until the artichokes are tender, about 25 minutes. Remove the artichokes from the pot, reserving the cooking water, and allow them to cool. The best way to do this is to turn them upside down on your drainboard—all the excess water will drain out and they'll cool quickly.

Boil the potatoes in the water in which the artichokes were cooked just until they're tender, about 35 to 40 minutes, reserving 1 cup of the water (or if most of the cooking water has evaporated, add enough water to measure 1 cup). Peel the potatoes and dice enough into $\frac{1}{2}$-inch cubes to measure 1 cup firmly packed; slice the remainder into $\frac{1}{2}$-inch-thick rounds. Set aside.

If you're like me, you may be tempted to eat all the artichokes yourself right now, but resist! Inside every leaf there's a small amount of pulp—the good part. To get it out, with your thumb on the back of a teaspoon, scrape the pulp off the inside of the leaf, always scraping away from yourself. Reserve the pulp and discard the leaves. Scrape out and discard the choke, the fuzzy section underneath all the little leaves, and be sure to get it all. Peel the stems and dice the hearts and stems into bite-sized pieces. Arrange the artichoke stems, hearts, and pulp and the potato slices in a 9 × 13-inch casserole, alternating layers of potato and artichoke. Set aside.

Preheat the oven to 350°.

Melt the butter in a 3-quart pot over high heat. When the butter sizzles, add the onions, ginger, serrano peppers, and seasoning mix. Stir and cook, and when the onions begin to brown, about 6 minutes, add the diced potatoes. Reduce the heat to medium if necessary to prevent burning. Cook, stirring and mashing the potatoes constantly, until the mixture becomes thick, fairly dry, and brown, about 4 minutes. Add the reserved cooking water and cook, continuing to stir, for 6 minutes. Add the tamari and cook for 5 minutes, stirring vigorously and mashing the potatoes until they disintegrate. The mixture should be a rich brown color. Stir in the heavy cream, bring to a boil, then add the mozzarella cheese. Stir and remove from the heat. Pour this sauce over the artichokes and potatoes in the casserole and top with the Cheddar cheese. Bake until the cheese is a beautiful golden brown, about 25 minutes. Serve hot.

Cauliflower Casserole

MAKES 4 SERVINGS

This is a simple, homey-looking dish, but the seasonings pack a wallop that elevate the cauli-flower well above the ordinary. Use the best-quality cheese you can find—the better the cheese, the better this casserole tastes.

Seasoning Mix

2 tablespoons lightly packed light brown sugar

1½ teaspoons salt

¾ teaspoon white pepper

½ teaspoon dried basil leaves

½ teaspoon cayenne

½ teaspoon onion powder

½ teaspoon black pepper

½ teaspoon dried thyme leaves

¼ teaspoon garlic powder

✳

1 large head cauliflower

¼ cup olive oil

1½ cups chopped onions

½ cup chopped celery

1 cup chopped green bell peppers

1 tablespoon plus 2 teaspoons minced fresh garlic

3 generous tablespoons lightly packed chopped fresh parsley

3 generous tablespoons lightly packed chopped fresh cilantro (see Notes, page 7, Glossary, page 293)

4 tablespoons unsalted butter

1 cup chicken stock (see Notes, page 10)

2 cups unseasoned bread crumbs

1 cup freshly grated Cheddar cheese

Combine the seasoning mix ingredients in a small bowl.

Cut the cauliflower into small florets, leaving behind as much of the stalk as possible. Remove a thin slice from the bottom of the stalk (which is usually tough and dry), then cut the stalk into ½-inch chunks (you should have about 2 cups of chunks).

Preheat the oven to 350°.

Heat the olive oil in a heavy ovenproof 3-quart pot over high heat just until the oil begins to smoke, about 4 minutes. Add the onions, celery, bell peppers, and cauliflower stalks and cook, stirring occasionally, until the vegetables are wilted and just beginning to brown, about 10 minutes.

Add the garlic, seasoning mix, parsley, cilantro, and butter. Cook, stirring frequently, for 4 minutes, then remove from the heat. Stir in the stock and scrape the pot bottom thoroughly. Transfer to a 9 × 13-inch casserole and bake uncovered for 15 minutes.

Remove from the oven, stir in the bread crumbs and florets, and mix completely. Sprinkle the casserole with the cheese, return to the oven, and bake until the florets are tender, about 20 minutes. Serve hot and smile.

Gingered Green Vegetables

MAKES ABOUT 7 CUPS

The combination of the most ordinary ingredients makes a fairly exotic vegetarian dish, perfectly at home at a simple family meal or complementing an array of unusual, maybe even international recipes. One bunch of broccoli should yield the quantities of stalk and florets you need.

Seasoning Mix

1½ teaspoons salt

¾ teaspoon ground ginger

¾ teaspoon onion powder

¾ teaspoon paprika

½ teaspoon ground coriander
    (see Glossary, page 293)

½ teaspoon white pepper

¼ teaspoon garlic powder

¼ teaspoon black pepper

⅛ teaspoon cayenne1 large egg

2 large egg yolks

12 ounces cream cheese

1 teaspoon vanilla extract

✳

2 tablespoons olive oil

1 cup chopped onions

1 medium potato, peeled and diced
    into ½-inch cubes
    (about 2 cups), in all

1 cup broccoli stalks, chopped into
    ½-inch pieces

1 teaspoon brown or yellow
    mustard seeds

1½ cups vegetable stock, in all
    (see Notes, page 10)

½ small coconut, shelled and grated
    (about 1½ cups)

1 cup unsweetened coconut milk
    (see Glossary, page 293)

2 cups broccoli florets

1 pound fresh green beans, tips
    removed and cut in half

2 cups chopped green bell peppers

1 tablespoon minced fresh garlic

1 tablespoon minced fresh ginger

¼ cup medium packed chopped fresh
    cilantro (see Notes, page 7,
    Glossary, page 293)

Combine the seasoning mix ingredients in a small bowl.

Heat the oil in a heavy 5-quart pot over high heat just until the oil begins to smoke, about 4 minutes. Add the onions, 1 cup of the potato cubes, the broccoli stalks, and the mustard seeds. Cover and cook, stirring occasionally, for 10 minutes.

Add $1/2$ cup of the stock and stir and scrape the bottom of the pot thoroughly. Cook, covered, for 3 more minutes, then add the seasoning mix and another $1/2$ cup stock. Scrape the pan bottom thoroughly, then add the remaining stock, the remaining potatoes, and the coconut. Cook, stirring occasionally, until the potatoes are tender, about 12 minutes. Blend in the coconut milk and add the remaining ingredients. Cover and bring to a boil, then reduce the heat to low and simmer, stirring occasionally, until the vegetables are tender but still retain their beautiful bright green color, about 9 minutes. Serve hot as a side dish or chill and serve on a leaf of lettuce as an unusual appetizer or salad.

Dinner Vegetables

MAKES 8 CUPS

The tender-crisp vegetables in this colorful medley make a perfect accompaniment to broiled or fried fish. We call for "small" eggplants, by which we mean 2 to 3 inches in diameter and about 4 to 5 inches long. If you can find only larger ones, use fewer of them to get the correct amount. Also notice that we tell you to place the boiled salt pork in a "room-temperature" pot. Normally I tell you to preheat the pot, but not this time because we want to render the fat before we brown the salt pork.

Seasoning Mix

2 teaspoons salt

1¹/₂ teaspoons dried oregano
    leaves

1 teaspoon ground dried ancho
    chile peppers (see Notes,
    page 6)

1 teaspoon ground dried chipotle
    chile peppers (see Notes,
    page 6)

1 teaspoon dry mustard

1 teaspoon onion powder

¹/₂ teaspoon dried basil leaves

¹/₂ teaspoon cayenne

¹/₂ teaspoon garlic powder

¹/₂ teaspoon black pepper

¹/₂ teaspoon white pepper

＊

1 pound salt pork, diced into
    ¹/₂-inch cubes

³/₄ pound whole okra

2 medium onions, peeled and
    quartered

1 green bell pepper, sliced into
    8 wedges

1 red bell pepper, sliced into 8 wedges

1 yellow bell pepper, sliced into
    8 wedges

2 large tomatoes, sliced into 8 wedges

5 small eggplants (preferably
    Oriental), sliced into 8 wedges

4 medium shiitake mushrooms
    (see Glossary, page 296)

1 ripe plantain, peeled and sliced into
    rounds ¹/₂ inch thick (see Glossary,
    page 297)

continued

Combine the seasoning mix ingredients in a small bowl.

Cover the salt pork with water, bring to a boil, boil for 10 minutes, and drain. Repeat 2 more times to boil for 30 minutes in all. Place the cooked salt pork in a room-temperature 5-quart pot over high heat to render its fat. When the salt pork begins to sizzle, reduce the heat, cover, and cook, uncovering to stir occasionally, until the salt pork is brown on all sides, about 15 minutes. Add all the vegetables and plantain to the pot, return the heat to high, and stir in the seasoning mix, making sure to coat the vegetables evenly. Reduce the heat to medium and cook for 15 minutes, stirring occasionally and more frequently toward the end of the cooking time. If the vegetables begin to stick, reduce the heat. The vegetables should be tender-crisp.

Serve with your favorite main course at dinner.

Hot Bittersweet Eggplant

MAKES ABOUT 9 TO 10 CUPS

Served hot or cold, this is an excellent side dish, and it makes a great dip when puréed in a food processor.

Seasoning Mix

2 tablespoons lightly packed light brown sugar

2 teaspoons ground cardamom

2 teaspoons onion powder

2 teaspoons ground dried pasilla chile peppers (see Notes, page 6)

2 teaspoons salt

1½ teaspoons ground cumin

1 teaspoon ground coriander (see Glossary, page 293)

1 teaspoon ground fenugreek (see Glossary, page 294)

1 teaspoon garlic powder

1 teaspoon ground ginger

1 teaspoon ground dried California Beauty chile peppers (see Notes, page 6)

1 teaspoon ground dried Perfecto chile peppers (see Notes, page 6)

1 teaspoon black pepper

1 teaspoon white pepper

✳

¼ cup olive oil

1 large green bell pepper, sliced 2 inches long by ¼ to ½ inch wide (about 1½ to 1¾ cups)

1 large red bell pepper, sliced 2 inches long by ¼ to ½ inch wide (about 1½ to 1¾ cups)

2 cups shallots, peeled and quartered (about 12 medium shallots), or 2 cups onions cut into bite-sized wedges about 1 inch long

1 small head garlic, cloves peeled (if cloves are small, leave whole; otherwise, cut into bite-sized chunks)

¼ cup thinly sliced fresh ginger

¼ cup medium packed chopped fresh cilantro (see Notes, page 7, Glossary, page 293)

Juice of 1 large lemon

2 (14½-ounce) cans diced tomatoes (see Notes, page 7)

2 (1-pound) eggplants, unpeeled but stem ends removed, cut into 1 × 1 × 1½-inch chunks (try to get a piece of peel on each chunk)

Combine the seasoning mix ingredients in a small bowl.

Heat the oil in a 5-quart pot over high heat just until the oil begins to smoke, about 4 minutes. Add the bell peppers, shallots (or onions), garlic, and ginger. Cover and cook, stirring frequently, until the vegetables begin to brown, about 10 minutes. Add the cilantro, seasoning mix, and lemon juice and stir vigorously to loosen any brown bits on the bottom of the pot. Cook, checking frequently and stirring if necessary, for 3 minutes, then add the tomatoes and eggplant. Stir to mix thoroughly and scrape the bottom of the pot. Cover and cook until the liquid comes to a boil, about 3 minutes. Reduce the heat to low and cook for 1 hour, stirring frequently and scraping the pot bottom if the mixture begins to stick. Remove from the heat and stir thoroughly. The vegetables should be soft and almost pasty. Serve at room temperature or chill and serve cold.

Mirliton Casserole

MAKES 9 GENEROUS SERVINGS

Ever since I can remember, I've been eating mirlitons, fixed a huge number of ways—pickled, fried, poached, broiled, and stuffed. There are a couple of things about mirlitons that are truly wonderful: one is the underlying sweetness they lend to whatever they're in, and the other is their unusual ability to take on tastes and improve anything they're cooked with. This casserole is certainly one of my favorite mirliton recipes.

Seasoning Mix

2 teaspoons paprika

2 teaspoons ground dried pasilla
    chile peppers (see Notes,
    page 6)

2 teaspoons salt

1 teaspoon ground cumin

1 teaspoon garlic powder

1 teaspoon ground ginger

1 teaspoon onion powder

1 teaspoon ground dried ancho
    chile peppers (see Notes,
    page 6)

1 teaspoon dried tarragon leaves

$\frac{1}{2}$ teaspoon ground allspice

$\frac{1}{2}$ teaspoon cayenne

$\frac{1}{2}$ teaspoon black pepper

$\frac{1}{2}$ teaspoon white pepper

2 bay leaves

*

4 mirlitons (see Glossary, page 296)

$1\frac{1}{2}$ pounds lean ground beef

2 tablespoons olive oil

2 cups chopped onions

2 cups chopped green bell peppers

$\frac{1}{2}$ pound crumbled feta cheese
    (see Glossary, page 294)

$\frac{1}{4}$ cup cornmeal

4 thinly sliced fresh jalapeño chile
    peppers (see Notes, page 6)

$\frac{1}{2}$ pound shredded soft farmers cheese
    (see Glossary, page 294)

Combine the seasoning mix ingredients in a small bowl.

Boil the mirlitons until they are tender when pierced with a fork, about 30 minutes. Cut them in half, remove the seeds, and dice them into $\frac{1}{2}$-inch cubes. Mix the ground beef with 2 tablespoons of the seasoning mix.

Preheat the oven to 350°.

Heat the olive oil in a heavy 5-quart pot over high heat just until the oil begins to smoke, about 4 minutes. Add the seasoned beef and cook, stirring to break up the lumps, until nicely browned, about 8 minutes. Add the onions, bell peppers, mirlitons, and remaining seasoning mix. Cook, stirring occasionally and enjoying the great fragrance, for 20 minutes, then stir in the feta cheese and cornmeal. Cover and cook for 3 minutes, then transfer the mixture to a 9 × 13-inch casserole dish. Layer the top of the dish evenly with the jalapeño peppers and sprinkle with the farmers cheese. Bake until the cheese is golden brown and bubbly, about 25 minutes. Serve hot.

Spinach and Cream Cheese Pie

MAKES 2 (9-INCH) PIES

We had a lot of fun in the test kitchen when we were topping this pie. The topping is so pretty that we couldn't resist making all sorts of squiggly shapes on the pie. Use a pastry bag if you have one, or improvise by putting the topping in a plastic zipper bag, snipping off a little corner, and squeezing the topping through the hole. If you're in a hurry, simply drizzle the topping on the pie with a spoon. Use your imagination and you'll be rewarded with a beautiful treat.

Wheat and olive oil pie crusts

2 cups all-purpose flour

1½ cups whole wheat flour

1 tablespoon sugar

2 teaspoons salt

1 teaspoon ground ginger

2 tablespoons chopped fresh jalapeño chile peppers (see Notes, page 6)

2 tablespoons chopped fresh serrano chile peppers (see Notes, page 6)

2 tablespoons grated Romano cheese

2 tablespoons grated Parmesan cheese

¾ cup very cold vegetable shortening

½ cup olive oil

½ cup plus 1 tablespoon very cold water

Filling

Seasoning Mix

1½ teaspoons ground dried chipotle chile peppers (see Notes, page 6)

1 teaspoon dried basil leaves

1 teaspoon black pepper

1 teaspoon salt

¾ teaspoon white pepper

½ teaspoon garlic powder

½ teaspoon ground cinnamon

½ teaspoon ground nutmeg

½ teaspoon onion powder

❋

2 tablespoons vegetable oil

2 cups tightly packed bok choy leaves, green parts only (see Glossary, page 292)

3 (10-ounce) bags fresh spinach, washed and stemmed

1 cup heavy cream

1 tablespoon sugar

1 large egg

2 large egg yolks

2 (8-ounce) packages cream cheese

1 teaspoon vanilla extract

½ teaspoon ground dried chipotle chile peppers

¼ teaspoon ground cinnamon

¼ teaspoon ground nutmeg

Topping

12 ounces cream cheese

½ cup heavy cream

CRUSTS: Combine the all-purpose flour, whole wheat flour, sugar, salt, and ginger in an electric mixer equipped with a dough hook. Blend at low speed for 30 seconds, then add the fresh chile peppers and the cheeses and blend for 30 seconds longer. Add the cold shortening and the oil and continue to blend at low speed, scraping the sides and bottom of the bowl, until the ingredients just come together and resemble very coarse meal or dried split peas. Gradually add the water and continue to process at low speed just until the water is absorbed, being careful not to overmix. As soon as the liquid is absorbed, gather the dough into a ball and refrigerate until cold, at least 4 hours, preferably overnight.

To make the crusts, divide the dough in half and form each half into a ball. Liberally flour your hands, the working surface, and the rolling pin. Place one of the dough balls on the floured surface and roll it out, keeping it as even and round as possible. Turn the dough as you roll, and dust with flour as necessary, until the circle is about 11 inches in diameter. Carefully fit the circle into a 9-inch pie tin and crimp the edges with your hands or with the tines of a fork. Repeat with the remaining ball of dough. Set the shells aside while you prepare the filling.

FILLING: Preheat the oven to 300°.

Combine the seasoning mix ingredients in a small bowl.

Heat the oil in a 4-quart pot over high heat just until the oil begins to smoke, about 4 minutes. Add the bok choy, spinach, and seasoning mix and cook, stirring frequently, until the vegetables are wilted, about 4 minutes. Add the heavy cream and sugar, bring to a boil, then remove from the heat and cool.

Combine the egg and egg yolks in a blender or food processor and process until frothy and light lemon yellow in color, about 1 minute. Add the spinach mixture, cream cheese, and vanilla and process until the cream cheese is completely combined into the mixture.

TOPPING: Combine the topping ingredients in a blender or food processor and process until the mixture is soft and fully combined.

Divide the filling between the pie shells, then pipe or drizzle on the topping. Bake until the filling is set, about 1½ hours. Cut into wedges to serve.

Sweet and Sour Kraut

MAKES ABOUT 10 CUPS

Homemade sauerkraut is so different from the canned and bottled kinds that you'll think it should have a different name! It goes great with roasts, especially Patricia's Pork Roast (page 224). When you buy the apples, select a crisp sweet-sour variety, such as Gala or Braeburn if you can find them, or use your favorite crisp type.

Seasoning Mix

1 teaspoon ground dried ancho chile peppers (see Notes, page 6)

1 teaspoon ground dried guajillo chile peppers (see Notes, page 6)

1 teaspoon salt

$^3/_4$ teaspoon garlic powder

$^1/_2$ teaspoon caraway seeds

$^1/_2$ teaspoon dry mustard

$^1/_2$ teaspoon black pepper

$^1/_2$ teaspoon onion powder

$^1/_2$ teaspoon white pepper

$^1/_4$ teaspoon cayenne

$^1/_4$ teaspoon ground mace

✳

2 tablespoons vegetable oil

4 cups julienne onions

1 medium head cabbage, cut into julienne strips $^1/_4$ to $^1/_2$ inch wide (about 10 to 12 cups)

2 large or 3 to 4 small unpeeled apples, cut into thin wedges

2 tablespoons minced fresh garlic

2 tablespoons minced fresh ginger

1 cup balsamic vinegar (see Glossary, page 299)

1 cup dry white wine

$^1/_4$ cup firmly packed dark brown sugar

Combine the seasoning mix ingredients in a small bowl.

Heat the oil in a 6-quart pot over high heat just until the oil begins to smoke, about 4 minutes. Add the onions and cook, stirring occasionally, until they start to brown, about 8 minutes. Stir in the cabbage, apples, garlic, and ginger and cook, stirring frequently, for 4 minutes. Add the vinegar and scrape up all the brown bits on the bottom of the pot. Stir in the wine, brown sugar, and the seasoning mix. Cover, reduce the heat to medium, and cook, stirring occasionally, until the cabbage is tender and cooked down very well, about 25 to 30 minutes.

Can be served hot or cold, almost anytime, almost anywhere.

Three-Squash Stew

MAKES 5 QUARTS, ENOUGH FOR 10 (2-CUP) SERVINGS

The zingy seasonings make these squashes come alive with flavor! Because the recipe uses vegetable stock, it's totally vegetarian. And it's hearty enough for a main dish, maybe with brown rice or wild rice for flavor and texture contrast, and it also makes a delicious accompaniment to your favorite roast.

Seasoning Mix

2 tablespoons lightly packed dark brown sugar

2 teaspoons dried basil leaves

2 teaspoons paprika

2 teaspoons dried thyme leaves

1 1/2 teaspoons onion powder

1 teaspoon garlic powder

1 teaspoon ground ginger

1 teaspoon dry mustard

1 teaspoon salt

1/2 teaspoon cayenne

1/2 teaspoon black pepper

1/2 teaspoon white pepper

2 bay leaves

*

1 spaghetti squash

1 turban squash or any other hard squash, such as acorn or butternut

2 tablespoons vegetable oil

1 cup chopped onions

3 finely diced fresh jalapeño chile peppers (see Notes, page 6)

3 cups vegetable stock (see Notes, page 10)

1/4 cup thinly sliced fresh ginger

2 large unpeeled zucchini, diced into bite-sized pieces

1 head garlic, peeled (about 20 to 22 cloves)

1 green bell pepper, cut into 1 1/2-inch squares

1 red bell pepper, cut into 1 1/2-inch squares

3 tablespoons tamari (see Glossary, page 299)

1/4 cup molasses

Combine the seasoning mix ingredients in a small bowl.

Bake the spaghetti squash in a 350° oven for 20 minutes. Cut in half and discard the seeds and membrane. Turn the halves on their sides and use a fork to scrape out the flesh into a bowl. (Now you'll see how it got its name!) Set aside.

continued

Boil the turban or other type of squash for 15 minutes. Peel and discard the seeds and membrane. Chop the flesh into 1-inch cubes.

Heat the oil in a heavy 6-quart pot over high heat just until the oil begins to smoke, about 4 minutes. Add the onions, turban or other type of squash, jalapeño peppers, and seasoning mix. Cover and cook, stirring occasionally, for 5 minutes. Add the stock, ginger, zucchini, garlic, and bell peppers and cook, covered, stirring occasionally, for 10 minutes. Reduce the heat to low and simmer, covered, for 5 minutes. Stir in the tamari and molasses and cook, covered, for 10 minutes. Remove from the heat and add the spaghetti squash to the pot. Stir to blend thoroughly before serving.

Sweet
Surrender

Paul's Pies

Syrup and Corn Bread Pie

Peach Nectar Pie

Banana Poppy Seed Pie

Custards

Basic Custard

Apple Raisin Custard

Brown Sugar Custard

Honey Mustard Custard

Pine Nut Custard

Rice Custard

White Cheese Custard

Paul's Pies

Syrup and Corn Bread Pie

MAKES 2 (9-INCH) PIES

This pie is very unusual, but oh, so satisfying! It has a taste that brings back visions of my childhood, and texture that is somewhere between corn bread and custard.

The most important secret of successful pie-crust making is to refrigerate the dough before baking. Another secret is not to overmix. Some little flecks of shortening should still be visible when you've finished mixing the dough. Always liberally flour all the working surfaces—table, hands, and rolling pin—to help prevent sticking.

Corn flour pie crusts
Seasoning Mix

1 teaspoon ground cinnamon

1 teaspoon ground cloves

1 teaspoon ground ginger

¾ teaspoon ground nutmeg

✳

1¼ cups yellow corn flour
(see Glossary, page 293)

1 cup plus 2 tablespoons yellow
cornmeal

1 tablespoon sugar

2 teaspoons salt

1¼ cups very cold shortening

½ cup plus 1 tablespoon very
cold water

Syrup and corn bread filling

3 large eggs

2 large egg yolks

½ cup cane syrup (see Glossary,
page 298)

2 teaspoons vanilla extract

½ teaspoon salt

4 tablespoons unsalted butter, melted

½ cup yellow cornmeal

½ cup corn flour

½ cup all-purpose flour

2 teaspoons baking powder

1½ cups heavy cream

CRUSTS: Preheat the oven to 350°.

Combine the seasoning mix ingredients in a small bowl.

Combine the corn flour, cornmeal, sugar, salt, and seasoning mix in an electric mixer equipped with a dough hook and process until well blended. Add the cold shortening and blend at low speed, scraping the sides and bottom of the bowl, until the ingredients just come together and resemble very coarse meal or dried split peas. Gradually add the water and continue to process at low speed until the water is absorbed, being careful not to overmix. As soon as the liquid is absorbed, gather the dough into a ball and refrigerate until cold, at least 4 hours, preferably overnight.

To make the crusts, divide the dough in half and form each half into a ball. Liberally flour your hands, the working surface, and the rolling pin. Place one of the dough balls on the floured surface and roll it out, keeping it as even and round as possible. Turn the dough as you roll, and dust with flour as necessary, until the circle is about 11 inches in diameter. Carefully fit the circle into a 9-inch pie tin and crimp the edges with your hands or with the tines of a fork. Repeat with the remaining ball of dough. Set the pie shells aside while you make the filling.

Preheat the oven to 300°.

SYRUP AND CORN BREAD FILLING: Process the eggs and egg yolks in a blender or food processor until the eggs are light lemon yellow-colored, about 2 minutes. Add the syrup, vanilla, salt, and melted butter, and process until combined, about 1 minute. Add the cornmeal, corn flour, all-purpose flour, and baking powder. Process again until combined, then add the cream and process briefly.

Divide the filling between the pie shells and bake until the filling is firm and slightly browned around the edges, about 45 minutes. Cool slightly and cut into wedges to serve.

Peach Nectar Pie

MAKES 2 (9-INCH) PIES

I love a good, honest, homemade pie—and I love interesting flavor combinations, so this recipe is a gem on both counts. The peach filling is a classic, and the blueberries add a flash of flavor and excitement.

The most important secret of successful pie-crust making is to refrigerate the dough before baking. Another secret is not to overmix. Some little flecks of shortening should still be visible when you've finished mixing the dough. Always liberally flour all the working surfaces—table, hands, and rolling pin—to help prevent sticking.

Pie crusts

Seasoning Mix

2 tablespoons grated orange peel

2 tablespoons lightly packed light brown sugar

1 teaspoon brown mustard seeds

1 teaspoon yellow mustard seeds

✳

2 cups all-purpose flour

1 1/4 cups yellow corn flour (see Glossary, page 293)

1 tablespoon sugar

2 teaspoons salt

1 1/4 cups very cold vegetable shortening

1/2 cup unsalted butter, softened

1/2 cup plus 1 tablespoon very cold water

Peach nectar filling

6 tablespoons cornstarch

1 quart peach nectar, in all

1 tablespoon vanilla extract

3/4 cup sugar

5 cups peeled, sliced fresh peaches

2 cups heavy cream

1/2 cup sour cream

3 tablespoons real maple syrup

4 ounces fresh blueberries

CRUSTS: Combine the seasoning mix ingredients in a small bowl.

Combine the all-purpose flour, corn flour, sugar, salt, and seasoning mix in an electric mixer equipped with a dough hook and process until blended. Add the cold shortening and butter and blend at low speed, scraping the sides and bottom of the bowl, until the ingredients just come together and resemble very coarse meal or dried split peas. Gradually add the water and continue to process at low speed just until the water is absorbed, being careful not to overmix. As soon as the liquid is absorbed, gather the dough into a ball and refrigerate until cold, at least 4 hours, preferably overnight.

To make the shells, divide the dough in half and form each half into a ball. Liberally flour your hands, the working surface, and the rolling pin. Place one of the dough balls on the floured surface and roll it out, keeping it as even and round as possible. Turn the dough as you roll, and dust with flour as necessary, until the circle is about 11 inches in diameter. Carefully fit the circle into a 9-inch pie tin and crimp the edges with your hands or with the tines of a fork. Repeat with the remaining ball of dough. Set the shells aside while you make the filling.

FILLING: Dissolve the cornstarch in 1 cup of the peach nectar and set aside.

Heat the remaining nectar in a 4-quart pot just until it starts to simmer, then add the vanilla, sugar, and cornstarch mixture. Stir vigorously to blend the cornstarch into the liquid, then simmer, stirring frequently, for 10 minutes. Add the peaches, bring to a boil, reduce the heat to very low and simmer, stirring occasionally, for 10 more minutes. Remove from the heat and cool to room temperature. Carefully divide the filling between the pie shells and refrigerate until set.

Whip the heavy cream and sour cream just until soft peaks form. Add the maple syrup and whip just until the peaks are firm, being careful not to overbeat, especially if using an electric mixer. Overbeating will make the whipped cream grainy and can also cause it to break and turn into butter. Refrigerate until ready to use.

When the filling is set, spread or pipe the whipped cream over the top of the pies and arrange the blueberries on top of the cream. Refrigerate until the cream is firm. Cut into wedges to serve.

Banana Poppy Seed Pie

MAKES 2 (9-INCH) PIES

You'll never want a store-bought banana pie after you have tasted this little jewel.

The most important secret of successful pie-crust making is to refrigerate the dough before baking. Another secret is not to overmix. Some little flecks of shortening should still be visible when you've finished mixing the dough. Always liberally flour all the working surfaces—table, hands, and rolling pin—to help prevent sticking.

Honey mustard pie crusts

3¼ cups all-purpose flour

1 tablespoon sugar

2 teaspoons dry mustard

2 teaspoons salt

1¼ cups very cold vegetable shortening

½ cup plus 1 tablespoon very cold water

¼ cup honey

Banana poppy seed filling

Seasoning Mix

½ teaspoon ground coriander (see Glossary, page 293)

½ teaspoon ground mace

½ teaspoon salt

½ teaspoon ground turmeric

＊

3 tablespoons poppy seeds, toasted (instructions follow)

4 medium bananas, peeled and thinly sliced

1 large egg

2 large egg yolks

¾ cup honey

1 teaspoon vanilla extract

2 cups heavy cream

CRUSTS: Combine the flour, sugar, mustard, and salt in an electric mixer equipped with a dough hook and process until well blended.

Add the cold shortening and blend at low speed, scraping the sides and bottom of the bowl, until the ingredients just come together and resemble very coarse meal or dried split peas. Gradually add the very cold water, then immediately add the honey and continue to process at low speed, being careful not to overmix. As soon as the liquid is absorbed, gather the dough into a ball and refrigerate until cold, at least 4 hours, preferably overnight.

To make the shells, divide the dough in half and form each half into a ball. Liberally flour your hands, the working surface, and the rolling pin. Place one of the dough balls on the floured surface and roll it out, keeping it as even and round as possible. Turn the dough as you roll, and dust with flour as necessary, until the circle is about 11 inches in diameter. Carefully fit the circle into a 9-inch pie tin and crimp the edges with your hands or with the tines of a fork. Repeat with the remaining ball of dough. Set aside while you make the filling.

FILLING: Combine the seasoning mix ingredients in a small bowl.

Toast the poppy seeds in a small skillet over high heat, stirring and shaking the pan constantly until the poppy seeds darken slightly and give off a toasted aroma, about 3 minutes. Set aside to cool.

Arrange half of the sliced bananas on the bottom of each pie crust. Sprinkle 1 tablespoon of the toasted poppy seeds over the bananas in each pie.

Preheat the oven to 300°.

Process the egg and egg yolks in a food processor or blender at high speed until they are light and frothy, about 30 seconds. Add the honey, vanilla, cream, and seasoning mix and process until combined, about 30 seconds to 1 minute. Divide the blended mixture between the pie shells, and arrange the remaining bananas on top. Sprinkle the remaining poppy seeds on top.

Bake until the outside 1 inch is set (the center will still be slightly liquid), about 35 minutes, and remove from the oven. Cool to room temperature, until completely set, before serving.

Custards

Basic Custard

MAKES 6 (½-CUP) SERVINGS

With this basic recipe, flavored as it is with a bit of vanilla, you can enjoy a simple custard or use one of the variations that follow for an interesting change of pace. Your custard cups will be more or less full, depending upon the size of the cups. A single large ovenproof bowl may be used instead of individual cups but will take a little longer to bake. In all these custard recipes, watch the temperature of the oven carefully throughout the cooking, as baked custard is rather delicate.

Caramel

    1 cup sugar

Custard

    1 cup milk

    1 cup heavy cream

    1 large egg

2 large egg yolks

4 tablespoons sugar

2 tablespoons unsalted butter

2 teaspoons vanilla extract

CARAMEL: Be sure to have 6 custard cups nearby before you caramelize the sugar—the caramel goes in the bottom, and you'll need to work very quickly.

Heat the sugar in a 10-inch skillet over medium heat, stirring constantly to prevent burning, until the sugar melts and turns golden brown. Don't worry if lumps develop—keep stirring and be sure the heat is not too high—and they will eventually melt. Immediately remove the skillet from the heat and place 2 teaspoons of the caramelized sugar in the bottom of each custard cup.

CUSTARD: Preheat the oven to 300°.

Place all the ingredients in a blender or food processor and process until well combined and smooth. Divide the mixture evenly among the custard cups. Place the filled cups in a large deep pan and fill the pan with enough hot water to come three-fourths of the way up the sides of the cups.

Bake until the custards are set, about 1 to 1½ hours. To test for doneness, insert a knife into a custard; if it comes out clean, the custards are done. Refrigerate before serving, but if you're like Mrs. Podunk you're going to want to eat it as soon as it is cool enough not to burn your mouth!

Apple Raisin Custard

MAKES 6 (½-CUP) SERVINGS

I've always thought apples and raisins go together perfectly and look for different ways to enjoy them. Here they are enclosed in a rich custard, offering a perfect contrast of texture as well as flavor. These custards are delicious as soon as they are cool enough to eat without burning your tongue, at room temperature, or chilled. I like to eat them right out of the cup, saving the caramel for last, but you may prefer to turn them out onto a dessert dish.

Caramel

  1 cup sugar

Custard

  ½ cup apple juice

  1 cup finely diced peeled apples, a sweet variety such as McIntosh or Delicious

½ cup raisins

1 cup milk

1 cup heavy cream

1 large egg

2 large egg yolks

2 tablespoons unsalted butter

2 teaspoons vanilla extract

CARAMEL: Be sure to have 6 custard cups nearby before you caramelize the sugar—the caramel goes in the bottom, and you'll need to work very quickly.

Heat the sugar in a 10-inch skillet over medium heat, stirring constantly to prevent burning, until the sugar melts and turns golden brown. Don't worry if lumps develop—keep stirring and be sure the heat is not too high—and they will eventually melt. Immediately remove the skillet from the heat and place 2 teaspoons of the caramelized sugar in the bottom of each custard cup.

CUSTARD: Reduce the apple juice to $^1/_4$ cup in a small saucepan over medium heat. Watch it carefully, as once it starts to reduce, it happens very quickly, and you don't want to end up with dark brown apple syrup in the bottom of your pan.

Preheat the oven to 300°.

Divide the apples and raisins among the custard cups, on top of the caramel.

Place the apple juice, milk, cream, egg, egg yolks, butter, and vanilla in a blender or food processor and process until combined. Divide the mixture evenly among the custard cups (the recipe will work just fine even if your custard cups are larger than $^1/_2$-cup capacity) and place the filled cups in a large deep pan. Fill the pan with enough hot water to come three-fourths of the way up the sides of the cups.

Bake until the custards are set, about 1 to $1^1/_2$ hours. To test for doneness, insert a knife into a custard; if it comes out clean, the custards are done. Serve at room temperature or chilled and enjoy.

Brown Sugar Custard

A simple change—brown sugar for white—in the basic recipe gives this version a completely different but equally delicious flavor.

Caramel

  1 cup sugar

Custard

  1 cup milk

  1 cup heavy cream

1 large egg

2 large egg yolks

4 tablespoons lightly packed dark brown sugar

2 tablespoons unsalted butter

2 teaspoons vanilla extract

CARAMEL: Before you caramelize the sugar, be sure to have 6 custard cups nearby— the caramel goes in the bottom, and you'll need to work quickly.

Heat the sugar in a 10-inch skillet over medium heat, stirring constantly to prevent burning, until the sugar melts and turns golden brown. Don't worry if lumps develop—keep stirring and be sure the heat is not too high—and they will eventually melt. Immediately remove the skillet from the heat and place 2 teaspoons of the caramelized sugar in the bottom of each custard cup.

CUSTARD: Preheat the oven to 300°.

Place all the ingredients in a blender or food processor and process until completely blended and smooth. Divide the mixture evenly among the custard cups. Place the filled cups in a large deep pan and fill the pan with enough hot water to come three-fourths of the way up the sides of the cups.

Bake until the custards are set, about 1 to 1½ hours. To test for doneness, insert a knife into a custard; if it comes out clean, the custards are done. Serve at room temperature or chilled.

Honey Mustard Custard

MAKES 6 (½-CUP) SERVINGS

This version of our basic baked custard has such an intriguing flavor that it's sure to become a favorite. Without seeing the ingredients list, a person might never guess what's in it. I won't tell if you don't. You can substitute 2 tablespoons of a good prepared brown Dijon mustard if you cannot find the whole mustard seeds. I think that this custard tastes best when the custard and caramel are tasted together.

Caramel

   1 cup sugar

Custard

   1 teaspoon yellow mustard seeds

   1 teaspoon brown mustard seeds

   1 cup milk

1 (12-ounce) container plain yogurt

1 large egg

3 large egg yolks

4 tablespoons unsalted butter

2 teaspoons vanilla extract

½ cup honey

CARAMEL: Be sure to have 6 custard cups nearby before you begin to caramelize the sugar—the caramel goes in the bottom, and you'll need to work quickly.

Heat the sugar in a 10-inch skillet over medium heat, stirring constantly to prevent burning, until the sugar melts and turns golden brown. Don't worry if lumps develop—keep stirring and be sure the heat is not too high—and they will eventually melt. Immediately remove the skillet from the heat and place 2 teaspoons of the caramelized sugar in the bottom of each custard cup.

CUSTARD: Grind the mustard seeds (see Notes, page 8), or use the Dijon mustard.

Preheat the oven to 300°.

Combine all the ingredients in a blender or food processor and process until smooth. Divide the mixture evenly among the custard cups (the recipe will work just fine even if your custard cups are larger than ½-cup capacity) and place the filled cups in a large deep pan. Fill the pan with enough hot water to come about three-fourths of the way up the sides of the cups.

Bake until the custards are set, about 1 to 1½ hours. To test for doneness, insert a knife into a custard; if it comes out clean, the custards are done. Serve at room temperature or chilled.

Pine Nut Custard

MAKES 6 (½-CUP) SERVINGS

Caramel

1 cup sugar

Custard

1 cup toasted pine nuts
(instructions follow)

1 cup milk

1 cup heavy cream

1 large egg

2 large egg yolks

4 tablespoons lightly packed dark
brown sugar

2 tablespoons unsalted butter

2 teaspoons vanilla extract

CARAMEL: Before you caramelize the sugar, be sure to have 6 custard cups nearby—the caramel goes in the bottom, and you'll need to work quickly.

Heat the sugar in a 10-inch skillet over medium heat, stirring constantly to prevent burning, until the sugar melts and turns golden brown. Don't worry if lumps develop—keep stirring and be sure the heat is not too high—and they will eventually melt. Immediately remove the skillet from the heat and place 2 teaspoons of the caramelized sugar in the bottom of each custard cup.

CUSTARD: Toast the pine nuts in an 8-inch skillet over high heat, stirring constantly, just until the pine nuts are golden brown—be careful not to let them burn! Spoon 1 tablespoon of the toasted pine nuts into each custard cup on top of the caramel.

Preheat the oven to 300°.

Process the remaining custard ingredients in a blender or food processor until smooth, then add the remaining toasted pine nuts and process just until combined. Divide the mixture evenly among the custard cups. Place the filled cups in a large deep pan and fill the pan with enough hot water to come three-fourths of the way up the sides of the cups.

Bake until the custards are set, about 1 to 1½ hours. To test for doneness, insert a knife into a custard; if it comes out clean, the custards are done. Serve at room temperature in the cup, or if you want to turn them out, refrigerate them until very cold, dip into hot water for a moment, then invert onto a serving dish.

Rice Custard

MAKES 12 (½-CUP) SERVINGS

Rice pudding has long been a favorite dessert all over the country. It originated with thrifty cooks looking for a way to use up leftover rice, then people realized how good it can be and began cooking rice just so they could make the pudding. Now rice custard may take its place!

Seasoning Mix

2 teaspoons ground cinnamon

2 teaspoons ground ginger

1¾ teaspoons ground allspice

1½ teaspoons ground nutmeg

½ teaspoon salt

＊

¼ cup real maple syrup

2¾ cups water, in all

¾ cup raisins

1 cup converted (preferred) or regular white rice

2 cups sugar, in all

6 large eggs

3 cups heavy cream

1 cup milk

Combine the seasoning mix ingredients in a small bowl and set aside.

Combine the maple syrup and ¾ cup of the water and soak the raisins in this liquid for 4 hours.

In a covered 2-quart pot, bring the remaining 2 cups water to a boil, then add the rice, and 2 teaspoons of the seasoning mix. Cover, reduce heat to low, and simmer for 20 minutes, or until the rice is cooked. Add the raisins and soaking liquid to the rice and cool to room temperature.

Have 12 custard cups nearby before you make the caramel, because the caramel goes into the bottom of each cup and you'll need to work very quickly. Heat 1 cup of the sugar in a heavy skillet over medium-high heat until the sugar melts and turns a rich brown. Don't worry if lumps develop—keep stirring, and be sure the heat is not too high—and they will eventually melt. Immediately remove the skillet from the heat and place 1 teaspoon of the caramelized sugar in the bottom of each custard cup.

continued

Preheat the oven to 300°.

Combine the eggs, cream, milk, remaining sugar, and remaining seasoning mix in a blender and process until well blended. Place a generous $1/4$ cup of the rice mixture in each custard cup, then pour in $1/2$ cup of the cream mixture. Place the custard cups in a large deep pan and fill the pan with enough hot water to come three-fourths of the way up the sides of the custard cups.

Bake until a knife inserted in one of the custards comes out clean, about 1 hour. Serve chilled or at room temperature and enjoy.

White Cheese Custard

My two favorites of the custard recipes we developed for this book are the Honey Mustard Custard and this one. I think the reason is that both are very unusual and really wonderful-tasting. If they don't give you an unmistakably refreshing and exciting experience, do it again—you did something wrong!

Caramel

1 cup sugar

Custard

1 cup milk

1 cup heavy cream

1 cup grated queso blanco cheese
(or other bland white cheese,
such as farmers cheese, white
Cheddar, or Neufchâtel)

1 large egg

2 large egg yolks

4 tablespoons sugar

2 tablespoons unsalted butter

2 teaspoons vanilla extract

CARAMEL: Before you caramelize the sugar, be sure to have 6 custard cups nearby—the caramel goes in the bottom, and you'll need to work quickly.

Heat the sugar in a 10-inch skillet over medium heat, stirring constantly to prevent burning, until the sugar melts and turns golden brown. Don't worry if lumps develop—keep stirring and be sure the heat is not too high—and they will eventually melt. Immediately remove the skillet from the heat and place 2 teaspoons of the caramelized sugar in the bottom of each custard cup.

CUSTARD: Preheat the oven to 300°.

Combine all the ingredients in a blender or food processor and process until combined. Divide the mixture evenly among the custard cups. Place the filled cups in a large deep pan and fill the pan with enough hot water to come three-fourths of the way up the sides of the cups.

Bake until the custards are set, about 1 to 1½ hours. To test for doneness, insert a knife into a custard; if it comes out clean, the custards are done. Serve at room temperature or chilled.

Glossary

One of the purposes of this book is to introduce good cooks like you to ingredients from all over the world that you might not have used before. This list gives you a quick reference to alternate names for these ingredients and tells you where to find them and how to prepare them. If you're like me, you'll enjoy the adventure of perusing this section even when you're not actually preparing a recipe. It's a little like taking a trip without leaving your comfortable chair!

Andouille Pronounced "ahn-DOO-ee," this south Louisiana favorite is Cajun smoked pork sausage. If genuine andouille is unavailable where you shop, use the best-quality smoked pork sausage you can find, and if you want a low-fat substitute, try smoked turkey sausage.

Bean Thread A product made from soybean which resembles a very thin vermicelli pasta. Sold in bundles at Asian markets, bean thread is softened by soaking in warm water. It is used in Asian dishes.

Bok Choy Also called Chinese cabbage, bok choy is recognizable by its thick white stems, which are crisp and juicy, and dark green leaves. The stems and leaves may be used together or separately, raw or cooked, and keep for at least a week in the refrigerator.

Burdock Root Also known by its Japanese name, *gobo,* this long, thin, brown root is used in Asian dishes. Considered a "yang," or earthy vegetable, by the Japanese, it is often cooked with other roots, such as carrots, onions, and lotus roots, and is thought to be helpful for diabetics. It is similar to nuts in its vitamin potential. Varieties grow all over the world, and burdock is common in the midwestern United States, where it is often seen along railroad tracks. The roots grow very deep into the ground and must be peeled of their rough skins before using.

Cabbage Turnip See Kohlrabi.

Cane Syrup See Syrup, Cane.

Cane Vinegar See Vinegar, Cane.

Chinese Cabbage See Bok Choy.

Chorizo A very garlicky sausage made of chopped pork and seasoned with ground dried peppers, including paprika and chiles, chorizo is especially popular in Old and New World Spanish-speaking countries. It adds an intense flavor to stews and bean dishes. The links are generally about 10 inches long and 3 to 4 inches in diameter.

Cilantro The leaves of the coriander plant (see also), cilantro closely resembles flat-leaf or Italian parsley in appearance but not in flavor, and is a staple of Latin American and some African cooking. There really is no substitute for the distinctive taste, but if you absolutely can't find cilantro, you can use flat-leaf parsley to balance the volume of the recipe.

Coconut Milk All of our recipes that specify coconut milk use the unsweetened canned variety. Made from fresh coconut and water, several brands are available in many large urban supermarkets and most Latin American or Asian markets. Two of the brands we use and like, both from Thailand, are AROY-D and Chaokoh. Be sure not to buy coconut cream, as that is a different product entirely and will not work in these recipes. Check the label—if there is added sugar, then it is not coconut milk.

Coriander An herb cultivated for its aromatic seeds; these seeds, when ripe and ground, are called coriander, and the plant's leaves are called coriander leaves in some cultures and cilantro in others.

Corn Flour Corn flour is simply cornmeal that has been milled to extra fineness. If you can't find corn flour, look for fish fry, because several brands of fish fry are pure unseasoned corn flour.

Corn Masa Also called masa or masa harina, this Mexican staple is made from ground dehydrated whole-kernel corn, plus trace amounts of lime, and may be enriched with various vitamins. It is used as the basis for tamales, tortillas, and other dough items.

Couscous This is Moroccan pasta, made from raw hard wheat that's ground into flour, rubbed into tiny particles (originally by dampening and pressing through a screen), then steamed.

Cracked Wheat Cereal This wheat product can be cooked as a cereal, but we like to use it to replace part of the flour in some of our recipes for the distinctive, slightly nutty flavor it adds. You should be able to find this product at health food or organic food stores.

Daikon, or Japanese Radish Unseen in ordinary grocery stores and supermarkets just a few years ago, daikon is widely available now. This root vegetable adds texture and a slightly sharp taste to soup, salad, and vegetable dishes, or it can be sautéed and served as a side dish. It looks like a large (sometimes huge!) white carrot and can be used raw or cooked.

Farmers Cheese This bland white cheese is readily available in supermarkets everywhere; it's used to add texture to dishes without affecting their flavor much.

Fenugreek The pungent, aromatic seeds of a cloverlike Eurasian plant, fenugreek is used as a flavoring, either whole or ground. The fragrance is wonderfully sweet and spicy and will probably seem slightly familiar to you, as it is used in almost all American curry mixes. You might be interested to know that fenugreek extract is used in butterscotch and imitation rum and maple flavorings.

Feta Cheese A crumbly soft white cheese, feta was originally made in Greece from goat's milk and pickled in brine. In this country it's usually made from cow's milk.

Filé Also called gumbo filé, filé powder is ground, dried sassafrass leaves, used primarily as a thickening agent and also for the slightly musty flavor it imparts.

Glutinous Rice See Rice, Glutinous.

Gobo See Burdock Root.

Hot Sauce Bottled hot sauces vary considerably in strength, so when using one in a recipe, be sure to taste carefully and not overdo the amount.

Japanese Radish See Daikon.

Jerusalem Artichoke See Sunchoke.

Jicama An ovoid vegetable with brownish-gray skin and crunchy off-white flesh, jicama (pronounced HEE-cah-mah) is popular in Mexican cuisine. It can be cooked or served raw, either grated or chopped.

Kohlrabi, or Cabbage Turnip This versatile root vegetable is pale green and has a mild turnip flavor. It can be peeled and boiled or steamed, or grated and used raw in salad. The leaves can be cooked like any other green.

Lemon Grass This dry, brittle reed has leaves that are green to yellow-green. The outer leaves should be used only for flavoring, as they tend to be too tough to chew, but the pale, almost white inner leaves can be eaten if finely slivered or minced. Many Asian cooks chop the stalks and enclose them in a bag made from something like cheesecloth, then remove the whole thing, bag and stalks, when the cooking is completed. That procedure imparts the wonderful flavor without the risk of an unpleasant texture. Another way to enjoy lemon grass is to roll it with your hand, then cut it into large pieces that can be removed easily from the dish after cooking. The aroma of this plant is astonishingly like lemon. Commonly available in Asian markets, lemon grass is becoming easily obtainable in supermarkets as well.

Mango There are many varieties, ranging in size and color, of mangoes. Most seen in supermarkets here are 5 or 6 inches long, with golden yellow flesh and skin, sometimes touched with red, when ripe. The seed is long and flat, and the flesh is sweet and juicy. All types of this tropical fruit are unripe if their color is green, so let them ripen on a sunny windowsill before using. For those few people whose skin is sensitive to mangoes, the use of protective gloves while handling them will solve the problem.

Masa, Masa Harina See Corn Masa.

Millet The white seed of a grass grown in Europe, Africa, and Asia as a grain and in the United States for fodder, millet is a strongly flavored grain that is ground for use as a cooked cereal and in flat breads.

Mirlitons A member of the squash family, mirlitons are also called chayote, vegetable pear, christophene, cho-cho, huisquil, and guisquil. The thin skin is bumpy and pale green, and the crisp flesh is very pale greenish-white.

Mushrooms, Black This tasty fungus is used all over Asia and has many names, including black fungus, cloud ear, wood ear, wood fungus, rat's ear, mouse ear, Judas' ear, and Jew's ear. Always sold in this country in dried form in cellophane packets, the fungus must be soaked in water before using—which causes it to expand up to five times its size. Records indicate that black mushrooms were used in Chinese cooking as early as the sixth century and are still highly regarded for their medicinal properties as well as their taste and texture. Their appearance has been described as similar to charcoal shavings. Sometimes available in supermarkets and commonly available in Asian markets, these mushrooms last indefinitely in dried form.

Mushrooms, Oyster Delicate and subtly flavored, this mushroom is named for its supposed resemblance to oysters. Sometimes you'll see specimens that look like the popular mollusk, and their color can certainly be called oyster white. More often they're shaped like irregular puffy leaves, generally 2 or 3 inches long. Oyster mushrooms are becoming so popular that many supermarkets have them on hand most of the time. If you can't get them, you can substitute any fresh young white mushroom.

Mushrooms, Portobello Possibly the largest mushroom variety commonly available in supermarkets, Portobellos can measure six or seven inches in diameter. Interestingly enough, their shape is standard mushroom—if you drew a picture of a mushroom, that's what a Portobello looks like, only bigger! They add a wonderful, rich flavor and color to sauces, meats, and rice dishes.

Members of the Agaricus family, these mushrooms are sometimes served as meat-substitute burgers in health food establishments, and British readers will recognize them as "breakfast flats." Smaller versions are sometimes sold as portobellini mushrooms.

Papaya, or Pawpaw A tropical fruit, usually 5 to 6 inches long, the papaya has bright golden orange skin and flesh and a soft texture when ripe. The numerous seeds are small and very shiny black. If your skin is sensitive to papayas, use vinyl or latex gloves when handling them.

Pine Nuts Also called pinoli and piñon nuts, pine nuts are the edible seeds of certain pine trees, particularly the piñon. Crunchy and flavorful, they are great as a snack, especially toasted and salted, and add a pleasant taste and texture to recipes.

Plantain A tropical fruit larger than but very similar to bananas, plantains are generally cooked before serving. Whether they are used green or ripe depends upon the particular recipe. Most Latin American markets keep a good supply of the popular fruit on hand.

Rice, Glutinous Gluten is the protein found in wheat that, when combined with yeast or baking powder, allows dough to rise; gluten is generally absent from rice, but some strains used all over the Pacific and in Southeast Asia do contain it. Other terms for glutinous rice are sweet rice and sticky rice, because when cooked, the exterior becomes sticky and starchy. Although not actually sweet itself, glutinous rice is a popular ingredient in desserts in Indonesia and Thailand. The brand we use is packaged by the Thai company Nep Thon Deo.

Rice Wine Not to be confused with rice wine vinegar, a true rice wine can be drunk, slightly warmed as the Japanese prefer, or at room temperature. There are two distinct types of rice wine: mirin (its name in Japanese) is used for cooking, and sake for drinking. We use rice wine in several of our recipes, and if you like the taste, why not experiment and see which of your favorite dishes would benefit from a few ounces? Just be sure that the variety you buy doesn't contain salt.

Saffron More expensive per ounce than gold, the world's finest saffron comes from Spain's fertile high plain, La Mancha. The three delicate, fragrant red stigmas produced by tiny crocus flowers growing there are what we call saffron. These stigmas must be picked by hand, and it is this labor-intensive production that contributes to the high cost. This spice imparts a distinctive rich yellow color, as well as subtle flavor, to the food in which it's used.

Sake See Rice Wine.

Spring Roll Wrappers Chinese wrappers, sold in refrigerated packages in Asian stores and many supermarkets, are rectangular soft sheets of dough. Vietnamese spring roll wrappers are circular, come in a variety of diameters, and are made from rice paper. Soften by immersing them quickly in warm water.

Sugar Snap Peas These wonderful sweet peas are very much like snow peas and can be used interchangeably, although they are a little smaller. And sweeter. Like snow peas, they are eaten pod and all and add great color, taste, and crunch to dishes. Do not overcook these delicate peas or they will lose their fresh color and crunch.

Sunchoke Also called Jerusalem artichoke, the sunchoke is the tuber from the sunflower. It can be eaten raw, grated, or chopped for salads, or it can be boiled or sautéed as a side dish. Its flavor is a cross between an artichoke and a potato.

Syrup, Cane Popular in the South, cane syrup is often used on pancakes and waffles instead of maple syrup. It's made by simmering pure sugarcane juice in open kettles until it reaches the desired color and consistency. It has a very distinctive flavor—rich, dark, and sweet—that can at times border on being bitter. We use Steen's 100% Pure Cane Syrup, distributed by the C. S. Steen Syrup Mill, Inc., P.O. Box 339, Abbeville, LA 70510, or call (318) 893-1654. There's no real substitute for the flavor, but in these recipes you can use maple syrup (about two-thirds of the amount of cane syrup called for); just be sure to buy pure maple syrup, not maple-flavored pancake syrup.

Tamari A kind of soy sauce, tamari is made with more soybeans and aged much longer than usual, giving it a rich, complex flavor that holds up well in cooking. The brand we use in the test kitchen is Mitoku Macrobiotic (Mansan Organic Tamari). If you can't find tamari where you shop, use the best kind of regular soy sauce available.

Tomatillo Also called *tomate verde* in Spanish, this fruit is firm and green even when ripe. Encased in a papery husk, the fruit itself is sticky, so wash thoroughly if using raw, such as chopped in salads. The stickiness disappears during cooking. Because tomatillos are very popular in Mexican and other ethnic cooking, especially in salsas, they're usually available in supermarkets. In spite of the similarity of their appearance and name to tomatoes, one cannot be substituted for the other.

Vinegar, Balsamic This vinegar, with both sweet and acidic characteristics, is made in Italy from the must of white grapes and aged for years in oak barrels. It is thought to be good for all kinds of ailments, from childbirth pain to hangovers.

Vinegar, Cane This Louisiana product offers a very slightly sweet touch to its tangy vinegar taste. If you want the real thing and can't find it where you shop, write to C. S. Steen Syrup Mill, Inc., P.O. Box 339, Abbeville, LA 70510, or call (318) 893-1654, and they will be happy to ship it to you. There really is no substitute, but you can complete your dish by using the same amount of cider vinegar plus 1 tablespoon of cane syrup.

Vinegar, Rice As you might guess, this is vinegar distilled from rice, and it is now available all over the country. There isn't a real substitute, but if you can't find it just when you need it, don't stress—just substitute another good-quality variety.

Vinegar, White Balsamic White balsamic vinegar is a blend of white wine vinegar and the boiled-down musts of white grapes. If you can't find it, use plain balsamic vinegar or any other of your favorite vinegar varieties.

Index

cheese:
artichoke, and potato
casserole, 255–256
custard, white, 289
farmers, 294
feta, 294
-filled muffin cups,
spicy, 57–58
chicken:
the best damned grilled
chicken I ever ate!,
151–152
with cabbage, 152–153
in cauliflower cream, 184–185
coconut, 176–177
coffee-nut, 160–161
dippin', 172–173
fenugreek, 186–187
frontier, 170–171
in a fruit sauce, 154–155
Jerry's lemon grass, 174
mango, 162–163
onion gingered, 164–165
with oyster mushrooms,
158–159
papaya, 156–157
red-eye, 168–169
Sean, 178–179
in tamari cream, 175–176
tomatillo and mushroom,
166–167
tomato cream, 181–183
and zucchini casserole, 180–
181
chickpea:
and pork pie, 215–217
spread, 102–103
chile peppers, 6–7
shrimp-stuffed poblanos,
132–133
sweet beef and fresh, 210–211
see also specific chile peppers
chili, Western, 87–88
Chinese cabbage, 292
chipotle chiles:
andouille and egg muffin
cups, 51–53
beans with chorizo, 250–251
broiled catfish, 145
broiled orange roughy, 146
chicken with oyster
mushrooms, 158–159
dinner vegetables, 261–262
elixir of portobello, 70–71

fennel and split pea soup, 76–
77
flank steak with black
mushrooms, 193–194
hot and sour beef, 191–192
hot and sour shrimp, 123–124
lima bean soup, 78
mango chicken, 162–163
peppery-sweet butter, 50
potato and daikon fritters, 93
shrimp-stuffed poblanos,
132–133
spicy cheese-filled muffin
cups, 57–58
spinach and cream cheese
pie, 266–268
sweet beef and fresh chiles,
210–211
sweet spiced lamb patties,
229–230
tomatillo and mushroom
chicken, 166–167
twice-fried plantain chips,
101
white bean fritters, 94–95
chips, twice-fried plantain, 101
chorizo, 293
beans with, 250–251
cilantro, 7, 293
coconut:
chicken, 176–177
cream, beef in, 199–200
milk, 293
coffee-nut chicken, 160–161
cookware, buying, 8
coriander, 293
corn:
flour, 293
masa, 294
corn bread:
jalapeño, 19–20
okra, 20–21
and syrup pie, 275–276
couscous, 294
cracked wheat cereal, 294
crawfish:
pie, 136–138
in tomato-sugar snap pea
gravy, 138–139
cream:
cauliflower, chicken in, 184–
185
chicken, tomato, 182–183
coconut, beef in, 199–200

mango, shrimp in, 128
portobello, sweet shrimp in,
134–135
rice, gingered, 237
tamari, chicken in, 175–176
cream cheese and spinach pie,
267–268
cucumber salad with yogurt
dressing, 109
curried shrimp, 121–122
custard:
apple raisin, 282–283
basic, 281–282
brown sugar, 284
honey mustard, 285
pine nut, 286
rice, 287–288
white cheese, 289

daikon, 294
and beet salad, 107–108
and potato fritters, 93
devilishly delicious black
beans, 244–245
dinner vegetables, 261–262
dipping sauce:
herbal brown sugar, 116
spring roll, 114
tamari ginger, 116
dressing, yogurt, for
cucumber salad, 109

egg:
and andouille muffin cups,
51–53
lemon custard soup, 68–69
eggplant:
fried, 100
hot bittersweet, 263– 264
and scallops, 119–120
elixir of portobello, 70–71
enchilada casserole, 206–207

farmers cheese, 294
fennel and split pea soup, 76–77
fenugreek chicken, 186–187
feta cheese, 294
filé, 294
filled breads, 31–43
apple raisin spice, 41–43
black bean, 31–33